P9-EFH-141

Introduction
2 1765 0001 9369 1

INTRODUCTION TO THE ENGLISH LANGUAGE

INTRODUCTION TO THE *English Language*

ALBERT H. MARCKWARDT

ASSOCIATE PROFESSOR OF ENGLISH, UNIVERSITY OF MICHIGAN

OXFORD UNIVERSITY PRESS

TORONTO NEW YORK

Printed in the United States of America

Introduction

In 1928 the National Council of Teachers of English, realizing that, 'for more than a century, *good English* has been one of the major concerns of our educational system,' appointed a committee of nine prominent linguistic scholars 'to study the problems of the English language courses in our universities and colleges.' The report of this committee, published in the December 1928 issue of the *English Journal*, made the following general statement of policy:

> It is clear that training [in the English language] is deficient unless it includes adequate study of the historical development of English pronunciation, grammar, and vocabulary. To acquire a scientific point of view toward language and a true conception of the real nature of language is of course far more important than learning any particular facts. A knowledge of the principles of general linguistics is of greater value . . . than a knowledge of the details of the history of the language. But general linguistics cannot be studied *in vacuo*, and a knowledge of the principles of general linguistics can only be acquired through the detailed study of linguistic facts.

Although agreeing with his colleagues in principle, Professor Robert L. Ramsay of the University of Missouri in an appended statement suggested certain modifications and additions to the specific recommendations made by the committee as a whole. These are indicated by the following excerpts from his minority report:

For . . . most students, I believe it desirable that Modern English, in its linguistic aspects, be studied distinctly and separately. The recognition of Modern English as a distinct field for language study, and its addition as an essential supplement to the traditional scheme which has so long confined the formal study of the English language to its two earlier periods, is in accordance with the most progressive tendencies of modern linguistic scholarship, and its insertion in the curriculum is long overdue.

I am disposed to question that part of the report which deals with the arrangement of subjects. The logical order, it is stated with obvious truth, is to take up first phonetics and then Old and Middle English, ending with Modern English. But what is good logically is not always good pedagogically, and few subjects have suffered more in the past from what may be called the 'curse of logic' than the teaching of English. I think much may be said in favor of beginning with Modern English and proceeding backward. It is perfectly true that a student who has already studied Old and Middle English will be better prepared to understand the problems of Modern English; but it is also true that a student who has first gained some insight into the nature of a living language will be more ready to realize that Old and Middle English were once living too. The four aspects of Modern English which I have listed as specially important, namely phonetics, vocabulary, dialects and language kinships, and grammar, can be fairly well approached without any previous study of Old or Middle English; and there is always a certain value in proceeding from the known to the unknown.

The present textbook has been planned to meet the needs of precisely the kind of course in the English language visualized by the members of this forward-looking committee. It is in keeping with the general spirit and educational philosophy expressed by the report of the whole group, and with the specific procedure suggested by Professor Ramsay. Consisting in large part of sets of exercises, directing the student to close observation and analysis of the facts of the language, it encourages him to formulate his own rules and generalizations about linguistic developments and the structure of present-day English. Modern English is given its due recognition as a field for language study in that fully one-half of the textbook is devoted to it. The crabwise progression from the English of the present day to that of King Alfred and his contemporaries constitutes the fundamental scheme of its organization.

The present work does not pretend to be a new 'history of the English language' or a definitive treatment of any single division of that broad subject. There are available at present several adequate and admirable works of that nature by scholars of eminent authority, and there would be little justification for adding to the already existing number. Frequently, however, such scholarly works, excellent though they may be, are lacking in a sufficient amount of exercise material to aid the student in grasping the linguistic principles which they so ably set forth. Moreover, they often proceed upon the assumption that the student has an unlimited amount of time to devote to historical language study.

This book pretends to little, if any, original contribution

to the total of our present linguistic knowledge. It is designed, rather, to present on a college classroom level a synthesis of the most important results of linguistic investigation and grammatical speculation. To a greater extent than most treatments of phonetics or Old or Modern English grammar, this book is based upon induction as the fundamental activity in the learning process, particularly in connection with the acquisition of languages and the formation of linguistic concepts. For this reason, every section devoted to a discussion of some particular topic is followed by a series of study questions which are designed not only to reinforce but to extend the conclusions which have just been presented. The student is encouraged to observe the language about him, that which he hears and that which he reads. Moreover, in connection with the study of earlier stages of the English language, a number of illustrative selections from Shakespeare, Chaucer, and Old English have been included to serve as material for observation.

Another important aim of the present work is to familiarize the student with the most authoritative books in every field of language study. Accordingly, there is appended to the discussion of every topic a list of references for further study, and not infrequently some of the study questions are based upon the material in the references. This may constitute a difficulty in colleges where the library facilities are limited. However, almost every reference list includes a reference to the Preface to Webster's *New International Dictionary*, which is a highly useful compendium of linguistic information, and there are few chapters where the Webster reference alone will not furnish a good part of the information needed. In fact, one of the specific aims of the author has been to impress upon students and teachers alike the value of the dictionary, not merely as a handy authority for pronunciation and meaning, but as a general source book for language study, a record not only of living speech but of the language of former centuries as well. It has been generally assumed also that a copy of the *Oxford English Dictionary* will be available.

In a treatment so comprehensive as this, designed at the same time to serve as an introduction to the study of the English language, a certain amount of simplification is necessary and, indeed, almost inevitable. This may be justified in part by the fact that a general statement formulated by the student as a result of his own observation will undoubtedly be retained longer and be of more service than the same rule with its possibly confusing exceptions presented in the conventional textbook manner.

In accordance with the policy of simplification just expressed, the phonetic alphabet adopted here is distinctly 'broad,' making use of a minimum number of characters. Because the form of the International Phonetic Alphabet employed by workers on the *Linguistic Atlas of the United States and Canada* and by the journal *American Speech* seems well on its way to universal acceptance throughout this country, it has been adopted here with one or two minor changes.

The first approach to the study of phonetics here is through the ear: that is, the student is given a command of a phonetic alphabet and is taught to transcribe not only isolated words but connected discourse before the problems of dynamic phonetics are considered. The phonetic definitions, conventional though they are, do not indicate any intention on the part of the author to overlook the extremely complicated nature of every speech sound that is uttered.) The individual teacher is left free to emphasize, to whatever degree he wishes, the work and conclusions of those experimental phoneticians who are inclined to quarrel with the conventional terminology.

In the amount of space given over to the subject, it is impossible to do adequate justice to Modern English grammar. In planning this material three considerations were constantly kept in mind. (First, it is necessary for every student of the English language, and particularly the prospective teacher of English, to master the traditional and conventional grammatical terminology which is still used in elementary and secondary school textbooks. Second, it is desirable that he be made aware of the newer approaches to grammar as exemplified in the works of Sweet, Jespersen, and others. Finally, he must be constantly impressed with the fact that there is a grammar of Spoken English as well as of Written English, and that the two will not coincide in all points.) The topics for discussion are sufficiently flexible so that the emphasis may be placed where it will best fit the needs of the particular class.

Unfortunately, however, considerations of time and space forbade the inclusion of those problems of diction and construction which are primarily rhetorical rather than linguistic. For example, the sources of our vocabulary and the meaning of our derivative prefixes and suffixes are essentially a part of the science of language. On the other hand, the question of the effectiveness, in a specific context, of a plurisyllabic word of Latin origin as compared with a shorter word of Teutonic derivation is a problem of rhetoric, of the art of language rather than the science, and accordingly was considered outside the scope of this book. So too were such problems as parallelism in sentence structure, the placing of sentence modifiers for stylistic effect, and types of procedure in paragraph writing, important as these topics are in other connections.

There is very little agreement, even among the most competent authorities, about the pronunciation of Early Modern English. Accordingly, the phonetic transcription of Hamlet's first soliloquy represents what appeared to the author to be a judicious combination of the views of Viëtor, Zachrisson, and Wyld. The amount of space devoted not only to the sounds but to the inflections and syntax of this period of our language constitutes one of the most striking departures from the conventional survey of the English language. Usually this period is slighted in favor of Old and Middle English, even though some of the most important phonetic and grammatical developments occurred at this time.

The material devoted to Middle English needs no explanation (however, see footnote 19, p. 247), but some aspects of the approach to Old English must be accounted for. Most of the illustrative selections are taken from the Old English translation of the Gospels, particularly those passages which can be comprehended with the aid of a Modern English Bible, and indeed the student should be encouraged to do this. This material does not aim to give the student a fully rounded vocabulary or a memorized knowledge of the details of Old English inflections. Some matters that may seem of considerable importance in a graduate Old English class are passed over rather hastily here. Everything is subordinated to the chief purpose of demonstrating to the student those grammatical features of Old English which have been retained in Modern English, those which have disappeared, those which may be present in sub-standard English but not in the standard language. In other words, those facts of Old English which have some bearing upon the evolution of the English language are constantly stressed. It must be borne in mind, moreover, that the illustrative selections from Old English, and from the subsequent periods as well, were chosen not on the basis of their literary merit, but because they contained apt illustrations of the significant features of the English language at the time at which they were written.

The thoroughness with which this book can be covered will depend, of course, upon the length of time which can be devoted to it and upon the intellectual maturity of the class. It is designed with the idea of a full year course for third and fourth year undergraduates. If it is used in a somewhat less leisurely manner, whole sections can be omitted, or only the broader and more significant questions of every exercise can be assigned. For example, in a single-semester course in Modern English, only the first three chapters need be used. Or for a one-semester historical survey, the instructor may, after a brief consideration of the phonetic alphabet, omit the first two chapters and confine himself to the last four. Although it is the general plan that each set of exercises constitutes a normal assignment for a single recitation, the difficulty of using the text with less advanced students can be met by parceling out the various questions of any one exercise for individual reports.

To sum up the whole matter, this is probably not the textbook that I should write if conditions for teaching the history of the English language were ideal. It is a book designed to help the instructor make the necessary adjustments for teaching, within the limits of a short space of time, a subject which might easily demand two or more years of study.

I wish to express my appreciation to Professor Albert Elsasser of Princeton University for the many suggestions which followed his careful reading of the manuscript, to Professor Howard Lowry, also of Princeton and formerly of the Oxford University Press, and to Mr. William M. Oman of the Oxford University Press for their encouragement and assistance in the preparation of the manuscript.

A.H.M.

University of Michigan
Ann Arbor, Michigan

Contents

Illustrative Selections

EARLY MODERN ENGLISH

MIDDLE ENGLISH

OLD ENGLISH

INTRODUCTION TO THE ENGLISH LANGUAGE

I

The Sounds of English

1. Sound and Spelling

The study of language is a science. The student of language, that is to say the grammarian in the broadest sense of the term, is a scientist. The method of all sciences is similar in that the scientist first observes the phenomena with which he is concerned; then, he classifies the results of his observation; and finally, he draws certain general conclusions from the material before him. This is the method of the botanist, the geologist, the chemist; it is necessarily also the procedure of the student of language.

The English language is to be our particular field of observation. We must begin then by observing it; but naturally we shall want to know what to observe and what there is about it to be observed.

Speech is one important aspect of language. It consists of sounds put together in such a way that they have significance for speaker and hearer. Our observation could, therefore, begin with the sounds of the English language —

or, to bring it even closer home, with the sounds of our own language, the sounds we use in our daily intercourse. What sounds do we use? How many sounds are there? How are they made? These are all questions which must be answered at the very outset of our work. The branch of language study which concerns itself with such questions is called *phonetics*.

In the exercises which follow, and which form the major part of this textbook, you will be asked to engage in exactly the same activities which occupy the scientist: to observe, to classify, and to generalize. You can learn more about the English language from your own observations, from the work you do yourself, than from what any author can tell you, because you are in a better position to examine your own speech. You must try to make yourself language-conscious in the best, the scientific, sense of the word.

You are to begin by examining a list of words that have been selected because they contain all the simple vowel and consonant sounds of present day or Modern English. Your task is to find out what these sounds are. You will have to pronounce the words aloud many times to determine which sounds are alike and which differ from one another. Remember that speech cannot be studied in silence.

Naturally you will also want to know something of the relationship of our system of spelling to these sounds, for we shall be writing and talking about language a great deal in the course of our observation. In doing so we must be certain that we all understand the same thing when a letter such as *e*, *i*, or *g* is referred to. It is important that we decide whether the ordinary system of spelling will answer our requirements in this respect.

EXERCISE I

1. What is the purpose or function of any system of spelling? Try to frame your answer into a simple and definite statement.

2. In an ideally constructed spelling system, what do you think would be the relationship between the number of sounds in the language and the number of letters or characters for those sounds?

3. From the following list of words, determine how many stressed vowel sounds there are in Modern English as it is spoken in your locality. Rearrange the list, putting words of similar vowel *sound* (not spelling) together: *i.e. soul* and *boat* although spelled differently have the same vowel sound and consequently belong together.[1]

soul	gnaw	full
food	bin	cough
great	book	leave
pass	word	bird
calm	top	bathe
rut	jerk	feed
let	son	rude
long	heard	turn
sham	boat	zinc
measure	chews	yet
think	hand	which

[1] The number of distinctive vowel sounds in Modern English is not the same in all localities in which the language is spoken; moreover, various students may not all have exactly the same groupings of the words in this list. One speaker may pronounce *pass* with the vowel of *sham*, whereas another may use the vowel sound of *calm*. The only correct answer so far as you are concerned is an accurate indexing and representation of your own sounds; we are not now concerned with what is right or wrong, but with what you normally and habitually use.

4. How many vowel characters does the English alphabet provide for these vowel sounds? What vowel characters do not always represent the same sound? What vowel sounds are not always represented by the same letter?

5. Determine, from the same list of words, how many consonant *sounds* (not characters) there are in Modern English.

6. How many characters does the English alphabet provide for these consonant sounds? What consonant characters do not always represent the same sound?

7. How many vowel sounds are represented in the following list of words:

taut	deep	pique
bead	piece	key
dawn	sought	people
balk	frost	quart
receive	eve	broad

8. What does this suggest as to the number of characters or character combinations per sound in the English alphabet?

9. How many different sounds are represented by the character *a* in the following list:

ale	tall	nap
ask	many	take
father	arm	water

10. What does this suggest about the number of sounds per character in the English language?

11. Various dictionaries have somewhat similar systems for marking the quality of sounds, most of them based essentially upon spelling. That in Webster's *New International Dictionary* may be considered typical of this method of recording sound quality. Consult that dictionary to discover the symbols which are employed in indi-

cating the stressed vowel sounds in the words under (3). How many stressed vowel symbols do you find in all? Are there any instances where more than one symbol is used to represent a single sound? Would you consider this a scientific method of recording sounds? Explain.

2. The Phonetic Alphabet

From our work in Exercise 1, it is clearly evident that Modern English spelling, although it may meet everyday requirements, is neither logical nor consistent. The same letters or characters often have more than one value, and any one sound may be indicated in a number of ways. Even the systems of diacritical markings employed by the dictionaries are somewhat unwieldy, chiefly because they are based so largely upon the conventional spelling system.

Yet, in order to study English or any other language scientifically, we must have a consistent method of recording speech sounds — one which will assure us that writer and reader will have the same sound in mind when any letter or syllable is employed. This is as important to the student of language as it is for all students of chemistry to agree that *H* stands for hydrogen and *O* for oxygen. We can attain this end only by employing an alphabet which arbitrarily assigns one and only one sound value to each letter in it, and in which each sound has but one symbol to represent it. The International Phonetic Alphabet was designed by linguistic scholars to perform such a function, and it is presented here in a modified form, especially adapted to the needs of American English. Note the value of each symbol as it is illustrated in the key word, and its use in the transcription which appears in the third column.

Phonetic Symbol	Key Word	Transcription
1. ɑ	balm	bɑm
2. æ	bat	bæt
3. e	bait	bet
4. ɛ	bet	bɛt
5. i	beat	bit
6. ɪ	bit	bɪt
7. ɔ	bought	bɔt
8. o	boat	bot
9. ʌ	but	bʌt
10. u	boot	but
11. ʊ	put	pʊt
12. ɝ	bird, word, turn	bɝd, wɝd, tɝn

(As pronounced with *r* coloring. For other varieties of this sound see Section 13.)

13. ə	above, custom	əbʌv, kʌstəm
14. ɚ	burglar, Herbert	bɝglɚ, hɝbɚt

(As pronounced with *r* coloring.)

15. b	bait	bet
16. d	date	det
17. f	fate	fet
18. g	gait	get
19. h	hate	het
20. k	cake	kek
21. l	late	let
22. m	mate	met
23. n	neat	nit

Phonetic Symbol	Key Word	Transcription
24. ŋ	ring	rɪŋ
25. p	pate	pet
26. r	rate	ret
27. s	same	sem
28. ʃ	shame	ʃem
29. t	tame	tem
30. θ	loath	loθ
31. ð	loathe	loð
32. v	van	væn
33. w	wait	wet
34. ʍ	whale	ʍel
35. j	yoke	jok
36. z	zest	zɛst
37. ʒ	vision	vɪʒən
38. tʃ	choke	tʃok
39. dʒ	joke	dʒok

The thirty-nine symbols listed above may be considered the minimum number which will represent adequately the speech sounds of the greater portion of the United States. A phonetic alphabet such as this, which uses the fewest possible number of symbols, is called *broad;* one which uses more than the minimum number of essential symbols or which modifies its symbols as a means of indicating slight differentiations in sound is called *narrow.*

This phonetic alphabet arbitrarily ignores many of the finer distinctions in our speech, such as that between the sound of *a* in *calm* as compared with the somewhat more fronted vowel used by some speakers in pronouncing the stressed vowel in *bath.* Nor is any attempt made to differentiate between the sound of the vowel in *lawn* and the more lax but nevertheless rounded vowel which is sometimes heard in such a word as *doll*. Therefore, if you observe that you pronounce the vowel of such words as *doll* or *fog* with any degree of lip rounding whatsoever (which may be easily ascertained by looking at a mirror as you say the word), it should be transcribed as [ɔ], *i.e.* [dɔl, fɔg]; if you pronounce the vowel without lip rounding, transcribe it as [ɑ], *i.e.* [dɑl, fɑg].

This alphabet does not provide a special character for the stressed vowel sound heard in some pronunciations of *care*, *marry*, or *Mary*. You must decide, in each instance, whether your pronunciation is closer to [ɛ], [æ], or [e] and transcribe the vowel accordingly.

Note that symbol 13 [ə] is used *only* when the vowel to be recorded is *unstressed*. It must not be used to transcribe a stressed vowel sound. Observe also that symbol 9 [ʌ] is never used in recording a sound which is relatively unstressed. Pay particular attention to the transcriptions of *above* and *custom*. Similarly symbol 12 [ɝ] is used only in stressed syllables; the corresponding unstressed sound is represented by symbol 14 [ɚ].

Observe especially the difference between the sounds indicated by symbols 30 [θ] and 31 [ð]. If the distinction between these sounds is not immediately apparent, pronounce the key words aloud several times until you comprehend the difference.

Henceforth all phonetic transcriptions and references to isolated sounds will be enclosed in square brackets. All conventionally spelled words used for illustrative purposes and references to spellings will be italicized.

It will be convenient to adopt some consistent scheme for referring to the symbols of the phonetic alphabet. It is most desirable to refer to the vowel characters by the sound they represent (ɑ = 'ah,' i = 'ee') for this will help you to learn their values. Symbols 12 [ɝ] and 14 [ɚ] may be distinguished by calling them 'stressed *er*' and 'unstressed *er*' respectively. Symbol 13 [ə] is frequently called *shwa* [ʃwɑ]. Those consonant symbols which are also in our conventional alphabet may be called by the names which we ordinarily give them: b = [bi], d = [di], f = [ɛf], etc. The remaining symbols may be named as follows: g = [ge], ŋ = [ɛŋ], ʃ = [ɛʃ], θ = [ɛθ], ð = [ɛð], ʍ = [ʍe], ʒ = [ʒi].

Exercise II

1. Using the phonetic symbols listed on pages 8 and 9, record your pronunciation of each of the following words. Do not allow yourself to be misled by spelling. In transcribing the last four words, pay careful attention to the unstressed syllables, following the practice indicated on page 10.

pill	fruit	foe	earth	luck
best	shave	cloth	yield	purpose
charm	meek	which	shock	lagoon
jaw	thud	bathe	quack	treasure
rang	shook	hose	seek	money

Note particularly the final sound of *money*, as you would use it in ordinary conversation. Put the word into a sentence: *e.g. Put the money there.* Is the final sound closer to [i] or [ɪ]? Make certain that your transcription indicates your actual pronunciation.

2. Pronounce aloud the words *don*, *din*, *dine; pot*, *put*, *pout; mitt*, *moot*, *mute; fall*, *fill*, *foil.* Listen carefully to the stressed vowel sounds in *dine*, *pout*, *mute*, and *foil.* In each of these four words attempt to prolong artificially the beginning of what seems to be the vowel sound; then

prolong the end of it. Now pronounce the whole group of words again, distinctly and slowly. How does the stressed sound in the words *dine*, *pout*, *mute*, and *foil* differ from the others? What happens when you prolong the stressed sounds in these last four words? Put all twelve words into phonetic transcription.

3. Define the term *diphthong*. May the combinations *ea* in *beat* and *au* in *maul* be considered diphthongs? Give reasons for your answer.

4. The stressed vowel sounds in such words as *date* and *note* are transcribed as diphthongs by many phoneticians, although for practical reasons they are considered as simple vowels in our alphabet. Say the two words over a number of times. Assuming them to be diphthongs, how would you transcribe them?

5. Transcribe the following list of words and phrases as they would sound if spoken conversationally. Exercise particular care in transcribing the unaccented syllables, not only in the separate words but in the last four phrases as well. Just as the syllables within a word may vary in the amount of stress or accent they receive, so the words in a phrase or sentence are similarly given different degrees of stress. For example, *or* in *Take it or leave it*, when spoken rapidly and informally, is not pronounced [ɔr] but [ɚ]; *the* in *Take the book* is normally spoken as [ðə], not as [ði]. The vowels of words with light sentence or sense stress are transcribed with the same symbols, [ə] and [ɚ], that are used for lightly stressed syllables within a word.

carpet	ethics	hydrophobia	auspicious
sublime	delusion	vertical	horoscope
business	phalanx	haphazard	woodchuck
shipment	bequeathe	multiplication	jointure
prestige	outrageous	pecuniary	whippoorwill

who's there	believe it or not	get out of the way
true to life	has he come yet	bread and butter

3. Transcribing Connected Speech

You are at a point now where you are ready to use the phonetic alphabet for the transcription of connected speech. From the work you have already done, the purposes and the advantages of this method of indicating spoken language are undoubtedly so clear that a detailed discussion will not be necessary. It is sufficient to say that any phonetic alphabet exists chiefly for the purpose of making an objective, graphic record of the spoken word, wherever such a record is necessary or desirable. This may be in the transcription of actual living speech, either for corrective or analytical purposes, or the linguistic scientist may wish to indicate his conception of the speech of some past generation.

The phonetic alphabet performs these tasks better than any other means short of a mechanical recording. First, the characters in such an alphabet consistently refer to actual sounds rather than to letters in a system of spelling. Second, the alphabet provides a way of indicating such neutral vowels as [ə] as well as consonants for which no actual spelling letter exists, as for example the character [x], which you will use later for the *ch* sound in such a word as Scotch *loch*. Moreover, by getting some distance away from the conventional alphabet, you are less likely to be deceived into thinking that you pronounce certain words in ways suggested by the spelling. It is not until one has employed some kind of phonetic alphabet that he comes to realize that the second sound in the word *ink* is actually [ŋ] and not [n], as the spelling would seem to indicate, or that the initial sound in *who* is [h] and not [ʍ].

Yet there are certain limitations of the phonetic alphabet which it will be advantageous for us to recognize before going any farther. First of all, it is obvious that although ordinary speech consists of sounds of widely differing qualities, such as [ɪ] compared with [ɔ], the factors of stress, pitch, and pause also play very important parts. These last, however, are so very finely graded, they permit such minute variations, that phonetic alphabets rarely do little more than to suggest the grosser differentiae of such phenomena, and more often ignore them altogether.

It must also be recognized that speech is a continuum: that is to say, the word *sake* [sek], does not in reality consist merely of a sound [s], a sound [e], and a sound [k]. Actually, the way we make the [s] in this word is very probably affected by the fact that it is followed by an [e] rather than an [ɑ] or an [o]. Moreover, the [e] sound is in turn influenced by the [s] which precedes it and by the [k] which follows. Finally, the [s] and [k] sounds in *sake* are by no means identical with what appear to be the same sounds in the word *case* [kes].

In addition, it is scarcely possible to tell, without the aid of laboratory instruments and techniques, the precise point at which the [s] leaves off and the [e] begins, or where the [e] leaves off and the [k] begins. These sounds merge into one another very gradually; that is part of what we mean by saying that speech is a continuum. Yet the person using the phonetic alphabet as a means of transcribing connected discourse must make the assumption what sounds may be delimited, that, in this instance, there are the three sounds, [k], [e], and [s], in the word *case*.

Speech, like any purely physical activity, consists of continuous motion. Yet a motion picture film of a baseball pitcher taking his windup is made up of a series of individual frames or still photographs, showing particular stages of the action in progress. Transcription is like the motion picture film: it catches a continuous action at certain points, and hopes, by a faithful reproduction of these stages, to suggest the action in its entirety.

Exercise III

1. Study the following passage. Be prepared to read it aloud as you think it should sound according to the transcription given here.

wʌnts ðɚ wʌz ə jʌŋ ræt hu kʊdnt mek ʌp ɪz mɑɪnd ʍɛnɛvɚ ðɪ ʌðɚ ræts æst ɪm ɪf hi wʊd lɑɪk tə kʌm ɑʊt wɪθ ðɛm hi wʊd æntsɚ ɑɪ don no ænd ʍɛn ðe sɛd wʊd jə lɑɪk tə stɑp ət hom hɪ wʊdn se jɛs ɚ no iðɚ   hi wʊd ɔlwɪz ʃɝk mekɪŋ ə tʃɔɪs

wʌn de ɪz ænt sɛd tə hɪm nɑụ lʊk hɪɚ no wʌn əl ɛvɚ kɛɚ fɚ ju ɪf ju kærɪ ɑn lɑɪk ðɪs   ju hæv no mɔɚ mɑɪnd ðən ə bled əv græs   ðə jʌŋ ræt kɔft ən lʊkt wɑɪz æz juʒwəl bət sɛd nʌθɪŋ dont jə θɪŋk so sɛd ɪz ænt stæmpɪŋ ɚ fʊt fɔɚ ʃi kʊdnt bɛɚ tə si ðə jʌŋ ræt so kol blʌdəd   ɑɪ dont no wəz ɔl ðə jʌŋ ræt ɛvɚ æntsɚd ænd ðɛn hid wɔk ɔf tə θɪŋk fɚ ən ɑʊɚ   ʍɛðɚ hi ʃəd ste ɪn ɪz hol ɪn ðə grɑʊnd ɔɚ go ɑʊt ɪn ðə lɔft   wʌn nɑɪt ðə ræts hɝd ə gret nɔɪz ɪn ðə lɔft   ɪt wəz ə vɛrɪ drɪrɪ ol lɔft   ðə ruf lɛt ɪn ðə ren ðə bimz ən ræftɚz wɚ ɔl rɑtn so ðət ðə ples wəz ræðɚ ʌnsef   æt læst wʌn əv ðə dʒɔɪs gev we ænd ðə bimz fɛl wɪð wʌn ɛnd ɑn ðə flɔɚ   (ðə wɔlz ʃʊk ænd ɔl ðə ræts hɛɚ stʊd ɑn ɛnd wɪθ fɪɚ ənd hɔrɚ)   ðɪs wont du sɛd ðə tʃif   wi mʌst liv ðɪs ples   so ðe sɛnt ɑʊt skɑʊts tə sɝtʃ fɚ ə nu hom ɪn ðə nɑɪt ðə skɑuts kem bæk ənd sɛd ðe əd fɑund ən old kup əv ə bɑɚn ʍɛɚ ðɚ wud bi rum ənd bɔɚd fɚ ðɛm ɔl æt wʌnts ðə tʃif gev ðɪ ɔɚdɚ fɔɚm ɪn lɑɪn ðə ræts krɔld ɑut əv ðɛɚ holz ənd stud ɑn ðə floɚ ɪn ə lɔŋ lɑɪn (dʒʌs ðɛn ðɪ old ræt kɔt sɑɪt əv jʌŋ grɪp) ðæt wəz ðə nem əv ðə ʃɝkɚ hi wʌznt ɪn ðə lɑɪn ænd i wʌznt ɪgzæktlɪ ɑutsɑɪd ɪt hi stud dʒəs bɑɪ ɪt ʍɑɪ dont ju spik sɛd ðɪ old ræt koɚslɪ əv kɔɚs ju ɑɚ kʌmɪŋ ɑɪ dont no sɛd grɪp kɑmlɪ ðɪ ɑɪdiə əv ɪt wɑɪ jə dont θɪŋk ɪts sef du jə ɑɪm nɑt sɝtn sɛd grɪp ʌndɔntɪd ðə ruf me nɑt kʌm dɑun jɛt wɛl sɛd ðɪ old ræt wi kænt wet fɔɚ ju tu dʒɔɪn əs rɑɪt əbɑut fes mɑɚtʃ ænd ðə lɔŋ lɑɪn mɑɚtʃt ɑut əv ðə lɔft ʍɑɪl ðə jʌŋ ræt wɔtʃt ðəm

ɑɪ θɪŋk ɑɪl go təmɑro hi sɛd tu ɪmsɛlf bʌt ðɛn əgɛn ɑɪ dont no ɪts so nɑɪs ən snʌg hɪɚ ɑɪ θɪŋk ɑɪl go bæk tə mɑɪ hol ʌndɚ ðə lɔg fɚ ə bɪt dʒʌs tə mek ʌp mə mɑɪnd

ðæt nɑɪt ðɛɚ wəz ə bɪg kræʃ dɑun kem bimz ræftɚz dʒɔɪs ðə hol ruf nɛkst mɔɚnɪŋ ɪt wəz ə fɑgɪ de səm mɛn kem tə luk ət ðə lɔft ðe θɔt ɪt ɑd ðət ɪt wʌznt hɔntɪd bɑɪ ræts bʌt ət læst wʌn əv əm hæpnd tə muv ə bɔɚd ænd i kɔt sɑɪt əv ə jʌŋ ræt kwɑɪt dɛd hæf ɪn ən hæf ɑut əv ɪz hol ðʌs ðə ʃɝkɚ hæd ɪz du[2]

2. How are the words *a*, *an*, and *then* consistently transcribed throughout the story? Explain these transcriptions in the light of the discussion to be found in connection with Question 5, Exercise II.

3. List the different transcriptions which you find for each of the following: *and*, *at*, *but*, *for*, *had*, *just*, *or*, *that*, *them*, *there*, *to*, *was(n't)*, and *would*. Read aloud the phrases or word groups in which these word groups occur, being

[2] The student should understand that this transcription does not in any way pretend to set up a model or standard of pronunciation. It is nothing more than a descriptive record, an indication of how one person might at some particular time tell this little story.

careful to give to your reading the exact quality indicated by the transcription.

4. What transcriptions do you find for the article *the?* Can you see any connection between the way this word is transcribed and the kind or class of sound which follows it? What transcriptions do you find for *her*, *he*, *him*(*self*), *why?* How do the stressed and the unstressed forms of these words differ from each other?

5. It is often difficult to know whether to transcribe certain *r* sounds as vowel or consonant. A detailed discussion of this question will be given later (p. 47). For the present, follow the practice illustrated by the transcription of the following words. Find them in the story and notice how the *r* sounds are treated.

Grip	floor	ever	carry	morning
rotten	bear	rafter	very	board
crawl	more	under	dreary	march

6. Transcribe the following passage of conversational English. Do not begin your transcription until you have read the selection aloud several times in a wholly natural manner and have listened carefully for the precise quality and stress of each word and syllable.

> I don't believe it will rain tonight. It has been cloudy today, but the wind was very strong. Was that thunder that I heard just now? Frances, run upstairs and close all the windows. You might know it would start to pour about the time we wanted to go out. We may have to postpone our trip after all. I don't see why it couldn't have rained last night. Listen to those terrible crashes and look at the lightning! You're not afraid of thunderstorms, are you? Put the car in the garage while he holds the doors.

Other passages of transcribed material may be found in the following works:

Krapp, *The Pronunciation of Standard English in America*, pp. 151–211.

Kenyon, *American Pronunciation*, 6th edition, p. 30.

Jones, *Phonetic Transcriptions of English Prose*, pp. 1–41.

American Speech. This quarterly journal devotes two or three pages of each issue to phonetic transcriptions. A collection of these has been published under the title *Phonetic Transcriptions from 'American Speech,'* edited by Jane Dorsey Zimmerman.

4. Production of Sound

So far we have considered speech sounds primarily from the acoustical point of view, from the standpoint of hearing. In order to understand this aspect of language more completely, we must also give some attention to the dynamics of speech sounds, to the way in which they are made.

The primary condition for the production of speech sounds is a steady outward flow of air through the vocal apparatus. This air is forced from the lungs by a co-ordination of chest and abdominal muscles, causing a rise and fall of the diaphragm in a kind of bellows-like fashion. It is then necessary for the steady stream of air to be broken into periodic, interrupted, and audible movements; that is, into those sounds which we recognize as significant and meaningful.

After leaving the lungs, the air passes through the trachea or windpipe into the larynx, which contains the vocal folds or vocal lips. (See Figure 1. The popular term *vocal cords* gives an inaccurate conception of the laryngeal mechanism.) These fleshy folds or lips, containing ligament and muscle fibre, extend from the front to the back

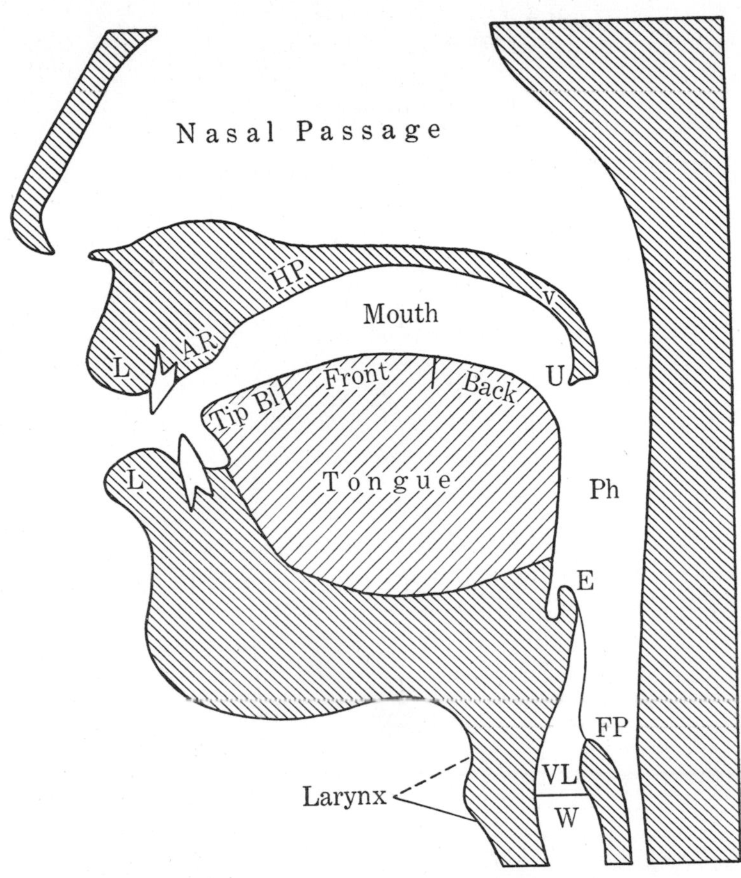

Fig. 1. DIAGRAM OF THE SPEECH ORGANS

LL — Lips. BL — Tongue Blade. AR — Alveolar Ridge.
HP — Hard Palate. V — Velum or Soft Palate.
U — Uvula. Ph — Pharynx. VL — Vocal Lips. W — Windpipe.
FP — Food Passage. E — Epiglottis.

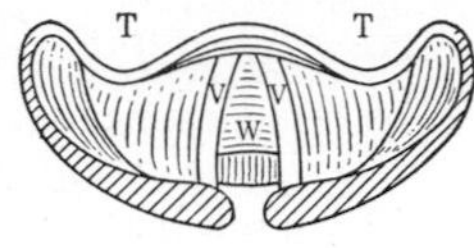

FIG. 2. THE LARYNX: Position for Breath or Voiceless Sound
VV — Vocal Lips, Open. TT — Tongue. W — Windpipe.

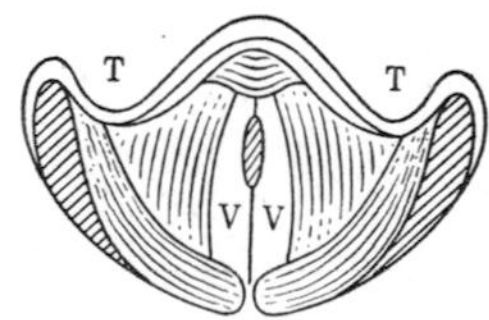

FIG. 3. THE LARYNX: Position for Voice
VV — Vocal Lips, Partly Closed. TT — Tongue.

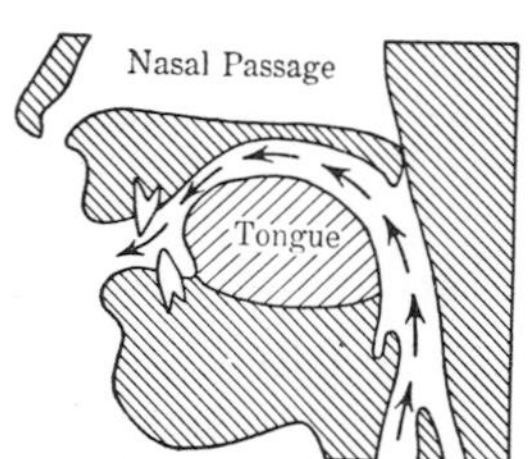

FIG. 4. Position of Velum for Oral Sound

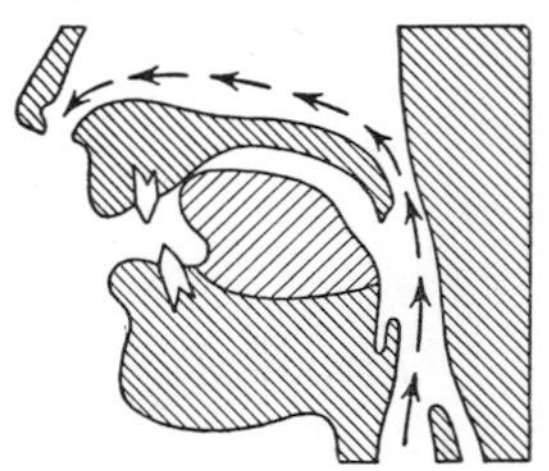

FIG. 5. Position of Velum for Nasal Sound

Arrows indicate course of breath stream

on either side of the interior of the larynx. (Figures 2 and 3.) When the vocal lips are parted or open, the air stream passes through them without obstruction, as in ordinary breathing or as in the sound [h]. When the vocal lips are drawn lightly together, the air stream in passing through causes them to vibrate, and the resulting sound is called *voice*.[3]

All our speech sounds are classified in terms of this quality of voice, that is as *voiceless* or *voiced*. Compare, for example, the voiceless sound [s], made with the glottis or vocal lips open, and the voiced sound [z], identical in every other respect, but made with the vocal lips or glottis partially closed. Make the two sounds several times, that you may be sure to recognize these qualities. Try such other pairs as [f] voiceless and [v] voiced, [k] voiceless and [g] voiced. If you are not certain that hearing alone enables you to distinguish between voiced and voiceless sounds, try pronouncing them with your thumb and forefinger pressed lightly against your larynx. You should feel vibration or movement in the larynx when you make the voiced sounds, but nothing at all when the voiceless sounds are produced. Another means of distinguishing them is to stop your ears as you pronounce the sounds aloud. You will hear nothing — or only rushing air — as you make the voiceless sounds, whereas when the voiced sounds are produced, you will hear the vibration of the vocal lips even though your ears are stopped.

[3] At the back wall of the larynx, the vocal lips are fastened to the arytenoid cartilages. It is possible to close the vocal lips, but to permit the escape of air between these cartilages — that is, through the cartilage glottis. When this is done, the result is whispered sound.

After leaving the larynx, the breath stream proceeds past the epiglottis, through the pharynx (see Figure 1), and finally into either the mouth or the nasal passage, or into both. The velum or soft palate determines whether the sound shall issue orally or nasally. When the velum is retracted or drawn up, as in Figure 4, the nasal passage is closed off, and the air must escape entirely through the mouth. If the velum hangs down or is lax, as in Figure 5, and if there is also a complete obstruction somewhere in the mouth passage, the air must necessarily escape through the nose. For example, when the sound [m] is made, the closed lips prevent any escape through the mouth, and the air is forced out nasally.[4]

The majority of our speech sounds, particularly the consonants, are formed with the tongue as the chief articulating organ. In phonetic descriptions, four regions or parts of the tongue are recognized. They are: (1) the tip or point; (2) the blade, including the tip and a little back of it; (3) the front, extending from the blade back to about the middle, or that part which is opposite the hard palate when the tongue is in normal resting position; (4) the back, or that portion which is opposite the soft palate. (See Figure 1.)

In addition to the tongue, the lips, teeth, and roof of the mouth play important parts in the production of sound. For purposes of phonetic description, three divisions of the roof of the mouth are recognized: (1) the teeth ridge or alveolar ridge, extending from the teeth to the

[4] With such nasalized vowels as French *-on*, *-en*, note that the velum is lax, but the mouth passage is not obstructed, thus allowing the breath stream to escape through both mouth and nose at the same time.

point where the roof of the mouth begins to be concave; (2) the hard palate; (3) the soft palate or velum.

Exercise IV

1. Pronounce aloud all the English vowels as indicated in the chart on p. 8. Are these sounds voiced or voiceless?

2. Pronounce aloud all the English consonant sounds. Make a list of those which you find to be voiceless.

3. Opposite each of the voiceless consonants in the list which you made for the preceding question, place the symbol for the corresponding voiced consonant, that is, the one which resembles it in every respect but that of vocal quality. For example: [k] voiceless — [g] voiced — and so on.

4. Are the English nasal consonants voiced or voiceless? If you find them to be voiceless, try to make the corresponding voiced sound for each; if you believe they are voiced, try to make the corresponding voiceless sounds. What happens when you try to pronounce the sound [m] aloud and hold your nose tightly closed at the same time? Why?

5. With what portion of the tongue is the [s] sound made? Which articulating organs operate in producing [v]? With what part of the roof of the mouth does the tongue come in contact in producing the sound [ŋ]?

5. Classification of Consonants

We have already seen that sounds may be divided into two categories, voiceless and voiced, in terms of the action of the larynx. We have also recognized another twofold classification, oral and nasal, in terms of where the breath stream ultimately escapes. Thus we have gone part way toward classifying the consonant sounds of English and toward understanding how they are made.

The next great division may be made in terms of the nature of the escape of air. If the sounds [s] and [t] are compared, it is readily seen that with the sound [s] the escape of air is continuous, that the sound may be produced as long as one's supply of breath holds out, and that the peculiar character of the sound arises from the friction of the rapidly escaping air against the narrow aperture through which it must pass. Sounds of such a nature that they may be produced indefinitely are called *continuants;* those continuants which, like [s], are also characterized by the friction of escaping air are called *fricatives.*

Although the sound [t] is made with the tongue-tip placed very nearly in the same position as it is for [s], its very different character is noticeable at once. In making the [t] sound, not only is the tongue-tip placed firmly against the alveolar ridge, but the sides of the tongue are placed against the lower surface of the upper teeth. This creates an air-tight pocket behind which the breath stream is completely stopped for an instant; then the tongue is suddenly released, and the air which has been condensing in this pocket escapes with a somewhat explosive sound. Consonants made in a fashion similar to [t] are classified as *stops* or *plosives.*

Most of our consonants may be classified either as stops or as continuants, but there are also two other minor groups. An *affricate* is a stop followed by a slow separation of the articulating organs, making the last part of the sound fricative in nature. The sounds [tʃ] and [dʒ] are affricates.

The characteristic quality of sounds such as [j] and [w] arises not from a single position of the articulating organs, but rather from their shifting from one position to another. In making the initial sound of the word *yawn* [jɔn], note that at the beginning of the [j] sound the tongue is high in the mouth and considerably forward. The shift or glide of the tongue from this high forward position to the low back position required for the vowel [ɔ] gives us the sound [j]. Such transitional sounds are called *glides*.

We have now four criteria for the classification and description of consonants. These are:

(1) Is the consonant voiced (glottis partly closed) or voiceless (glottis open)?

(2) Is the consonant oral (velum retracted) or nasal (velum lax)?

(3) Which articulating organs are employed in making the sound: lips, teeth, tongue-tip, -blade, -front, -back? What portion of the roof of the mouth is involved?

(4) What is the nature of the articulation: stop, continuant (fricative or non-fricative), affricate, or glide?

All consonants may be described in terms of these criteria. For example, [f] is a voiceless, oral, labio-dental (lip-teeth) fricative. That is, the vocal lips are open, the velum is retracted, and the breath stream escapes in a continuous flow between the upper lip and the lower teeth. In the same fashion, the sound [g] might be called a voiced, oral, velar stop. The advantages of such a classification are obvious; with a little training you will be able to describe any sound which you make, and conversely, you should be able to produce a sound from a description of the processes which go into its production.

EXERCISE V

1. Take the list of voiceless consonants which you made in connection with Question 2, Exercise IV, and further classify them into *stops*, *fricatives*, and *affricates*.
2. Take the list of voiced consonants which you made in connection with Question 3, Exercise IV, and classify these into *stops*, *fricatives*, and *affricates*.
3. From a list of all the English consonant sounds, subtract those which you have already classified in the two preceding questions. Those sounds which remain will consist of some glides, some oral continuants, and the nasals. Divide the remaining sounds among these categories and complete the classification.
4. Are the English nasal sounds stops or continuants? Try to make a bilabial nasal stop; a velar nasal stop.
5. Are the glides voiced or voiceless? Oral or nasal?

6. STOPS OR PLOSIVES

The English language has three pairs of stops. One pair [p, b] is bilabial, *i.e.* made with the two lips; one pair [t, d] is linguo-alveolar, *i.e.* made with the tongue tip against the teeth ridge; the third pair [k, g] may be palatal or velar, *i.e.* made with the tongue-back against the hard or the soft palate. Of each pair, one member is voiceless, the other is voiced.[5]

[5] A glottal stop, produced by the complete closure and rapid opening of the vocal lips, also may occur in English, and is found regularly in certain dialects. The symbol for this sound is [ˀ].

There are two phases in the production of every stop: the closure and the opening. As explained in section 5, p. 24, the closure is made by forming an air-tight pocket behind which the breath stream is condensed. This air-tight position is held momentarily, and then is suddenly released. The resulting outburst of the condensed air which has been collected while the closed position was being maintained gives a slightly explosive character to the sound. Accordingly, some phoneticians call these sounds *plosives*.

Notice, however, that both closure and opening need not necessarily be present in every stop which is uttered in actual speech. When a stop occurs finally, as in the word *stop* itself, the opening or plosion may not be heard, especially if a pause immediately follows the final stop. When a stop occurs at the beginning of a word, as in *pan*, *tan*, *can*, we hear only the release or plosion, because the sound has been initiated from a closed mouth position. When the stops are intervocalic (between vowels), as in *rapid*, *city*, *making*, both closure and opening are audible.

When two stops occur in succession, as the [dk] combination in *woodcraft*, instead of successive closures and releases for each of them, there is a tongue-tip alveolar closure for [d], then a shift to the tongue-back velar position for [k], and the release or plosion is from the latter position. In such a combination as [td] in *outdo*, where no shift of the tongue is necessary to transfer from the first stop to the second, the vocal lips are open when the closure is made, but they have partially closed at the time of the plosion.

Notice also that a doubled *b*, *d*, *g*, *k*, *p*, or *t* in the spelling of a word does not necessarily indicate two stops or a doubled stop, phonetically considered. There is no essential difference between the medial stops in the words *ditty* and *city*, the spelling notwithstanding.[6] In fact, even in such word groups as *black cap* or *ripe pears*, there is but a single closure and opening for the [k] and [p] sounds. The [k] in *black cap* differs from that in *blacker* or *black out* only in that the closure is held for a longer period of time; it is a lengthened rather than a doubled stop. We shall be more concerned with length when we come to study the vowels, but length in any sound is indicated in phonetic transcription by means of two dots following the character; thus, *black cap* = [blækːæp].

Two other phonetic phenomena must be observed in connection with the stops. The first of these may be called *intrusion*. In such words as *length*, *something*, *fence*, which require a shift from a nasal to a voiceless fricative, it is not uncommon for many speakers to insert whatever voiceless stop is made in the same position as the nasal, between it and the following fricative: [lɛŋkθ, sʌmpθɪŋ, fɛnts]. In the word *length*, for example, the position of the vocal organs for the sounds [ŋ] and [θ] is indicated in columns (1) and (3) below:

	(1) [ŋ]	(2) [k]	(3) [θ]
glottis	partially closed	*open*	open
velum	lax	*retracted*	retracted
tongue	-back on velum	*-back on velum*	-tip between front teeth

[6] Often a single [t] between vowels, or between a vowel and [ɚ] or [l], is so brief in duration that the glottis scarcely has time to open and close again, and moreover, very little aspiration is heard. Compare a

It is evident, from columns (1) and (3), that the transition from [ŋ] to [*θ*] requires three important changes in the organs of articulation: (*a*) the glottis must open; (*b*) the velum must retract; (*c*) the tongue must move forward. If all these changes occurred at precisely the same instant, there would, in all probability, be no intrusion of a [k] or of any other sound. But generally the vocal apparatus does not make these shifts with perfect co-ordination; frequently, one or two of the changes necessary for such a transition take place a fraction of a second before the others. Assuming, for example, that the glottis opens and that the velum retracts an instant before the change of tongue position, we should then have a situation as outlined in column (2), which is obviously that of the closure for [k]. When the tongue is then moved forward to the interdental position, a slight [k] plosion results.

Under certain other conditions, a medial consonant may be *syncopated* or omitted from pronunciation. For example, in Modern English, the *t* in *glisten* is no longer pronounced, although there is no question that this sound was present so long as there was a vowel of some length between the *t* and the *n*. The reason for the disappearance of the *t* becomes apparent upon observing the movements of the tongue necessary for making the [stn] combination. For the [s], the tongue-tip would be in very light contact with the alveolar ridge; for [t], a firm contact is required for the closure, a withdrawal for the opening; for [n], the

rapid pronunciation of *ditty* with *did he*, or of *latter* with *ladder*. Some phoneticians classify such a *d*-like *t* as a voiced *t* and transcribe it as [t̬]: [læt̬ɚ]. ˬ is the diacritic used to indicate voicing.

tongue would again have to be in firm contact with the alveolar ridge. Very likely because of economy of effort, we tend to make a single transition from loose to firm contact suffice for the three movements just outlined; the result is, of course, the omission of the [t] sound, as the tongue withdrawal necessary for the plosion has been eliminated.

ADDITIONAL READING:

Jones, *Outline of English Phonetics*, Chapter XVII.
Kenyon, *American Pronunciation*, pp. 117–26.
Webster's New International Dictionary, Guide to Pronunciation, §§ 97–9, 101, 111–13, 138, 164, 205, 206, 230–32.

EXERCISE VI

1. (*a*) Transcribe the following list of words as they would sound if spoken conversationally. In transcribing the word list at the beginning of every lesson, you must be careful to record each word as you customarily pronounce it in connected conversation. In doubtful cases frame a sentence using the word in question, so that the pronunciation may be free from any taint of unnaturalness or undue stress. Above all, record the pronunciation you use, not the one you think you should use.

1. pose	11. lobbed	21. nymph
2. cause	12. flag pole	22. mustn't
3. dumb	13. black dirt	23. thistle
4. wipe	14. note book	24. dense
5. lad	15. hold tight	25. marked
6. break	16. head rest	26. played
7. eager	17. head dress	27. famed
8. happy	18. stop pat	28. laughed
9. mettle	19. milk can	29. baited
10. medal	20. warmth	30. waded

(*b*) Transcribe the following passage as you think you would normally utter it:

Stop thief! That man took my pocketbook. Chase him and get it away from him. Will you please call the police? No, there wasn't much in it except some small change and my driver's license. I banked all my currency yesterday.

2. Describe in detail the actions of the speech organs involved in the production of each of the following sounds: [p, b, t, d, k, g]. For example, the phonetic description for [b] would be somewhat as follows: The glottis is partially closed, the velum is retracted, the lips are closed, fully stopping and condensing the breath stream for a moment. Then the lips are opened, allowing the condensed breath to escape with a slight explosion.

3. The detailed description illustrated in the previous question may be put into a convenient short form, which we shall call a phonetic definition. The phonetic definition for [b] is: Voiced bilabial stop. Give the corresponding definitions for the other stops. You may wish to make a regular practice of consulting the list of phonetic definitions on pages 76–78 in connection with each of these exercises.

4. Does the term *stop* describe precisely the same action of the vocal organs in respect to condensation and explosion in the words numbered 1, 2, and 3 (Question 1 *a*) that is implied in Nos. 4, 5, and 6? What can you say about the stops in Nos. 7 and 8 in connection with this same problem? How does the stop in No. 9 compare with that in No. 10? Point out the peculiarity of the stop combinations in Nos. 11–15.

5. Do you observe any difference between the point of contact for [k] in *break* and *cost?* Between *key* and *coo?* Can you give a reason for this? Does observing the tongue positions for [i] and [u] when pronounced in isolation help you frame an explanation? Would the term *palatal* or

velar be a more accurate description for the [k] in *key?* Frame similar pairs of words containing [g] sounds which would illustrate the same phenomenon.

6. Do the doubled consonant characters in Nos. 8, 9, and 11 actually indicate doubled consonants considered phonetically? How does the [d] in No. 16 differ from that in No. 17?

7. What consonant tends to appear after the [m] in Nos. 20 and 21? Using as a pattern the explanation of the intrusion of [k] in the word *length*, outline the phonetic processes giving rise to the intrusions in these words. Can you now explain why, four or five centuries ago, *tremble* was frequently spelled *tremle* and *thunder* was normally spelled *thunor?* How is the word *handsome* often pronounced? Why? Give an explanation for the omission of the [t] in *often*.

8. What is the pronunciation of *-ed* in No. 11 and in Nos. 25–30? Determine the phonetic value of this inflection in the past tense forms of any other regular verbs that may occur to you. Draw up a series of statements which will explain this variation on phonetic grounds. To what inflection of the verb other than the simple past tense would your series of statements apply? What does this suggest about the necessity of phonetic descriptions for grammatical phenomena?

7. Fricatives

There are four pairs of fricatives in English: the labiodentals [f, v], the interdentals [θ, ð], the alveolars [s, z], and the alveolopalatals [ʃ, ʒ]. As with the stops, one member of each pair is voiceless, the other is voiced.

The labiodental (lip-teeth) fricatives are produced by allowing the air to escape between the upper front teeth and lower lip. For the interdentals, the tongue-tip is thrust between the teeth. The [s] and [z] sounds are made either with the tongue-tip at the alveolar ridge or behind the lower front teeth. If the tongue-tip is in the latter position, the breath stream escapes between the tongue blade and the upper alveolar ridge. The sounds [ʃ] and [ʒ] are characterized by the escape of air through a lengthened channel rather than at a precise point, which gives them their particular quality. Compare, for example, the sounds of air escaping through a tire valve with the core removed, with the escape of air through a pin-prick in a toy balloon (assuming, of course, that the balloon has been punctured when deflated). To make [ʃ] and [ʒ], the tongue-tip is fairly well back on the alveolar ridge, and the blade of the tongue is placed somewhat more lightly against the extreme front portion of the hard palate; this forms the lengthened trough or channel, *alveolopalatal* in position, through which the breath stream must escape.

Such words as *special* and *nation* suggest that the [ʃ] sound has a variety of spellings; to understand this, we must pay some attention to the history of this sound. If you will pronounce in rapid order the words *force you*, it is almost impossible to avoid saying [fɔɚʃu]. The reason for this development is almost immediately apparent. The tongue position for [j], the initial sound of *you*, is just behind that for [ʃ], that is to say, the blade and front are loosely palatal. In transferring from [s] to [j], the tongue-tip remains at the alveolar ridge and acts as a pivot for the blade to swing upward. In so doing, it forms the lengthened channel which is the particular configuration necessary for the production of [ʃ].

Originally, such words as *special* and *nation* were trisyllabic, with the heaviest stress on the last syllable: [ˌspɛsɪˈɑl, ˌnɑsɪˈuːn], as they had been pronounced in French, the language from which they had been borrowed. In the course of time, as with other French loan words, the stress shifted to the first syllable, conforming to the English pattern, resulting also in neutralization of the final vowel: [ˈspɛsɪəl, ˈnɑsɪən].[7] Next, the [ɪ], preceding a lightly stressed vowel, became the glide [j], collapsing the original three syllables into two, after which the [sj] combination developed into [ʃ] in the manner just described.

In connection with the stops, some attention was given to the intrusion of sounds. In certain situations sounds may also be added at the end of a word; when they are, we speak of them as *excrescent*. Words ending in [s], for example, not infrequently add an excrescent [t]; this has occurred in *against*, earlier *agains*, *amongst*, earlier *amongs*, *betwixt*, earlier *betwix*, and in British English *whilst*. For [s], as for [t], the tongue-tip is at the alveolar ridge, although the contact is normally firmer for [t]. If, however, when phonation ceases, the tongue is withdrawn rapidly even from a light contact alveolar position, there will be a slightly plosive sound.

The fricatives offer some further illustrations of the way in which the English language employs phonetic devices to accomplish grammatical purposes. In a num-

[7] Note that in the phonetic transcription, the stress marks *precede* the syllable to which they are applied: [ˈspɛʃəl, ˌʌnˈlɑɪklɪ]. Primary or heavy stress is indicated by a vertical stroke above the line; secondary stress is indicated by a vertical stroke below the line.

ber of words ending in fricative sounds, we distinguish noun from verb, or adjective from verb, according to whether the fricative is voiced or voiceless.

1. abuse	noun [əbɪus]	verb [əbɪuz]
2. close	adjective [klos]	verb [kloz]
3. loath(e)	adjective [loθ]	verb [loð]
4. grief, grieve	noun [grif]	verb [griv]

Possibly twenty-five words in the English language regularly maintain this type of distinction (see Webster's *New International Dictionary*, Guide to Pronunciation, §§ 220, 235) and certain others maintain it only in part of the English-speaking world.

Stress may be employed to exercise a similar function in plurisyllabic words, where the verb will have heavy stress on the second syllable, the noun on the first.

convert	noun ['kɑnvɚt]	verb [kən'vɝt]
digest	noun ['daɪdʒɛst]	verb [dɪ'dʒɛst]
incline	noun ['ɪnklaɪn]	verb [ɪn'klaɪn]

At the same time, the position of the stress may affect the quality of a fricative, and when stress is employed as a means of indicating functional differences as well, we find such related pairs as: *dissolve* [dɪ'zɑlv], *dissolute* ['dɪsəˌlut]; *exert* [ɪg'zɝt], *exercise* ['ɛksɚˌsaɪz], where a variation in voice quality parallels a variation in stress. The explanation for this seems to be that voiceless pronunciations require a greater expenditure of energy than do the voiced. Remember that initial and final fricatives in such regularly lightly stressed words as *the*, *that*, *is*, *has* are almost invariably voiced. Also, compare *used* as a verbal auxiliary with its pronunciation as a full or independent verb:

I used to go. [just]
I used it three years. [juzd]

Note that *have* in such a phrase as *We have to eat* also devoices the final fricative to [hæf].

ADDITIONAL READING:

Jones, *Outline of English Phonetics*, pp. 165–78.
Kenyon, *American Pronunciation*, pp. 126–41.
Webster's *New International Dictionary*, Guide to Pronunciation, §§ 137, 217–29, 233–6, 259, 265–8.

EXERCISE VII

1. (*a*) Transcribe the following list of words as they would sound in actual conversation.

1. fill	11. patient	21. knees
2. phantasy	12. associate (*verb*)	22. places
3. vivid	13. associate (*noun*)	23. leeches
4. faith	14. censure	24. screens
5. southern	15. device	25. garages
6. science	16. devise	26. noses
7. conscience	17. execute	27. cloaks
8. wisdom	18. executive	28. brushes
9. mirage	19. luxury	29. mobs
10. azure	20. luxurious	30. cuffs

(*b*) Transcribe the following passage as you think you would normally speak it:

How many courses are you taking this semester? I elected five, but one of my classes meets only once a week. All my classes are in different buildings though, and I have to rush from one to another, so I'm late most of the time. It's good exercise, especially since I never exert myself in any other way. It's all in getting used to it.

2. Describe the action of the speech organs in producing each of the following sounds: [f, v, θ, ð, s, z, ʃ, ʒ]. Give the phonetic definition appropriate to each of these sounds. What is the meaning of the term *fricative?* What more commonly used word has the same first syllable?

3. Which of the fricatives does not occur initially in Modern English?

4. The words *vision* and *measure* were once pronounced [ˌvɪzɪˈuːn] and [ˌmɛzɪˈuər]. Can you reconstruct the various stages in their development which resulted in their present pronunciation? Does the rapid and connected pronunciation of the two words *praise you* throw any light on the problem? What may be concluded about the correctness, propriety, or necessity of retaining the [s] pronunciation in No. 14, or in such a word as *appreciate?* Do your replies to the preceding questions throw any light on the differences between the pronunciation of *sc* in Nos. 6 and 7?

5. What is the phonetic difference between Nos. 15 and 16? What grammatical purpose does this serve? Answer the same question in respect to possible forms of the words *house*, *mouth*, and *leaf*. What are your pronunciations of *rise* (noun) and *grease* (verb)? Are these in keeping with the phonetic pattern indicated by the preceding pairs of words? What information does Webster's *New International Dictionary* give you concerning the last two words?

6. Describe phonetically the variations in the pronunciation of *x* in Nos. 17–20. In your transcription of each of these words, place an accent mark *before* the syllable receiving the greatest amount of stress. What is the apparent cause for the variation in consonant quality in these words? The adverb *off* and the preposition *of* were once the same word, pronounced with final [f]. Can you account for the present differentiation in the quality of the final fricative?

7. What is the pronunciation of -(*e*)*s* in Nos. 21–30?

Determine the pronunciation of this inflection in the plurals of any other nouns that may occur to you. Construct a 'law' or general rule which will account for the distribution of these pronunciations upon phonetic grounds. Might your observations for noun plurals be applied to any other inflection of the noun? To any inflection in the verb? How does this set of rules compare with that established in connection with Question 8, Exercise 6?

8. What frequently happens when you try to pronounce the plural forms of *mouth* and *moth* with some rapidity? Explain why, in terms of the movements of the articulating organs. Can you employ these observations in accounting for the development of our present pronunciation of *clothes?* From what singular noun would both *cloths* and *clothes* seem to be derived? Verify your guess by looking up the derivation of *clothes* in the Oxford English Dictionary.

9. Account, on phonetic grounds, for such pronunciations as [wʌnst] for *once* and [əkrɔst] for *across*.

10. How would you transcribe the word groups *half fed, these zones?* What phonetic phenomenon is illustrated here?

11. What sound substitutions may be said to comprise the chief bases of lisping? What further substitutions for fricatives are frequently characteristic of baby talk? What do these substitutions signify in terms of the movements of the speech organs?

8. Non-Fricative Continuants and Affricates

Three of the four English non-fricative continuants are nasals. These are made with the same series of lip and tongue positions as are the stops: bilabial [m], tongue-point alveolar [n], and tongue-back velar [ŋ].

The remaining non-fricative continuant is [l], also a tongue-point alveolar, but one which acquires its distinctive character from the escape of the breath stream at one or both sides of the tongue. It is classified, therefore, as a *lateral* continuant. Although the tongue-point has a set position for the [l] sound, the rest of the tongue is free to assume various positions, depending upon the character of the adjacent sounds and the position (initial, medial, or final) in the word. The type of resonance found in such a word as *leek* [lik] is called clear, and the sound is classified as a clear *l*. A sound with the resonance of a back vowel, as in *toll* [tol], is described as dark.

The affricates have already been defined (p. 24) as stops which open so slowly as to give the impression of a stop followed by the corresponding fricative, and indeed this impression is fortified by the compound symbols which many phonetic alphabets, including ours, employ for the English affricates: [tʃ, dʒ]. Note, however, that in pronouncing *flat shoe* [flæt ʃu] the tongue shifts from the point alveolar position for [t] to the point and blade alveolopalatal position for [ʃ], whereas the affricate in *may chew* is produced entirely with the tongue-point and -blade at the alveolopalatal position.

A phonetic phenomenon which frequently occurs in connection with the nasals is *assimilation*, the full or partial conformation of one sound to a neighboring sound. Illustrations of this process are afforded by Modern English *ant*, earlier *amet* [æmɛt, æmət]. When the unstressed [ə] disappeared, leaving the sound [m] and [t] in juxtaposition [æmt], the bilabial [m] developed into alveolar [n] because of the influence of the following [t], also alveolar. Conversely, earlier *henep* became *hemp;* here the bilabial [p] changed the preceding *n* into a bilabial [m]. Even in present English, such a pronunciation as [pæŋkek] *pancake*, shows the influence of the velar *k* upon the preceding sound.

A somewhat different type of assimilation was discussed in the preceding section in connection with the development of [ʃ] from an earlier [sj] combination, as in *nation*. A corresponding change can be observed in connection with the affricates, where [tj], rapidly uttered, often becomes [tʃ] *e.g. can't you* [kæntʃu]. Here again the shift of the tongue from the alveolar to palatal position has resulted in the establishment of the alveolopalatal affricate. Historically this may be illustrated by the successive stages in the pronunciations of the words *feature* and *soldier*, both originally trisyllabic, with heavy stress on the first and third syllables. First they lost their final heavy stress, becoming disyllabic; the [ɪ] became [j]; finally, the stop and following [j] combined to produce the appropriate affricate:

'fitɪ'ur > 'fitɪɚ > 'fitjɚ > fitʃɚ
'soldɪ'ur > 'soldɪɚ > 'soldjɚ > soldʒɚ

We are ready at this point to discuss a problem of transcription which could not be broached until you had a fairly complete knowledge of the processes involved in making the various consonants. This is the question of the unstressed vowels in such words as *mutton*, *reason*, *nation*, *bottle*, and *buckle*. Note that our system of spelling has preserved vowel characters between the two final consonants in the first three words, but not in the last two. Yet if we take into account the position of the speech organs for making the sounds [t] and [n], as in *mutton*, it is clear that both of these require virtually the same tongue position — the point on the alveolar ridge. Ordinarily the tongue is not withdrawn from the alveolar ridge in transferring from [t] to [n]; the dropping of the velum, causing the transition from oral to nasal breath escape, is all that takes place within the oral cavity (it is necessary, of course, for the glottis to become partially closed). Accordingly, it is quite proper to transcribe this word as [mʌtn]. In *reason*, almost the same situation prevails; for [z] the tongue is already at the alveolar ridge, though the contact may be light, so again [rizn] is entirely appropriate to the facts. With *nation*, however, the tongue must shift upward and forward from the alveolopalatal position, allowing time usually for the intervention of a very brief vowel while the transition is being made: [neʃən].

Note also that the [t] and [l] in *bottle* are homorganic (made in the same position), whereas in *buckle* a shift forward must again be made, often allowing time for the insertion of an unstressed vowel. Hence, [bɑtl, bʌkəl].

With a little practice you will be able to train your ear sufficiently to catch the presence or absence of these very short unstressed vowels, and you should use your knowledge of the way in which the sounds are made to reinforce your observations in this particular.

Additional Reading:

Jones, *Outline of English Phonetics*, pp. 145–50, 154–64.
Kenyon, *American Pronunciation*, pp. 141–51.
Webster's *New International Dictionary*, Guide to Pronunciation, §§ 104, 139, 161, 167–75, 177–8.

Exercise VIII

1. (*a*) Transcribe the following list of words as they would sound in conversational speech:

1. button	11. monkey	21. little
2. vacation	12. conclave	22. not sure
3. mineral	13. concrete	23. moisture
4. longing	14. concord	24. heard you
5. longer	15. incongruous	25. verging
6. strength	16. pumpkin	26. creature
7. range	17. steeple	27. nature
8. engulf	18. knuckle	28. verdure
9. distinct	19. halt	29. grandeur
10. junction	20. least	30. individual

(*b*) Transcribe the following passage as you think you would normally speak it:

> What are you going to do now? Don't you want to go down town? There's a feature picture on at the Majestic. If you can't leave right away, maybe we can go to the second show.

2. Describe the action of the speech organs in making the sounds [m, n, ŋ, l, tʃ, dʒ]. Give the appropriate phonetic definition for each sound.

3. What sound is ordinarily associated with the *ng* spelling? How many sounds are represented by the letters *ng* in Nos. 4–8? Can the [ŋ] sound occur in every possible position (initial, final, medial) in a word?

4. Are the [l] sounds in Nos. 17–21 identical in quality of resonance? If not, which of the sounds are 'clear' and which are 'dark'? Can you explain the occurrence of each with reference to the adjacent sounds?

5. Observe carefully your practice in forming the medial consonants in Nos. 22–5. Are the two members of

each pair identical in nature? If not, explain how they differ. Make a voiceless bilabial affricate; a voiced bilabial affricate; the corresponding velar affricates.

6. What is the sound represented by the letter *n* in Nos. 9–11? Explain what happens here on phonetic grounds. What name is given to the process which is illustrated? Is your practice in respect to the pronunciation of the final *n* in the *con-* prefix, Nos. 12–15, consistent or otherwise? If it is not, can you see any reason for the inconsistency?

7. Many speakers give an [ŋ] pronunciation to the first nasal in *pumpkin*. Can you account for its development? Trace the successive stages in the change from the standard English *heaven* to the Negro dialect form *heb'm*. How might the word *can* in Question 1 (*b*) be pronounced? Why?

8. When a speaker says *goin'* instead of *going*, he is often accused of 'dropping his *g*'s.' Is this an exact statement of the phonetic difference between the two pronunciations?

9. What sound substitutions are ordinarily made by speakers who have a cold? In the light of the phonetic character of these substitutions, is it correct to say that a speaker with a cold 'talks through his nose'? Explain.

10. Some dictionaries and teachers of elocution and diction appear to insist upon the pronunciation [tɪu] and [dɪu] in *literature*, *education*, as well as for the words numbered 26–30 in Question 1 (*a*). From your knowledge of phonetic processes, would you say that this insistence was justified?

11. Review your practice in respect to indicating the final syllables of Nos. 1, 2, 3, 17, 18. Justify each of your transcriptions. In view of this, how would you transcribe *often*, *oven*, *chasm*, *chicken?*

9. The Glides and [h]

Although the sound [h] is most often classified as a fricative, it has certain features which make it more advantageous to consider it along with the glide sounds. It is voiceless, of course; it can be produced as long as there is sufficient air supply. At the same time it is characterized by a friction-like quality which proceeds from the outrush of air through the glottis. These are the grounds for its classification as a voiceless glottal fricative.

Two characteristics of the [h] sound serve to set it distinctly apart from the other fricatives. First, with the help of a mirror and small flashlight, observe your lip and tongue positions in pronouncing the series: *heel*, *hale*, *ham*, *hard*, *haunt*, *hope*, *hook*. Note that so far as lip and tongue position is concerned, there is no set configuration of these organs for [h]. They merely assume the position for the following vowel, even before phonation begins.

The second peculiarity of the [h] lies in the positions in a word in which it may occur. From the series of words just observed, it is clear that (1) it may occur in initial position before a vowel. From such words as *Jonah*, *behave*, *John*, we can further conclude (2) that although it may be spelled, [h] is not pronounced when final; (3) that it may occur medially before vowels, (4) but not before consonants. It is possible to condense these four observations into a single statement, to the effect that [h] occurs only initially and medially before vowels.

A final characteristic of the [h] sound has already been made clear in the course of our transcriptions of connected speech: initial [h] in lightly stressed words tends not to be pronounced. This is illustrated by such forms as [ɪz] and [ɚ] for unstressed [hɪz] and [hɝ].[8]

The glides proper have already been defined (p. 25) as sounds whose characteristic quality arises not from a single position of the articulating organs, but rather from their shifting from one position to another. In pronouncing the [w] sound in *wet*, the speaker begins with the tongue high in the mouth, bunched toward the back, and the lips rounded; the transition from this position to that of the following vowel [ɛ] produces the sound which we recognize as [w]. The high back position of the tongue and rounded lips constitute the normal configuration for the [u] sound. Even if, as in *woo*, the [u] sound is to follow the glide, notice that the tongue and lips will assume a starting position somewhat higher and closer than is normally demanded by [u].

The [w] sound may accordingly be defined as a voiced labiovelar glide, the term *labiovelar* suggesting the part that the lips and high back tongue position play in its production. However, since the starting point for [w] is really a vowel rather than a consonant position, but since the characteristic quality of the sound is not, like that of a vowel, capable of continued production, [w] is frequently classified as a semi-vowel, and more completely defined as a voiced labiovelar semi-vowel.

An examination of such words as *wake*, *wring*, *always*, *jowl*, *saw*, *grew*, *sow*, *cow* will indicate that the conclusions concerning the positions in a word in which [h] may occur

[8] Medial [h] also tends to disappear in certain situations: *exhaust* [ɪgzɔst], *vehement* [viəmənt]. For a discussion of French loan words with initial *h*, *heir*, *honest*, *honor*, *humble*, etc., see page 251.

are equally applicable to [w]; the sound occurs only initially and medially before vowels, that is to say in a pre-vocalic position.

The sound [ʍ], as it is ordinarily made in American English combines the glottal affrication of [h] with the labiovelar opening of the [w]. It is voiceless at the outset, when tongue and lips are still in the high back round position, but soon after the transition to the next sound begins, voice is also introduced, a process which might be illustrated graphically by [hw].

Like [h], the sound [ʍ] tends not to appear in unstressed situations, where [w] is frequently substituted for it. Compare ˈ*where can he be?* [ʍɛɚ] with ˈ*that's where it is!* [wɛɚ]. There is also some difference between British and American practice in respect to [ʍ] in such words as *whine*, *whether*, *whale*, Southern British tending to employ [w] to a greater extent.

Just as [w] represents a downward opening glide from the position for [u], so the sound [j] has [i] as a starting point. Compare [iɛt] with [jɛt]. Since the tongue is high and near the hard palate for [i], and since the shifting of the tongue rather than the lips seems to contribute most to the particular quality of this sound, it may be defined as a voiced linguopalatal glide or semi-vowel.

Consonantal [r] is also produced by a shifting of the tongue, but in this instance the glide is from an inverted or retroflex position of the tongue. Where [r] occurs between vowels, a movement to the inverted position is first necessary to put the tongue in place for the down glide. Note the acoustical difference of the [r] in *run* as compared with *foreign*, and observe the difference in tongue movement with the aid of flashlight and mirror. Like the other glides, consonantal [r] occurs only in prevocalic position; the sound [ɚ], final in *car* and *butter*, and preconsonantal in *ford* and *bark*, is produced with an upward movement of the tongue, and for a number of reasons is more conveniently classified as a vowel. Consonantal [r] may be defined as a voiced retroflex tongue glide.[9]

Additional Reading:

Jones, *Outline of English Phonetics*, pp. 179–88, 190–96.
Kenyon, *American Pronunciation*, pp. 137–41, 152–61.
Webster's *New International Dictionary*, Guide to Pronunciation, §§ 44 (8), 45, 149, 150, 211–16, 255–8, 261–4.

Exercise IX

1. (*a*) Transcribe the following list of words and phrases as they would sound in conversational speech:

1. Utah	11. once	21. onion
2. behoove	12. wretch	22. familiar
3. huge	13. awkward	23. uniform
4. John	14. which	24. ready
5. warrant	15. whole	25. fair
6. swagger	16. whether	26. guard
7. blow	17. who	27. pour
8. grew	18. whooping cough	28. orate
9. anguish	19. whine	29. martyr
10. choir	20. yawn	30. rhetoric

[9] A more complete analysis of this sound would have to recognize many different varieties, among which are the fricative type as in *train*, and the flap or tap *r* of British English *very* (often spelled *veddy* by writers wishing to suggest this type of speech).

(*b*) Transcribe the following passage as you think you would normally speak it:

'You didn't tell me about John's accident.' 'Why, I didn't realize that you knew him.' 'Yes, I met him when he was working at that summer camp near Durham.' 'Well, I don't know who was with him or when it happened. He ran off the highway into a drainage ditch. I don't think he had been working late, so he couldn't have fallen asleep at the wheel. Anyway, he has some bad cuts on his hand and his head, and a welt across his face.'

2. Describe the action of the speech organs in making the sounds [h, w, ʍ, j, r]. What is the phonetic definition appropriate to each sound?

3. Examine the words in Question 1 (*b*) that begin with *h*. In how many instances is the *h* present in pronunciation? In the light of the discussion of the [h] sound in the preceding paragraphs, be able to justify your transcriptions.

4. In times past, certain phoneticians classified [h] as a glide. In the light of your observations and your knowledge of this sound, what reasons can you adduce for and against such a classification?

5. The sound [ʍ] is at times defined as a voiceless *w*. Is this an accurate description of your pronunciation of the sound? Can you see any relationship between the mechanism of producing the initial sound of *Hugh* or *huge* and that required for [ʍ]?

6. Judging from Nos. 20–23, what are your conclusions about the positions in which the sound [j] may occur? Can you think of any words in which [j] occurs before the sound [i]? What can be said about the starting point for [j] in these sounds?

7. What would you assume about the British and eastern American loss or retention of *r* in Nos. 24–30? In which words would it be retained? What is substituted

for it when it is 'lost'? Formulate a rule for the pronunciation of *r* in these regions. Is consonantal [r] affected by this regional variation?

8. From your knowledge of the mechanism for the production of glide sounds, does it seem reasonable that these sounds as a class should not occur in final position? Why? Taking into consideration the fact that the tongue position for consonants is generally higher than that for vowels, does it seem reasonable that glide sounds should occur only in pre-vocalic position? Why?

10. Classification of Vowels

Criteria for the classification of consonants included (1) the condition of the vocal lips, (2) the position of the velum, (3) the nature of the escape of the breath stream, and (4) the position of the organs of articulation in the mouth. In respect to the first three of these, vowels are all alike: they are all voiced, for practical purposes they are all oral, and they are all continuants. Obviously, then, a new system of classifying the fourteen vowels of our English must be sought.

Although it is difficult, and indeed unnecessary for our purpose, to draw a scientific line of demarcation between vowels and consonants, it is true that vowels generally have a lower tongue position than that required for consonants. Their tone quality is dependent upon the particular conformation of the resonance chamber, rather than upon friction attending the complete or nearly complete stoppage of the air passage. The oral resonance chamber may be modified in a number of different ways, but those which seem to influence most profoundly the quality of vowel sounds are:

(1) The height of the jaw.
(2) The position of the tongue.
(3) The configuration of the lips.

If the sounds [i, e, æ] are uttered in succession, it will be noticed that the jaw, and with it the tongue, assumes a lower position for [e] than for [i], and that it drops again when [æ] is pronounced. The series [u, o, ɔ] will also result in successive dropping of the jaw as each new sound is spoken. In classifying and describing vowel sounds, three degrees of jaw height are recognized:

(1) High — the level usually assumed for [i] and [u].
(2) Mid — the level usually assumed for [e] and [o].
(3) Low — the level usually assumed for [æ] and [ɔ].

In pronouncing the series [i, u, i], it may be observed with the aid of a small flashlight and mirror that in transferring from [i] to [u] the tongue moves backward, and that when the change from [u] to [i] is made, the raised part of the tongue again resumes its position in the front of the mouth. A similar shift [o, e, o], will move the high point or concentration of the tongue from the back to the front and back again. It is convenient to recognize three degrees of tongue position also:

(1) Front — as for [i, e, æ].
(2) Back — as for [u, o, ɔ].
(3) Central — representing an intermediate position between front and back.

Pronounce the series [i, u, i] before a mirror and observe the movement of the lips. In shifting from [i] to [u], the lips assume a closely rounded position; in returning from [u] to [i], they are again spread wide. The series [o, e, o] will illustrate the spreading necessary for the shift to [e], and then the rounding required for the return to [o]. In terms of lip configuration, vowels are classified as *round* or *unround*. If you are uncertain about the lip configuration for any particular vowel, place a pencil between and across the teeth and try to make that vowel. If it is rounded, [u] for example, you will feel pressure of the corners of the mouth against the pencil; an unround vowel, [i], will not produce this sensation.

By combining the descriptive criteria just discussed, it is possible to suggest the normal configuration of jaw, tongue, and lips for each of the vowels. For example: [i] is made with the jaw high, the tongue advanced, the lips unrounded; thus it may be characterized or defined as a high, front, unround vowel. A low position of the jaw, retraction of the tongue, and rounded lips are characteristic of [ɔ], which is accordingly defined as a low, back, round vowel. The characteristic positions for the English vowels may be suggested by the diagram on page 52, the rounded vowels being enclosed in parentheses.

It will be observed from this diagram that the divisions representing the high front, the mid front, and the high back positions contain two vowels each. To distinguish between the otherwise similar members of these pairs, we may classify [ɪ], [ɛ], and [ʊ] as lower high-front, lower mid-front, and lower high-back respectively. (The mid-central category, containing four vowels, will be treated in detail later.) There are, indeed, certain other differences between such pairs as [i] and [ɪ], but we may, for the purposes of our classification, recognize the difference in height as the most significant.

In the diagram of the positions for the various vowels, a trapezium instead of a rectangle was purposely chosen to suggest that such terms as *high*, *low*, *front* are essentially relative in nature. The term *high* in respect to the front

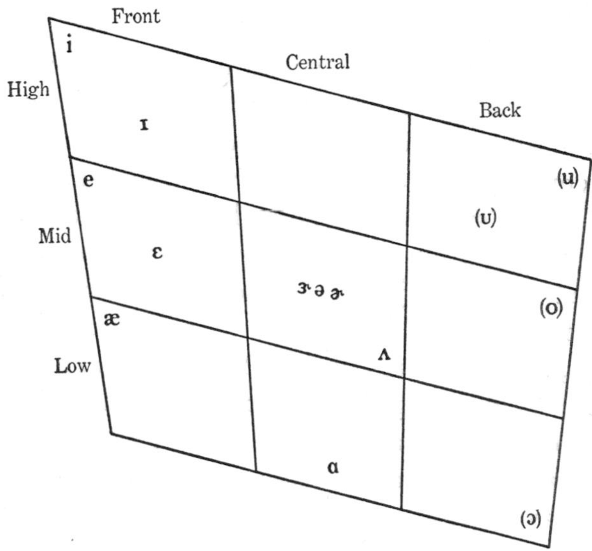

vowels actually indicates a somewhat higher position than it does when applied to the back vowels; moreover, the tongue is farther advanced for a high-front vowel than for a low-front vowel.

It is true also that this systematization by no means tells the whole story of vowel production. It neglects, among other things, the extremely important part which the pharynx may play in modifying the resonance chamber, thus influencing the quality of the sound produced. Moreover, not all speakers pronounce the same vowel with exactly the same tongue and jaw positions. It is possible, for example, to produce recognizable varieties of both the sounds [æ] (low-front unround) and [u] (high-back round) with a pencil held between the teeth, assuring a high jaw and unround lip position. That is to say, in both cases, compensatory adjustments are made by the tongue, pharynx, and the cheek walls. Yet, the classification presented here has been found to be useful both for the purpose of describing the normal production of the sounds of present-day English and for understanding the changes in pronunciation which have taken place from one period of the English language to another.

Additional Reading:

Jones, *Outline of English Phonetics*, pp. 23–35, 36–40.
Kenyon, *American Pronunciation*, pp. 60–65.
Webster's *New International Dictionary*, Guide to Pronunciation, §§ 27–35.

11. Back Vowels

The relative height of the four back vowels [u, ʊ, o, ɔ] has already been indicated in the vowel diagram, p. 52. Observe that they are all produced with the lips rounded, the rounding being markedly closer for the high vowels than for the mid and low varieties.

Some phonetic alphabets provide characters for two low-back vowels, [ɔ] and [ɒ], the first of these being considered higher low-back. For example, the vowel of British English *water* has a much more *o*-like quality than that which is heard in such words as *hot* and *fog*. In contrast, General American has but one variety of low-back vowel, therefore it did not seem advisable to provide two symbols; [ɔ] was chosen in preference to [ɒ] as the symbol for our single low-back vowel because it may be written more quickly and easily. In General American the low-back vowel is generally very low in position, which explains the placing of this sound on the vowel chart, p. 52, as compared with the position assigned to [ɔ] in such a work as Jones's, where it represents a quite different sound.

One phonetic concept at variance with popular terminology must be considered here: that of vowel length. Not infrequently such paired vowels as [o] in *home* and [ɑ] in *knot* are spoken of as 'long' and 'short' *o* respectively. Likewise the vowel sounds of *food* and *book* are similarly labelled.

The terms *long* and *short* naturally imply a difference in, or a measure of quantity. The term *long* as applied to a vowel should appropriately suggest, then, the same kind of sound as in a short vowel, but more of this same. Just as the [f] in *half fed* is held for a longer period of time than the [f] in *effect*, so the [o] in *dome* is longer than that in *dope*, and the same sound in the word *dough* is the longest of the three, so far as the actual length of time consumed by that sound is concerned. But the difference between [u] in *food* and [ʊ] in *foot* is one of quality or kind of sound, not one of quantity, or amount or length of sound. When necessary, length or half length in a vowel may be indicated as follows: [dop, doˑm, doː].

From our exercises in transcription, we have already familiarized ourselves with the common phenomenon often called *gradation*. This may be further described as the tendency of vowels in unstressed positions to become obscured in sound. Note the unstressed vowels in *assume* [əsum], *obscure* [əbskɪuɚ], *fortune* [fɔɚtʃən]. Now, by referring to the chart, p. 52, indicating the normal position of the jaw, tongue, and lips for producing the different vowels, we can interpret this obscuration in terms of movement and position of the articulating organs. Obviously, gradation is to be interpreted as centralization, for the vowel [ə] is shown to be a mid-central vowel, occupying the halfway or center position of the whole diagram. At times, however, the process of centralization is not completely carried out, as for example in *project*, verb, where in many speakers the vowel of the lightly stressed first syllable is still recognizable as [o], although very brief, rather than as [ə].

In considering vowel sounds, we become increasingly aware that the same word is not pronounced in exactly the same fashion by every speaker of English. Often the difference between two pronunciations is one of height, as in [brum] versus [brʊm]; at other times one pronunciation is diphthongal where the other is monophthongal, [nɪu] versus [nu]. Finally, one type of pronunciation may employ a rounded vowel, and the other may be characterized by lack of rounding, [fɔg] versus [fɑg]. Many such differences are regional; others may represent social levels of speech. For the present we shall not concern ourselves with the question as to which of two variant pronunciations is 'correct.' You should, however, develop a sensitive ear, one which will catch pronunciations differing from your own, and whenever you hear them, you should try to determine the difference in terms of the movements of the organs of articulation.

Additional Reading:

Jones, *Outline of English Phonetics*, pp. 75–83, 97–100.
Kenyon, *American Pronunciation*, pp. 179–90.
Webster's *New International Dictionary*, Guide to Pronunciation, §§ 179–85, 198, 199, 242, 243.

Exercise X

1. (*a*) Transcribe the following list of words as they would sound if spoken conversationally:

1. hoof	11. immune	21. protest (*verb*)
2. hoop	12. possible	22. protest (*noun*)
3. room	13. not	23. proceed (*verb*)
4. roof	14. doll	24. proceed (*noun*)
5. root	15. pond	25. propose
6. new	16. sorry	26. proposition
7. blue	17. foreign	27. morn
8. assume	18. swamp	28. mourn
9. tumor	19. water	29. course
10. crude	20. watch (*verb and noun*)	30. coarse

(*b*) Transcribe the following passage as you think you would normally speak it:

> What book are you reading now? Lou wants to read it too, but she has lost her glasses. I always hate to lose anything, don't you? Hand me the shoes that are on the floor in front of the stool. No, those are both for the same foot.

2. Describe the position of the speech organs, with particular reference to jaw, tongue, and lips, in making the sounds [u, ʊ, o, ɔ]. Give the phonetic definition for each of these vowels.

3. What is the configuration of the lips for all these back vowels? Try making the series of back vowels with your lips unrounded.

4. Do you pronounce Nos. 1–5 with the same vowel? Have you heard pronunciations for these words which vary from the one you use? Is the variation a matter of tongue position, jaw height, configuration of the lips, or diphthongization? Do you associate any of the variant pronunciations with particular regions or social levels? What other words presenting the same problem might be added to the list?

5. Answer Question 4 with respect to Nos. 6–9. Is there ever a similar variation in Nos. 10 or 11, or with such words as *cruel*, *cruise*, *ruse*, *croup*, *brute*, *beauty*, *mule*, *few*, *futile?* Taking these words into account, can you form a series of generalizations which will indicate those situations where there is little or no variation, and those where the variation is most marked?

6. Apply Question 4 to Nos. 12–20.

7. What is the function of the stress shift in Nos. 21–4? How complete is the gradation of the unstressed vowels in these words, and in Nos. 25 and 26?

8. Do you use the same vowel for both Nos. 27 and 28? For Nos. 29 and 30? Can you think of other pairs of words which might be used to illustrate the same point?

9. Pronounce the following words, giving careful attention to the length which is normally given to the vowel: *doom*, *groove*, *loop*, *crew*, *truth*, *juice*, *food*, *loon*. Which word seems to you to have the longest vowel? Which the shortest? Can you frame a series of generalizations indicating the effect of various classes of adjacent sounds upon vowel length?

12. Front Vowels

The relative height of the front vowels has already been indicated in the diagram on p. 52. Note that the front vowels are all pronounced with unrounded lips.

Although the central vowel [ə] appears as the unstressed

form of most of our vowels, such words as *funny*, *elect*, *indicate* show that there is also a high-front vowel which is used in many unstressed or lightly stressed situations. That the quality of this vowel corresponds exactly neither to [i] nor to [ɪ] is evident when the unstressed vowels in *ditty* and *sleepy* are compared with the stressed vowels in the same words. In fact, this unstressed front vowel has a range of variation from the lower high [ɪ] to a quality almost as high and as tense as [i]. In some speakers the words *candid* and *candied* are homophones (*i.e.* the same in sound); in the speech of others, the unstressed vowel is higher than [ɪ] but retracted to a central position. The symbol for a lower high-central vowel is [ɨ] and may be used to transcribe your pronunciation of these unstressed vowels if you are convinced that you do retract them. Ordinarily the symbol [ɪ] will suffice for this purpose, if writer and reader will understand that [ɪ] used in the transcription of unstressed vowels is to have a certain latitude of interpretation.

Upon several occasions variations in the stress of disyllabic words have been noted. Usually these have served the purpose of indicating grammatical function. That the same phenomenon may occur in words of three or more syllables has been demonstrated by such a word as *associate*, which normally preserves primary stress on two syllables for the verb [ə'soʃɪ'et], but has only one for the adjective [ə'soʃət]. This is true for all those *-ate* derivatives which may serve both as adjective and as noun.

Derivatives ending in *-ary*, *-ery*, and *-ory* also show an interesting variation — this time a regional difference between British and American English. In American

English a distinct secondary accent has remained on the penultimate syllable ['nɛsəs,ɛrɪ]; in British English this syllable has lost its secondary stress and has been at least partly syncopated ['nɛsəsrɪ, 'dɪkʃənərɪ].

ADDITIONAL READING:

Jones, *Outline of English Phonetics*, pp. 62–71, 96, 97.
Kenyon, *American Pronunciation*, pp. 161–71.
Webster's *New International Dictionary*, Guide to Pronunciation, §§ 77–80, 89, 90, 114–19, 127, 154, 155.

EXERCISE XI

1. (*a*) Transcribe the following list of words as they would sound if spoken conversationally:

1. creek	11. hair	21. bonnet
2. clique	12. carriage	22. way
3. sleek	13. nippy	23. always
4. breeches	14. creepy	24. declaration
5. been	15. burying	25. declare
6. berry	16. fistic	26. rebel (*noun and verb*)
7. happy	17. phases	27. subject (*noun and verb*)
8. merry	18. bleakness	28. separate (*adjective and verb*)
9. marry	19. village	29. intimate (*adjective and verb*)
10. bare	20. braided	30. initiate (*noun and verb*)

(*b*) Transcribe the following passage as you think you would normally speak it:

I wonder how many people there will be at the game? I don't care if I go or stay at home. Next week's is bound to be more exciting. I never do enjoy a game when the weather is cold.

2. Describe the action of the speech organs, with particular reference to tongue, jaw, and lips, in making the sounds [i, ɪ, e, ɛ, æ]. Give the appropriate phonetic definition for each of these vowels.

3. What is the configuration of the lips for all the front vowels? Try making the series of front vowels with rounded lips. Do you know any languages which have some of these sounds?

4. Do you pronounce Nos. 1–5 with the same vowel? Have you heard pronunciations for any of these words which differ from yours? Is the variation a matter of jaw height, tongue position, or configuration of the lips? Do you associate any of the variant pronunciations with particular regions or social levels? Has frequency of use or familiarity with the words anything to do with the problem?

5. Observe carefully the stressed vowel which you normally use in pronouncing Nos. 9–12. How does it compare with your pronunciation of Nos. 6, 7, and 8? Have you heard pronunciations other than the one you use? What other words can you think of which would present the same problem?

6. Listen carefully for the precise quality of the unstressed vowel you use in Nos. 13–16. Is it closer to [i] or to [ɪ]? Are your unstressed vowels in Nos. 17–21 closer to [ɪ] or to [ə]? Is there anything about the adjacent consonants which might account for the nature of the unstressed vowel in this last group of words?

7. What is the quality of the unstressed vowels in the words *always*, *declare*, *rebel* (verb), and *subject* (noun)? Does this lead you to any possible conclusion about the vowels which have [ɪ] as their unstressed forms and those which have [ə]?

8. What is the difference in the way functional change is indicated by Nos. 26 and 27, as compared with Nos. 28–30?

13. Central Vowels

The central vowels in American English are [ɑ, ʌ, ɝ, ɚ, ə]. Of these, the vowel [ɑ] is low central and is frequently made with the tongue retracted almost to the position for a back vowel. The remaining four vowels are all made in a mid-central position, although American [ʌ] may be described as a lowered and retracted mid-central vowel, that is to say, with the jaw somewhat lower and the elevation of the tongue somewhat farther back than for [ə]. See the position of [ʌ] in the vowel diagram, p. 52.

The vowel [ə] is variable in quality, depending in part upon the character of the adjacent sounds, the way in which they are made, and sometimes also upon the nature of the vowel from which the sound has been graded or reduced. We have already seen that in such words as *stated* and *salad*, where the adjacent consonants are alveolar, the [ə] is likely to be raised somewhat above an absolute mid position, and it may have an [ɪ] or [ɨ]-like quality.

When [ə] is final, it is often lowered almost to the position for [ʌ], as in *Cuba*, *sofa*. Then too, an [ə] representing an unstressed [o] as in *proposed* may be slightly rounded; one representing unstressed [ɛ], *moment*, is often somewhat fronted. In connection with this sound, the really important thing is your willingness to recognize it as a wholly natural occurrence when it does exist. There is no ground for the feeling that there is something undesirable or reprehensible about this sound; in fact, any speaker who neglected to employ it would scarcely be able to take advantage of the prominence which the English stress system gives to certain syllables at the expense of others; accordingly, the efficiency of his speech as a means of communication would be reduced. In this connection, see Kenyon, *American Pronunciation*, pp. 198–200.

The vowels [ɝ] and [ɚ] differ from all our other sounds in that they are characteristically *retroflex*, that is, made with the tongue in an inverted position. The practice of considering stressed vowels as [ɝ] and the unstressed as [ɚ] has already been established in our transcriptions. Those speakers, chiefly in southern England and along the Atlantic coast in North America, who do not 'pronounce their *r*'s' employ in place of [ɝ] in *word*, *learn*, *bird*, a mid-central unround vowel produced with the tongue in normal, that is in non-retroflex position. The symbol for this sound is [ɜ]. For a discussion of the various diphthongal qualities of this vowel, as the supposed *oi* of *boid* (bird) in the speech of New York City, see Webster's dictionary, Guide to Pronunciation, § 120, last paragraph.

Like [ə], the unstressed [ɚ] may represent the reduction of a number of vowel combinations with *r*, as in *friar*, *butter*, *Oxford*, *augur* [frɑɪɚ' bʌtɚ, ɑksfɚd, ɔgɚ]. Speakers who do not pronounce their *r*'s, normally use the mid-central unstressed [ə] in place of [ɚ]: [frɑɪə, bʌtə, ɑksfəd, ɔgə]. Here, as with the stressed *r* vowel, the difference between those speakers who do 'pronounce *r*' and those who do not, phonetically considered, is that the former employ retroflex vowels; the latter employ non-retroflex vowels made with the tongue and jaw in the same mid-central position.

It is important to recognize that even those speakers who do not normally 'pronounce their final *r*'s' — that is, those who use [ə] in place of [ɚ] — will pronounce final *r* before a word beginning with a vowel. A New England or Southern British speaker would pronounce the word *more* in isolation as [mɔə] but the expression *more ice* would be heard as [mɔrɑɪs]. This is known as the *linking r*, and constitutes merely an extension of the principle that *r* like any other glide may occur medially between vowels.

From the fixation of this habit of linking two adjacent vowels with an *r*, it is but a short step to the actual insertion of *r* between vowels, especially in short phrases which are spoken as a unit:

LINKING R: *fire and sword* [fɑɪr ən sɔəd], but [fɑɪə] in isolation
better off [bɛtərɔf] but [bɛtə] in isolation

INTRUSIVE R: *law on him* [lɔr ɑn ɪm] or [lɔɚ ɑn ɪm]
diphtheria and scarlet fever [dɪfθɪɚjɚ ən skɑlɪt fivə]

It is this tendency carried to its utmost extreme that has led to the regular addition of *r* to such words as *idea* by some Eastern American speakers, although the practice is frequently deprecated.

ADDITIONAL READING:

Jones, *Outline of English Phonetics*, pp. 72–5, 83–94, 182, 183.

Kenyon, *American Pronunciation*, pp. 158–61, 171–8, 191–203.

Webster's *New International Dictionary*, Guide to Pronunciation, §§ 81–3, 91, 92, 120, 121, 126, 191, 213, 214, 244, 245, 250.

Exercise XII

1. (*a*) Transcribe the following list of words as they would sound if spoken conversationally:

1. father	11. mongrel	21. shirk
2. garden	12. constable	22. foreword
3. rather	13. obscure	23. forward
4. dance	14. produce (*verb*)	24. demurrer
5. advance	15. chorus	25. shirring
6. master	16. villa	26. blurring
7. half	17. condense	27. clearer
8. smother	18. churn	28. patter
9. bunion	19. adjourn	29. actor
10. couple	20. pert	30. zephyr

(*b*) Transcribe the following passage as you think you would normally speak it:

> 'Are you going out of town tomorrow?' 'I don't know. We are all ready to go if our friends come from the South. We have not heard from them for some time, though. I surely hope they get here in good time, so that we can all start out on our trip. It is much nicer driving in the early part of the day. But most of the road has been oiled anyway, so it won't be very dusty.'

2. Describe the action of the speech organs, with particular reference to jaw, tongue, and lip position in making the sounds [ɑ, ʌ, ə, ɝ, ɚ]. Be able to give the appropriate phonetic definition for each vowel.

3. Do you pronounce the stressed vowels of Nos. 3–7 as [æ] or as [ɑ]? Name some other words in which the same problem arises. Some dictionaries recommend the use of a vowel midway between [æ] and [ɑ] in these and similar words. What would be the phonetic definition of such a vowel? The symbol for this sound is [a].

4. From Nos. 8–10, and also such words as *blood*, *flood*, what do you conclude about the possible ways of spelling

the sound [ʌ]? How do you pronounce Nos. 11 and 12? Do you know another pronunciation for these words? Which do you think might be the older? Does this suggest to you what might be meant by the term *spelling pronunciation?* Consult the index of Kenyon for treatments of this topic.

5. Compare the unstressed vowels of Nos. 13–17. Are they exactly identical in sound? Can you detect any differences in the position of the tongue as you pronounce them?

6. What is the difference in your transcriptions of Nos. 22 and 23? Be able to justify your practice. How does the final sound of No. 24 differ from that immediately preceding it?

7. What particular problems in transcription are represented by Nos. 25–7? Be able to justify your practice, and to trace in complete detail the movements of the tongue in pronouncing these words.

8. Transcribe Nos. 18–30 as they would be pronounced in Southern British or New England speech.

9. Transcribe the following as you would assume them to be pronounced in British and Eastern American speech: *poor fellow*, *poor old fellow*, *here I am*, *hear the car*. Be able to justify your transcriptions. How does your observation in these instances serve to explain the addition of [r] in such phrases as *China and Japan*, *Is Emma over there?*

14. DIPHTHONGS

Usually a diphthong is defined as a combination of two vowel sounds within a single syllable. This serves to distinguish such combinations as [ɑɪ, ɑʊ, ɔɪ, ɪu] in *file*, *foul*, *foil*, and *fuel*, where the vowel combination plays the role of a unitary speech sound occurring regularly within the language, from purely accidental combinations as [iɛ] in *pre-empt*, [oi] in *coeval*, or [uɑ] in *nuance*. In the last three words note that the syllabic division comes between the two vowels, whereas in such a diphthong as [ɑɪ] there is a continuous gliding sound, beginning at the position for [ɑ] and concluding at the position for [ɪ]. In fact, the concept of [ɑɪ] — usually spelled *i* — as a diphthong frequently comes as a surprise to the beginning student of phonetics, who has always thought of the English language in terms of spelling.

It is also customary to distinguish between *falling diphthongs*, which place the heaviest stress on the first element [ɑɪ], and *rising diphthongs*, with heavier stress on the second [ɪu].

Moreover, upon listening closely, you will discover that almost all the English vowel sounds, especially those popularly and inaccurately termed the 'long vowels,' are somewhat diphthongal in character. That this is true of the sounds [e] and [o] has already been suggested in Question 4, Exercise II, and they are, indeed, regularly transcribed as [ei] and [ou] by Daniel Jones. But even in the [i] and [u] sounds of *beet*, *bean*, *boot*, *boon*, there is almost always a distinct up-glide in their pronunciation, which might be variously suggested by such transcriptions as [ɪ˄^{i}, i^{j}, ʊ˄^{u}, ʊ^{w}] in which the initial symbols [ɪ˄] and [ʊ˄] represent sounds somewhat higher than normal [ɪ] and [ʊ], but lower than the highest conceivable varieties of [i] and [u]. Some writers classify the four diphthongs [ɑɪ, ɑʊ, ɔɪ, ɪu] as *full* diphthongs and those we have just discussed as *partial* diphthongs.

It is true also that our conventional uniform transcriptions for the full diphthongs are more often symbolic rather than actual descriptions of the sounds which are really uttered. Many speakers begin the [ɑɪ] diphthong in *rise* with a vowel which might be more accurately suggested by the low front [a] than by the central vowel [ɑ], whereas in *bite* or *nice*, the initial sound is frequently somewhere between [ɑ] and [ə], possibly a higher low-central vowel. Likewise, *down* may begin with an [a] first element, and *out* with an [ʌ]. The pronunciation of the diphthongs also varies in different parts of the country, as is evident from the Southern American pronunciation of [ɑɪ].

Finally, there is also the group of sound combinations heard in the words *mar*, *mare*, *more*, *mere*, *moor*, in which the second element is the sound [ɚ] or [ə], depending upon whether the speaker has a retroflex or non-retroflex *r:* [mɑɚ, mɑə, mæɚ, mæə, mɔɚ, mɔə, mɪɚ, mɪə, mʊɚ, mʊə]. These are often called *centering diphthongs*, since the second element is some kind of mid-central vowel, in contrast to the high front or back vowels constituting the second elements of the other four diphthongs.

The most notable characteristic of these centering diphthongs is the tendency in a number of them to lower the jaw position for the first element. Note that such words as *tier*, *pier*, *here*, etc. actually begin with an [ɪ] vowel instead of the [i] which would be historically regular for them, and that *poor* and *bore* begin their diphthongs with the sounds [ʊ] and [ɔ] respectively.

Additional Reading:

Jones, *Outline of English Phonetics*, pp. 57–59, 100–114.
Kenyon, *American Pronunciation*, pp. 203–29.
Webster's *New International Dictionary*, Guide to Pronunciation, §§ 36–8, 152, 197, 202–4, 240–42.

Exercise XIII

1. (*a*) Transcribe the following list of words as they would sound if spoken conversationally:

1. trite	11. boil
2. thyme	12. join
3. sleight	13. geared
4. ice	14. hero
5. eyes	15. serial
6. mouse	16. period
7. pout	17. brew
8. plowed	18. brewer
9. town	19. more
10. shroud	20. mower

(*b*) The following selections from James Russell Lowell's *Biglow Papers* are a representation of Yankee Dialect. With the departures from conventional spelling as a guide, put in phonetic transcription your conception of the pronunciation Lowell had in mind. Pay particular attention to the treatment of *r*.

She jedges by herself; she's no idear
How't stiddies folks to give 'em their fair sheer:
The odds 'twixt her an' us is plain 's a steeple, —

. . . .

Th' ain't nut a face but wut she's shook her fist in,
Ez though she done it all, an' ten times more,
An' nuthin' never hed gut done afore,
Nor never could agin', 'thout she wuz spliced
On to one eend an' gin th' old airth a hoist.

. . . .

I ha'n't no patience with sech swellin' fellers ez
Think God can't forge 'thout them to blow the bellerses.

2. Would the diphthongs [ɔɪ] and [ɑʊ] be classified as rising or falling diphthongs? Why?

3. How is the diphthong [ɑɪ] modified in what is popularly conceived to be Irish dialect, especially as suggested by such spellings as *foine*, *toime?* State the difference in phonetic terms. Do the same for the traditional Southern pronunciation of this diphthong. Look up in an unabridged dictionary the etymology of the word *hoist.* What has happened to it?

4. How is the diphthong [ɑʊ] often modified in certain types of American English? Transcribe and state the difference in phonetic terms.

5. What modification of the [ɔɪ] diphthong is suggested by such spellings as *p'int* for *point*, *b'ile* for *boil*, *'ile* for *oil?* Do you know of any other spellings for *roil?*

6. Some years ago many teachers of elocution and diction used to insist upon an [i] pronunciation for the stressed vowel of Nos. 14–16. Give an opinion as to the phonetic justification of this insistence.

7. What frequently happens to the pronunciation of the word *poor* in Southern American? Is this development in keeping with any phonetic tendencies you have seen manifested here?

15. The Dictionary

It is a frequent experience with all of us to settle an argument about the correct pronunciation or meaning of a word by referring the question to the dictionary. It is noteworthy also that we are generally inclined to accept without question the information that is given there. A cursory analysis will suffice to show that this procedure is based upon two assumptions: first, that there is a single correct pronunciation or a proper meaning for every word, definitely preferable to other pronunciations and meanings; second, that the dictionary is the one authoritative source for these pronunciations and meanings.

It is true, incidentally, that this second assumption is encouraged by the publishers of dictionaries, who are fond of using such phrases as *standard authority* and *final authority* in their advertisements. Nevertheless, it will be worth our while to examine both these assumptions in the light of how dictionaries are made, and the attitudes of their editors toward these questions.

Recall that on the very first page of this book the study of language was called a science, and the grammarian or student of language was likened to a scientist, whose primary task was the collection of all the facts pertaining to his subject. This is precisely the method employed by the dictionary maker or lexicographer. We are told, for example, by the editors of Webster's *New International Dictionary:*

> Since 1924 the editors have systematically received chosen cross sections of contemporary printed materials, including many thousands of books, pamphlets, magazines, newspapers, catalogues, and learned, technical, and scientific periodicals. From these sources have been collected about 1,665,000 citations. Besides these, the editors have also examined about 2,000,000 citations in other dictionaries, and have utilized as required, selections from the millions of citations contained in concordances to the English Bible, and to Spenser, Pope, Gray, Shelley, and other English writers. . . . In the technical and scientific fields, the problems being of a somewhat different kind, terms have been also collected extensively from indexes and lists.[10]

The great *Oxford English Dictionary*, without question the most monumental undertaking of its nature in any

[10] Introduction, p. vii. By permission. From Webster's *New International Dictionary*, Second Edition, copyright, 1934, 1939, by G. & C. Merriam Co.

language, reproduces on page xiv of its Preface a typical citation slip, of which there were more than six million in its files.

It is clear, then, that any authority on any phase of language which a dictionary may possess is derived directly from the language itself, from usage. With this in mind, let us see what the dictionaries themselves have to say about our original assumption of the 'single correct form.'

After quoting a number of competent scholars, such as Daniel Jones, who writes, 'I am not one of those who believe in the desirability or feasibility of setting up any one form of pronunciation as a standard for the English-speaking world,' and A. Lloyd James, Linguistic Adviser to the British Broadcasting Corporation, to the effect that, 'It is quite evident that we are not entitled to concede that there is *one* standard pronunciation, *one* and *only one* right way of speaking English,' the editors of Webster's Dictionary state:

> When the essential facts are considered, 'correctness of pronunciation' must be a flexible term. It is perhaps as accurate a definition as can be made to say that a pronunciation is correct when it is in actual use by a sufficient number of cultivated speakers. This is obviously elastic, depending both on knowledge — not always obtainable — of the number of users, and on judgment as to the cultivation of the speakers.
>
> The standard of English pronunciation, then, so far as a standard may be said to exist, is the usage that now prevails among the educated and cultured people to whom the language is vernacular; but, since somewhat different pronunciations are used by the cultivated in different regions too large to be ignored, we must frankly admit the fact that, at

> present, uniformity of pronunciation is not to be found throughout the English-speaking world, though there is a very large percentage of practical uniformity.[11]

It seems quite clear, therefore, that the first assumption which frequently prompts our references to the dictionary, that of the single correct form, is in large part unwarranted in the eyes of those who compile the dictionaries. Let us now examine the second of our initial assumptions, the fitness of the dictionary to furnish us with information about meanings and about pronunciation.

We have already seen that in order to know what words to include, every dictionary editorial staff must make an exhaustive investigation of the English language, which will provide it ultimately with millions of citation slips. Naturally the editors base their conclusions about the meanings of words upon those slips in which the words occur. An interesting description of the time and labor involved in organizing the definition of a single word is given on pp. xvii and xviii of the Introduction to the *Oxford English Dictionary*.

Pronunciation, characterized by the Oxford Dictionary editors as 'the actual living form or forms of a word,' naturally could not be adduced from such citations. It is necessary, then, for the lexicographer to make a second survey, this time of the spoken language, to secure a supply of information adequately extensive to permit him to draw valid conclusions. The method employed by one dictionary is here outlined in brief:

[11] Guide to Pronunciation, p. xxvi. By permission. From Webster's *New International Dictionary*, Second Edition, copyright, 1934, 1939, by G. & C. Merriam Co.

> Inquiries regarding thousands of individual words have been addressed to leading scholars, and, in the case of technical words, to specialists and experts; and lists of words, both general and technical, of doubtful pronunciation have been referred to cultivated speakers in various parts of the English-speaking world, in order that they might indicate the pronunciations preferred in the cultivated speech of their locality.[12]

Even so, of course, the task of gathering the variant pronunciations of nearly a half-million words as they are pronounced by well over two hundred million speakers is a task that can only be approximated, and it is of interest to note the frank admission of this in a subsequent statement (§ 7) in the Webster Guide to Pronunciation:

> The function of a pronouncing dictionary is to record as far as possible the pronunciations prevailing in the best present usage, rather than to attempt to dictate what that usage should be. In so far as a dictionary may be known and acknowledged as a faithful recorder and interpreter of such usage, *so far and no farther may it be appealed to as an authority*. [Italics mine.]

Note too the stress upon the concept of the dictionary as a *record* of pronunciations which exist, rather than as a dictator of what pronunciation should be.

We may thus gather from the words of the men who compile dictionaries and from the way in which dictionaries are made that the two assumptions with which we began — a single correct form for each word, and the infallibility of the dictionary to give us that form — are by no means tenable. This does not mean that the dictionary is not a useful tool. Properly employed and

[12] Webster's *New International Dictionary*, Introduction, p. xii.

interpreted it is the greatest single help to the student of language because it is based upon millions of individual observations and specific instances.

Unfortunately, the dictionary is all too frequently misused, primarily because those who consult it have never given any thought to the way in which it is compiled, and demand of it many things that its makers never intended it to furnish. It is the purpose of the exercise which follows to help you understand and interpret more accurately and intelligently the information, particularly about pronunciation, which the larger dictionaries have to offer. In preparing this exercise you should use Webster's *New International Dictionary*, second edition. Do not use an edition with a date earlier than 1934 on the title page.

Exercise XIV

1. Read § 5, p. xxvi, of the Guide to Pronunciation in Webster's *New International Dictionary*. What class of writers are quoted there in support of the opinion which the editors appear to maintain? Is a single standard of correctness for the English language considered a desirable end? Is it considered possible? When is a pronunciation correct?

2. Read page xii and §§ 7–10, page xxvi, of the Guide. Where does the dictionary secure its pronunciations? What do the editors say about the function of a pronouncing dictionary? In this connection, read also paragraphs 1 and 2 of the Introduction to Daniel Jones, *An English Pronouncing Dictionary*. Is the attitude toward correctness and toward the function of a pronouncing dictionary in these works the same as that implied in such a title as *Five Thousand Words Often Mispronounced?*

3. Note also in § 7, page xxvi, of Webster's Guide the statement of the editors concerning the extent to which their work may be appealed to as an authority. Keeping this self-imposed limitation in mind, look up the Webster pronunciation of the following words: *absolutely*, *altimeter*, *cerebral*, *caries*, *data*, *quintuplets*, *status*. Convert the pronunciations which you find recorded there into standard phonetic notation. Are you familiar with any pronunciations of these words which do not appear in this dictionary? In the light of the editorial statement referred to in this question, what is the reasonable attitude to take toward the pronunciations which are not recorded there?

4. Of the several varieties of spoken English, what kind did the Webster editors choose to record? See page xii of the Introduction. Compare the Webster practice with that of Daniel Jones, explained in paragraph 7 of the Introduction to *An English Pronouncing Dictionary*. Does this statement of the Webster practice place a further limitation upon your interpretation of the pronunciations which you find there? Explain.

5. Look up the meaning of the word *colloquial* in Webster. See also §§ 8–10, page xxvi, § 61, page lxxxviii. On the basis of these statements, would the label *colloquial* after a word or a pronunciation in the dictionary appear to imply a condemnation?

6. When two pronunciations of a word are given in the dictionary, what attitude is generally taken toward the second of these? In view of the method of gathering the material and the attitude of the editors toward it, frame a statement which will define precisely the status of a second pronunciation. See also § 7, second paragraph, § 10, page xxvi, § 277, page lix, § 11, page xciii. In view of the possible ratio between the number of consultants for the dictionary and the total number even of cultured English speakers, what is the probable validity of the 'slight preponderance of evidence,' mentioned in § 11,

page xciii? What is the importance of § 277 in this dictionary?

7. Consult § 83, page xl, to determine the exact quality of the diacritical symbol *ȧ*. How is it described? Does the discussion of this symbol suggest that the diacritical markings in Webster have a fixed or a relative value? What is the attitude of the editors concerning the desirability of generally adopting the 'broad' *a* sound?

8. Answer the first three questions under 7 in respect to the *ŏ* symbol. See § 184, page xlviii.

9. Read §§ 66–8, pages xxxv–xxxvi. Do the editors consider word stress definitely fixed? What factors influence it? In the light of this discussion, what would be your attitude toward the pronunciation of *finance?*

16. Definitions of the English Speech Sounds

The following table of phonetic definitions is inserted to aid you in your review of English sounds and the way in which they are made. With both the consonants and the vowels, this list of definitions proceeds from those sounds made in the front of the mouth toward those made in the back. Notice to what extent the English sounds present a symmetrical pattern considered from the point of view of where the sounds are made.

CONSONANTS

1. Voiceless bilabial stop	p
2. Voiced bilabial stop	b
3. Voiced bilabial nasal continuant	m
4. Voiceless labiodental fricative	f
5. Voiced labiodental fricative	v
6. Voiceless interdental fricative	*θ*

7.	Voiced interdental fricative	ð
8.	Voiceless alveolar stop	t
9.	Voiced alveolar stop	d
10.	Voiced alveolar nasal continuant	n
11.	Voiced lateral alveolar continuant	l
12.	Voiceless alveolar fricative	s
13.	Voiced alveolar fricative	z
14.	Voiceless alveolopalatal fricative	ʃ
15.	Voiced alveolopalatal fricative	ʒ
16.	Voiceless alveolopalatal affricate	tʃ
17.	Voiced alveolopalatal affricate	dʒ
18.	Voiceless (palatal) (velar) stop	k
19.	Voiced (palatal) (velar) stop	g
20.	Voiced velar nasal continuant	ŋ
21.	Voiceless glottal fricative	h
22.	Voiced labiovelar glide	w
23.	Voiced linguopalatal glide	j
24.	Voiced retroflex tongue glide	r
25.	Voiceless glottal fricative accompanied by a voiced labiovelar glide	ʍ

VOWELS

26.	High-front unround	i
27.	Lower high-front unround	ɪ
28.	Mid-front unround	e
29.	Lower mid-front unround	ɛ
30.	Low-front unround	æ
31.	Mid-central unround (unstressed)	ə
32.	Mid-central unround retroflex	ɝ
33.	Mid-central unround retroflex (unstressed)	ɚ

34. Mid-central unround, lowered and retracted ʌ
35. Low-central unround ɑ
36. High-back round u
37. Lower high-back round ʊ
38. Mid-back round o
39. Low-back round ɔ

II

English Grammar

17. Language and Grammar

We have completed our observation of the speech sounds which we normally use. Continuing the scientific approach which was briefly outlined in Section 1, we must now fix our attention upon other aspects of language. First, however, some general yet fundamental questions about language and grammar must be considered.

We may well begin with the question of the function of language, not that our conclusions will be at all startling, but because it is a matter which should never be lost sight of. Some years ago Edward Sapir, the great philologist, defined language as 'a purely human and non-instinctive method of communicating ideas, emotions, and desires by means of a system of voluntarily produced symbols.'[13] This definition is so carefully framed and so packed with meaning that it merits close analysis.

The core of the definition, the phrase *method of communi-*

[13] Sapir, *Language*, p. 7.

cation, suggests communication as the primary function of language. It is often argued, however, that situations may arise where expression rather than communication is the primary aim of linguistic activity. 'When a person talks at length to a cat or a dog (even a china one on a mantelpiece, as does a character in one of Barrie's plays), it is quite certain that he does not talk in order to be understood by his ostensible interlocutor, or even, necessarily to set his own thoughts in order. Quite often he talks, as the infant does when he babbles meaningless sounds, or the grown-up when he recites nonsense jingles, for the pure enjoyment of utterance.'[14] It is undoubtedly important that we recognize the expressive as well as the communicative side of language, if only for the implication that language is psychological as well as logical in nature.

In this same connection, it must be observed that according to Sapir's definition, language communicates not only ideas, but emotions and desires as well. Again, a system or method of communicating ideas only, complicated though it might be, might well have a certain logical regularity, comparable, let us say, to the symbolic system which we know as algebra. If the content of language is to be emotional as well as ideational, this clearly necessitates a highly complex, extra-logical system of communication.

Two other aspects of the definition deserve mention. The qualification *purely human and non-instinctive* raises

[14] Robertson, *Development of Modern English*, p. 2. This same question of the relative importance of the expressive and the communicative function in respect to art has been discussed at length by Croce in his *Aesthetic*.

language far beyond the sphere of yelps, grunts, and cries of pain and hunger, which constitute nearly the sum total of animal communication below the human level — and the term *voluntarily produced symbols* reinforces this distinction.

Finally, there is the important word *system* — 'a system of voluntarily produced symbols.' Anthropologists, too, from their point of view often define language as a behavior pattern. Both of these words, *system* and *pattern*, are valuable in that they suggest a sphere for the activities of the grammarian, namely to describe the details and organization of such a system or pattern.

This is precisely what we have already done with one aspect of the English language, the speech sounds which it employs. First we set about to discover what they were; then we tried to find out how they were made. Next, we classified the various ways of making sounds, recognizing such paired categories as *voiced* and *voiceless; oral* and *nasal; labial*, *alveolar*, and *velar*. We saw that our back vowels were generally rounded whereas our front vowels were unround. Even in analyzing such a problem as the alternation between [æ] and [ɑ] in words of the *pass*, *dance*, *bath* group, it was observed that the variation occurred chiefly in words of a given phonetic environment — chiefly when the vowel in question preceded nasals or voiceless fricatives. From one point of view, all this analysis may be considered as an attempt to define a system or describe a pattern.

The system to which we give the name *English language* obviously consists of more than just speech sounds, and it is thus the function of the linguistic scientist or grammarian to examine it from as many points of view as possible. English, like most languages which we know, employs sets of suffixes to indicate certain changes in meaning: *boy*, *boys*; *eat*, *eats*, *eating*, *eaten*; *he*, *his*, *him*, and so on. The suffixes *-s*, *-en*, *-ing*, and others employed in this manner are known as inflections, and the branch of language study or grammar which seeks to describe the part they play in the system or pattern is often called *morphology* (study of form).

In addition to the arrangement of the phonetic or inflectional elements which go to make up the word unit, there is also the problem of the arrangement of words into larger units. Such arrangements are also a vital part of the system of communicating meaning: *Did he* usually means something quite different from *he did; age old* is not the same as *old age; the Indian killed the bear* and *the bear killed the Indian* depend for their meaning also upon the sequence of the three important words in the group. The description of such patterns and the definition of them in the light of the meanings they normally convey is a large part of the field of *syntax*, another division in the study of grammar.

This concept of grammar, as the description of a system of communication, is somewhat remote from what the average person means when he speaks of grammar; nevertheless the broader concept is fundamental to the narrower one. The popular notion of grammar as a collection of rules which will enable one to speak and write correctly makes it a sort of Emily Post of language. Yet from our brief glance into the ways that dictionaries are compiled, we know that dictionary statements about pronunciations can come only from a careful observation of the way in which words are actually pronounced. Moreover, we have discovered that the very words which the dictionary includes, and the meanings which it assigns to those words are determined from usage, from the language itself.

The grammarian, perforce, must work in the same way as the lexicographer — which is the way of any scientist. He must observe and examine his material, classify and organize it, and draw whatever conclusions or general statements this observation and classification may permit. When the student employs such conclusions, either in learning a new language or in attempting to increase the mastery of his own, he is likely to refer to the conclusions or general statements as *rules*, for they do serve to guide his conduct. But considered in the light of their source and origin, these rules are actually descriptive generalizations, broad statements about the organization and behavior of the system or pattern which we call a language.

Nor is it conceivable that the rules of grammar can have any source other than the language itself, any more than a law of physics can arise from a source outside the behavior of matter. We would not accept as valid the generalities of an economist who had not observed the operations of economic forces, or of a sociologist who had not troubled to draw his conclusions from case studies. The grammarian occupies the same position in respect to language.

Additional Reading:

Curme, *Syntax*, Preface.
Fries, *American English Grammar*, p. 4.
Grattan and Gurrey, *Our Living Language*, Chapter 1.

Jespersen, *Essentials of English Grammar*, pp. 15–21.
Modern English Grammar, I, Preface, pp. v–vii.
Philosophy of Grammar, pp. 17–57.
Sweet, *New English Grammar*, pp. 1–10.

Exercise XV

1. From a careful reading of the definitions in the *Oxford English Dictionary* and in Webster's *New International Dictionary* can you reach any conclusion about the differences in meaning or implication of the terms *speech* and *language?*

2. Would you consider the method of grammar, as it has been explained in the preceding section, to be primarily inductive or deductive? Justify your answer. Is the method of science in general assumed to be inductive or deductive?

3. Consult the *Oxford English Dictionary* (definition 1) and Webster's *New International Dictionary* (definition 6) for their treatment of the word *grammar.* In what respect do these definitions alter your conception of the meaning of this word? Does *grammar*, as they define it, include anything which you had not before considered a part of the subject?

4. Considering the origin and early history of language, would you say that speaking or writing is the more fundamental linguistic activity? Consequently, which would be of primary importance to the grammarian, as we have defined him and his functions in the preceding section?

5. Observe carefully all the spoken English you hear before the next meeting of the class, and attempt to classify the various ways in which it differs from written English. Are certain types of sentences more prevalent in spoken than in written English? Are there any contractions in the spoken language which do not appear on certain levels of the written language? Can you think of any

phonetic differentiations characteristic of the spoken language which cannot be indicated by our conventional spelling? Can you think of any words which you use in informal speech but not in formal writing? Can you think of any words or expressions which you might write but rarely speak?

6. What difference is there in purpose and approach between studying the grammar of a foreign language and that of one's own language? Would the approach in studying a foreign language, French or Spanish, let us say, be primarily deductive or inductive?

7. From the point of view of the material or subject matter of language, how does the grammarian differ from the lexicographer in his approach to, and his treatment of, his material? In what respects are their working methods similar?

8. From the dictionary definitions and the discussions in Sweet and in Jespersen's *Philosophy of Grammar*, define the scope of each of the following: historical grammar, comparative grammar, universal grammar.

9. If your reading has not supplied it, consult the dictionary for the meaning of the following terms: phonetics, phonology, accidence, morphology, syntax.

18. Principles of Classification

In the study of language, as in any other science, the collection of relevant facts is but the initial step. Once collected, these facts must be sorted and classified in order that significant conclusions may be drawn from them. Before the sorting can begin, however, certain classes or categories into which the material may be gathered must be recognized; to do this, we must determine upon what bases such classes are to be chosen.

Since most of the languages we know anything about indicate changes in meaning by altering the outward form of words or sentences, either meaning or form may be used for a starting point in the determination of classes. That is, all those words which are capable of adding the ending *-ed* might be considered as one class. Such a class or collection, being based upon a consideration of form, would naturally be known as a *formal category*. The category once having been established, we could then proceed with our examination. We might find, for example, that this *-ed* ending was applied only to a certain kind of word, which we call a verb, according to one already established scheme of classification. We might discover further that not all verbs employ or acquire this ending, that the ending has a variety of phonetic values, and that finally and most important, it has something to do with the time of action indicated by the words to which it is applied.

It would be equally possible to employ meaning as the basis for a classification. To select a simple example, we might begin by asking ourselves how the idea of more than one, of plurality, was indicated. If the English language were serving as the subject of our observation, we should discover that most of those words which we call nouns added an *-(e)s* inflection, but that there are also other ways of indicating this idea: *sheep*, *oxen*, *geese*. We should also find that the pronouns had their ways of indicating this change in idea, but that in adjectives, contrary to the practice in Greek, Latin, German, Spanish, French, and Italian, there was little or no provision for it. Since we are here beginning with a possible modification of idea, we naturally speak of this more-than-one-ness as an *ideational category* (some grammarians call this a *logical category*).

For individual words, the basic scheme of classification for some two thousand years or more has been into what we call *parts of speech.* Because we have employed such terms as *noun*, *verb*, *adjective*, and *preposition* since our grammar school days, both in our study of English and in our learning of foreign languages, we may have come to feel that they are part of a permanent, inviolate, and wholly satisfactory systematization. Such is not the case.

Throughout the history of language study, grammarians have not always recognized the same number of classes, nor have they always given these classes the same names. For example, grammars of the sixteenth century did not consider the adjective as distinct from the noun. At various other times, articles, infinitives, participles, and expletives have all been recognized as separate parts of speech. This is not particularly surprising if we remember that any such scheme represents a merely human endeavor toward the classification of a highly complex organism. It is inevitable that as time goes on, our points of view will necessarily change, as they have changed, for example, in respect to the number of elemental substances recognized by the chemist.

Moreover, there is not, at present, wholly complete agreement among authorities on the English language about the number of parts of speech we should recognize, or on the appropriate designations or definitions for these parts. The Danish grammarian Jespersen, recognizing the impossibility of eliminating all the traditional names which have been in use throughout the centuries, attempts to superimpose upon the familiar scheme a hierarchy of what he calls ranks of words 'according to their mutual relations as defined or defining.' Thus, in such a phrase as *very old coat*, the word *coat* would be classified as the primary or principal; *old*, because it defines *coat*, is a word of secondary rank or an adjunct; *very*, which defines *old* is a tertiary word or a subjunct. An interesting corollary of this scheme of classification lies in the fact that the degree of specialization in meaning varies directly with rank: 'Primaries are more special (apply to a smaller number of individuals) than secondary words, and these in their turn are less general than tertiary words.'

Jespersen's scheme cuts across the conventional part-of-speech classification in a number of different ways: for example, the possessive noun *John's* in *John's coat* would be considered a secondary just as would the adjective *old* in *old coat*, even though nouns are generally ranked as primaries. 'Poor, in *the poor people* as well as in the combination *the poor*, is an adjective, though in the former case it is an adjunct and in the latter a principal; but (*the*) *blacks*, though derived from the adjective *black*, shows by its plural ending *-s* that it has become a substantive as well as principal.'[15] He also considers the verbs in a clause or sentence as occupying a special type of secondary relationship to the subject or primary.

This system of ranks is based chiefly upon logic or meaning; they are ideational categories. Still another scheme of classification is possible, one which proceeds

[15] *Modern English Grammar*, II, 5.

according to function or use in the sentence. Employing such a basis, another grammarian, Janet R. Aiken, has conceived of a six-class system, recognizing the following categories: absolute, verb, subject, complement, modifier, and connective. In it nouns may serve as absolutes, subjects, or complements; adjectives and adverbs are placed together in the category of modifier; prepositions, conjunctions, and possibly even the relative pronouns in certain constructions would be considered as connectives.

Mrs. Aiken's analysis of the traditional classification of the parts of speech is interesting because it indicates very plainly why so many students of the English language have become dissatisfied with this system, and have been led to attempt new classifications of their own.

> The eight traditional parts of speech, the pillars of the grammatical arch, are seen under logical analysis to be shaky. One, the verb, is a really functional concept. The noun is not one but two functions (subject and complement), while the adjective and adverb together make one (modifier). Prepositions and conjunctions may be combined as constituting the connective function. But the greatest anomaly is the pronoun, which is by no means 'a word used as substitute for a noun,' as it is usually defined. Pronouns are simply a set list of specific words, more or less arbitrarily chosen, which may fulfill any of the six grammatical functions with the exception of the verb. And the term *interjection* is equally misleading from the functional aspect; ordinarily the interjection is functionally an absolute, but occasionally it has a modifier function. In itself it is not a function; there is simply a list of words which are called interjections because they often have an exclamatory use.[16]

[16] Aiken, *New Plan of English Grammar*, pp. iii, iv. Henry Holt and Company, New York, 1933. Quoted by permission.

We may state the case in somewhat different terms: in order to have scientific validity, the various classes in any scheme of classification must be organized on a consistent basis, and they must be mutually exclusive. If you were sorting a quart of beans, it would not do to try to classify them as large beans, small beans, white beans, and kidney beans. *Large* and *small* imply classification according to size, *white* according to color, and *kidney* according to shape. It is easily possible to conceive of your finding both small and large white beans; the bin or category into which these would be placed is not clear according to the scheme which has been set up. That this is often true when we try to sort individual words into the traditional parts of speech classification is suggested by Mrs. Aiken's statement, and will appear in greater detail later.

Yet, none of the attempts at changing or adding to the familiar classification has won sufficient support to justify the belief that it will be generally adopted. They have been described here chiefly to show what possible directions a new scheme of classification might take. Throughout the remainder of this text, we shall use the traditional scheme with its familiar terminology of noun, adjective, verb, and so on, because that is the one to which we are accustomed, and much of our thinking about language is habitually done in these terms. At the same time, whenever the traditional classification seems to be contradictory, when the terms are not mutually exclusive, such shortcomings will be recognized. Moreover, when such a concept or term as *adjunct* appears to fit a particular situation better than the more familiar *adjective*, it will be employed, and the reasons for the choice will be stated.

Additional Reading:

Grattan and Gurrey, *Our Living Language*, Chapter xv.
Jespersen, *Essentials of English Grammar*, Chapters vii, viii.
Modern English Grammar, ii, pp. 1–12.
Philosophy of Grammar, Chapters iv–vii.
Sweet, *New English Grammar*, pp. 11–48.

Exercise XVI

1. Consult Webster's *New International Dictionary* for the definitions of each of the parts of speech: noun, pronoun, verb, adjective, adverb, preposition, conjunction, and interjection. In each instance decide whether the phraseology of the definition bases the concept of that part of speech upon form, function, or meaning. In each instance also, note the etymology of the word, observing whether the derivation corresponds to the way in which the word is used at present.

2. On the basis of the definitions which you have found for the various parts of speech, classify each of the words in the following sentences:

(1) We went to the polls to vote for Charles, but he was not elected.
(2) Not a single vote was cast for him, except our two.
(3) Everyone but us knew how to use the voting machine.
(4) Possibly that is why your candidate won, whereas ours was defeated.
(5) We told him that he should try again next time.
(6) He willingly agreed to that.
(7) He ups and tells me to get out of here.

3. Look up the word *round* either in Webster or in the *Oxford English Dictionary*. How many part of speech entries are given for it? What does this suggest about the

possibility of a single word occupying more than one category? If you use the *Oxford Dictionary* for this question, note the date of the earliest citation in each entry. What other words can you think of which might be used to illustrate this same point?

4. Read the definitions of the term *part of speech* given in the *Oxford English Dictionary* (s.v. *part*, sb. 19) and in Webster (s.v. *part of speech*). Do these definitions employ form, function, or meaning as a basis for classification?

5. If you were constructing or inventing an artificial language, what would be the probable relationship in it between formal and ideational categories? Is this relationship always present in English? Be able to illustrate your answer.

6. If one were using form as a basis of classification, how many parts of speech might be recognized in English? For example, nouns might be considered as one class because, with a few exceptions, they have a plural in *-s*. Find similar formal manifestations which will serve as a clue to other classes or categories.

7. For what parts of speech would the criterion suggested in the preceding question prove unworkable? What was meant by the term *form word* or *function word* as it was used in several of the suggested references? What parts of speech are considered form words in contrast to full words?

19. Nouns: Gender and Number

We are now ready to consider the parts of speech in detail. We have already seen that the same units of language may be classified either on the basis of form or of meaning, Obviously, then, we shall have to follow a somewhat standardized, or at least a consistent procedure in dealing with them.

It will be most advantageous to begin with the physical or outward aspect, and to proceed from it to what appears to be the inward content. That is to say, our general method will be to proceed from *form* to *meaning*. In connection with each part of speech we shall ask ourselves the following three questions:

1. What formal modifications (*i.e.* of inflection or of position) does this class of words undergo?
2. What functional or grammatical categories are indicated by such variations in form?
3. What modifications in meaning are suggested by these grammatical functions?

The problem of gender in nouns offers a brief but cogent illustration of the application of this approach. We take our first step by observing that possibly sixty or more words in the English language are capable of adding the ending *-ess* [əs]: *hostess*, *princess*, *waitress*, *shepherdess*, etc., and that the resulting new word indicates a change of gender from masculine to feminine. Thus, in this first observation, we have begun with a formal aspect of certain words and have noted its functional implication.

We must not forget, however, that this same functional shift may be indicated by certain other changes in form: *-ine*, *heroine*, *Ernestine; -a*, *sultana*, *Louisa; -ix*, *aviatrix*. The possibility of compounding by means of a gender-defining first element, as in *she goat*, *girl friend*, *woman doctor*, *manservant*, must also be considered, as well as the existence of such pairs as *drake:duck*, *buck* or *stag:doe*, *cock:hen*, *father:mother*, *husband:wife*, *widower:widow*. If any of these methods of constructing related pairs are confined to certain groups or classes of words (as the dissimilar pairs last listed are almost limited to animal names or terms of family relationship, and as the *-a* suffix is limited to personal names and titles of nobility), that is also pertinent to our observation.

Having concluded that one major formal modification and several less extensively used devices may be employed to indicate a shift from masculine to feminine gender, we must turn to our next task, namely, to inquire what changes in meaning may arise from the operation of this grammatical category or function of gender.

A cursory observation of our material will suggest and permit the statement that gender is the grammatical property of a noun which corresponds to the sex of the object named. By developing this preliminary statement and noting the behavior of the personal pronouns as they are used to refer to nouns, we may recognize the following relationship between function and idea:

Function — Gender	Idea — Sex
Masculine	Male
Feminine	Female
Neuter	Without special sex-defining characteristics

Nevertheless, we must not overlook certain special situations where the relationships suggested in the foregoing table do not hold. The use of feminine pronouns in reference to ships, motor cars, and even railway trains comes to mind almost at once. The way in which personification as a literary device intrudes itself into the problem of gender is also germane: 'Now the bright morning-star . . . comes dancing from the East and leads with *her* the flowery

May' (Milton). Another pertinent matter is the use of the neuter gender as a diminutive, which often is shown by the use of the pronoun *it* to refer to a baby — 'Did *it* hurt *its* little finger?' — or to communicate a sense of disparagement: '*It* has an idea occasionally.'

Finally, we must also note certain difficulties which arise out of the complications or deficiencies of the mechanism with which the English language provides us. Possibly the chief problem comes from the lack of personal pronouns which might indicate masculine and/or feminine as distinct from neuter, forcing us into the unsatisfactory use of *his* with a possible feminine application or the cumbersome *his or her:* Every teacher must observe the language of (*his*) (*his or her*) pupils.

The subject of gender has by no means been covered completely, but enough has been said to indicate the method which must be employed in our grammatical analysis of present-day English. (As yet we have not allowed historical considerations to intrude themselves, nor have we compared the situation in respect to gender in English with that which prevails in other languages.) But even from this short view, we can readily see that the difficulties of adequate description arise from the circumstance that the relationship among the factors *form*, *function*, and *meaning* is highly complex and does not admit of simple and dogmatic generalization. Yet to overlook these complexities in favor of a few deceptively easy generalizations would result in quite divorcing grammar from language and in rendering it ineffective as a means of understanding how the English language is put together and how it works.

In the next two exercises, devoted to a consideration of number in nouns, we shall follow the same general procedure which has just been illustrated. The first questions will deal with the ways in which the grammatical function of number is formally indicated; the next group will be concerned with whatever changes in meaning may result from the employment of the various number categories; finally, certain conflicts between form and meaning in respect to the indication of number will be considered.

Additional Reading:

Curme, *Parts of Speech and Accidence*, pp. 112–27.
Grattan and Gurrey, *Our Living Language*, Chapter xxvi.
Jespersen, *Essentials of English Grammar*, Chapter xx.
Modern English Grammar, ii, Chapters ii, iii.
Webster's *New International Dictionary*, s.v. *plural*, sections iv, v.

Exercise XVII

1. How do you form the plurals of the following nouns: *cup*, *pan*, *dish*, *bowl*, *crow*, *edge*, *tree*, *skate*, *place*, *maze?* Review the conclusions concerning the pronunciation of the plural inflection which were reached in Question 7, Exercise vii.

2. What is the phonetic nature of the irregularity in the plurals of the following: *life*, *calf*, *house*, *path*, *wreath?* What other words can you think of which form their plurals in similar fashion? What type or class of final consonant seems to be subject to this irregularity? Do all the consonants of this type or class permit the same irregularity? Do all nouns ending in *f*, *s*, *th*, form their plurals in the same irregular fashion? Be able to illustrate your answer.

3. Are the words with which the preceding question was concerned relatively new importations in the English language, or have they been in the language a long time? Look up a number of them in the *Oxford English Dictionary* and note the date of the earliest citation for them. Can you conclude from this whether the age of a word might have anything to do with the likelihood of its having an irregular inflectional form? What has the *Oxford Dictionary* to say about the plural form of the word *scarf?*

4. Look up *-en*, suffix 3, in the *Oxford English Dictionary*. What words in Modern English form their plurals by adding *-en* instead of the regular plural inflection? Are the words which still employ this suffix relatively old or new in the language? Are they common or rarely used words? How many nouns can you think of which add no inflection at all, but alter the stressed vowel instead? Answer the two preceding questions in respect to these words.

5. What is peculiar about the plural form of the following words: *sheep*, *swine*, *deer*, *grouse*, *perch*, *brace* (of animals), *head* (of cattle), *gross*, *hundredweight*. What classes of ideas or spheres of life are represented by these words? Can you name other nouns in each group that form their plurals in the same way? Look up the word *dozen* in Webster. What do you find about the plural form of this word?

6. What languages appear to have been the source of most of the words listed under IV in Webster's treatment of *plural?* Consult both the *Oxford English Dictionary* and Webster for the plurals of the following: *antenna*, *encomium*, *formula*, *narcissus*, *sarcophagus*. Do the two dictionaries differ in any instances? Can you give any explanation for these differences? Why should the form of the plural constitute more of a problem with these words than with words borrowed from the French? From the citations in the *Oxford English Dictionary*, trace the history of the plural form of *dogma*.

7. What is our general practice in forming the plural of such compound words as *fountain pen*, *gold piece*, *chain store*, *cigar lighter?* What parts of speech are combined to form these particular compounds? Is there any psychological reason why the plurals should be formed in this way? What are the plural forms of the compounds listed under V in Webster's treatment of *plural?* Can you see any reason for this in view of the way in which these compounds are formed?

8. How many compounds can you think of which have as their second element the adjective *full?* Do they all form their plurals in the same way? Look up *spoonful* in the *Oxford English Dictionary*. What was the earlier form of the plural? Can you account for the change?

9. What are the plural forms of *break down*, *passer-by*, *cut off*, *going on*, *go-between*, *set back?* Of what parts of speech are these compounds formed? Is the difference in plural inflection traceable to a difference in their formation?

Additional Reading:

Curme, *Syntax*, Chapter xxvi.
Grattan and Gurrey, *Our Living Language*, Chapters xix, xx.
Jespersen, *Essentials of English Grammar*, Chapter xxi.
Modern English Grammar, Volume ii, Chapters iv, v, vii.
Webster's *New International Dictionary*, s.v. *plural*, sections ix–xi.

Exercise XVIII

1. What is the usual distinction in idea implied by the terms *singular* and *plural?* Formulate a statement indicating the difference in idea between the singular and plural of the noun *coal* as it is used in the two following sentences:

a. Much coal was stored in the bin.
b. Many coals were glowing on the hearth.

What is the distinction between *much food* and *many foods?* Look up the definition of *mass word* in Webster.

2. From the point of view of number, what is peculiar about such words as *alms*, *means*, *measles*, *hysterics*, *tongs?*

3. What difference in idea is there between the singular and the plural of the following pairs: *ground*, *grounds; grit*, *grits; sweeping*, *sweepings?* Answer the same question in respect to the following: *brain*, *brains; color*, *colors; quarter*, *quarters*. Are the plurals of the last group of words really plural in meaning?

4. How does Webster define a collective noun? Does a collective noun require a singular or a plural verb? See also Jespersen's and Curme's treatments of this problem. Do you know of any differences between British and American English in this respect? See Kennedy, *Current English*, p. 495. Does grammatical form or the idea implicit in the collective noun seem to be the more important factor in determining the number of the verb?

5. Not long ago, many school textbooks used to consider as incorrect the plural forms *falls*, *ways*, *woods*, and would recommend the use of the singular *fall* (= waterfall), *way* (as a measure of distance), *wood*. In what constructions would an awkward discrepancy in number be likely to arise with the plural of these nouns? Why should there be a tendency to use the plural? Consult the treatment of each of these nouns in Webster. Is the plural form always acceptable, or is it, in some instances, confined to certain language situations? How do British and American usage compare in the phrase *out of the woods?*

6. The constructions *these kind of apples* and *those sort of people* are often condemned as incorrect. Consult the *Oxford English Dictionary*, s.v. *sort*, definition 7. Does this expression appear to be in use? Has it ever been used?

For how long? By reputable writers? How might you explain the development of such a construction?

7. Very frequently a plural verb or a plural pronoun of reference is insisted upon with the word *data*. What do you find concerning this in Webster? See also Horwill, *Modern American Usage*. What circumstances and processes were probably responsible for this word acquiring singular force?

20. Nouns: Case

We shall begin our study of noun relationships with the following Latin sentences:

Naut*ae*	stell*a*	vi*am*	mōnstrat.
To the sailor	the star	the way	shows.
Ar*a*	de*ae*	corōn*ā*	ornātur.
The altar	of the goddess	with a wreath	is adorned.

Notice that each Latin sentence contains four words, three of which are nouns. In reading or translating such sentences, the principal problem is to determine the relationship of the nouns to one another. This is done by means of the endings or inflections which are attached to the roots of these words. We must, however, first become familiar with the inflectional pattern of such nouns, which may be summarized as:

Nominative	*-a*	Accusative	*-am*
Genitive	*-ae*	Ablative	*-ā*
Dative	*-ae*		

This paradigm gives us the necessary clues for the determination of meaning. In the first sentence, *stella* has the nominative inflection: one of the functions of the nominative case is that of subject of the verb, therefore *star*, in the absence of other words with such an inflection, may be assumed to be the subject. *Viam* has the accusative inflection; one of the accusative functions is that of direct object. We are now at the point where we recognize our sentence to read: *The star* (subject) *shows the way* (direct object). The third noun *nautae* has an inflection which might, from our table, be either genitive or dative. The principal genitive function is possession; the chief dative function is that of indirect object. By the trial and error method we decide that the indirect object function, *to the sailor*, is a more likely translation than one which would place either the way or the star in the possession of the sailor, so we finally conclude with the English translation that is written immediately under the Latin. By the same method, the nouns in the second sentence are recognized as nominative, genitive, and ablative respectively.

Thus in Latin the relationships of nouns to one another, and to the other full words in the sentence, are indicated primarily by means of inflection, which, if it is not simple in itself, at least permits a relatively simple analysis.

Let us compare this briefly with the situation in English. Inflection is employed in such combinations as *the cat's paws*, *John's book*, *Mr. Clark's creditors*, *water's edge*. But in a number of these instances, the very relationships indicated by the inflection *-'s* may also be expressed by reversing the order of the two words and connecting them with the function word *of*, which thus acts as a substitute or a replacement for the inflection: *the paws of the cat*, *the creditors of Mr. Clark*, *edge of the water*. Because the *of*-phrase here expresses the same relationship which is otherwise indicated by the genitive inflection *-'s*, this construction is sometimes called a *periphrastic genitive* (*i.e.* a genitive by means of a phrase). Moreover, certain other relationships, as the locative or the instrumental, which in Latin, Greek, or other highly inflected languages may be indicated through inflection, are capable of being expressed in English only by means of prepositional phrases: *at Rome* (Lat. *Romae*), *with wreaths* (Lat. *corōnis*).

In addition to this interplay of inflectional suffixes and prepositional constructions in English, there is also the operation of word order. For the present it is sufficient to say that we derive meaning from such a succession of words as *The Indian killed the bear* by referring it to an established word order pattern which may be summarized as ACTOR — ACTION — GOAL. In terms of this we conclude that it was the Indian who did the killing (actor) and the bear who was killed (goal). Furthermore, we would derive precisely the opposite meaning from the sequence *The bear killed the Indian.*

Upon certain occasions we may agree to deviate from this pattern (*Him the Almighty Power hurled* . . . [Milton]), and in certain other situations this pattern may come into conflict with some other equally well established word pattern or sequence. Yet the practice in English is in marked contrast to that in Latin where the first of the sentences quoted at the beginning of this section might be expressed in at least four different ways:

Stella nautae viam mōnstrat.
Nautae stella viam mōnstrat.
Viam stella mōnstrat nautae.
Mōnstrat nautae viam stella.

These changes in word order would have no essential effect upon the relationship of the nouns to one another: so long as *viam* has the *-am* inflection, it will be interpreted as the object of the verb; so long as *stella* has the nominative ending, it will be understood to be the subject. The difference resulting from a shifting about of the words is a secondary one of emphasis rather than the primary factor of relationship.

Thus the problem of noun relationship in English requires a more extended analysis than the same phenomenon in Latin. It is quite possible also that, as we finish, we shall have a synthesis or organization of categories quite different from that which would serve to describe a language which indicated such relationships chiefly by means of inflection.

We shall begin our study of case with a study of the one function, variously called possessive or genitive, where inflection still plays an active part. As with number, we shall proceed from form to function to meaning. After we have finished with this active inflectional form, we shall then consider those noun relationships which are indicated by the use of function words and by word order.

In connection with the exercise following this section, you will be asked to use three reference books which will be new to you. These are Fries, *American English Grammar*, J. Lesslie Hall, *English Usage*, and S. A. Leonard, *Current English Usage*. As their titles indicate, each of these works attempts a survey of a certain sector of English usage; that is why they are important for our purpose. We have discovered, however, that a complete survey of the whole of the English language is a task beyond possible fulfillment even by the most extended of dictionaries based upon millions of citations.

In order to place the proper evaluation upon the materials from more limited surveys, like those of Fries, Leonard, and Hall, we must know what sector or level of the language they purport to cover, how the material is gathered, and the method of arriving at conclusions. Only in the light of such knowledge can the material in any survey of the English language be properly interpreted.

Additional Reading:

Curme, *Syntax*, pp. 71–88, 109–11.
Parts of Speech and Accidence, pp. 133–6.
Fries, *American English Grammar*, pp. 26–39, 72–8.
Grattan and Gurrey, *Our Living Language*, Chapters XXVII, XXIX.
Hall, *English Usage*, pp. 22–6.
Jespersen, *Essentials of English Grammar*, pp. 138–46.
Modern English Grammar, III, pp. 12–23.
Leonard, *Current English Usage*, pp. 1–12, 95–9. (If the original edition is not available, pp. 95–9 may also be found in Marckwardt and Walcott, *Facts About Current English Usage*, pp. 65–70.)
Webster's *New International Dictionary*, s.v. *genitive*, *possessive*.

Exercise XIX

1. From your reading of the introductory sections of Fries, Hall, and Leonard (both the punctuation and the usage survey), be able to answer the following questions about each:

(1) What sections or levels of language usage are covered by the survey?
(2) What kinds of materials were studied?

(3) How was the material selected?
(4) What types or groups of usage questions were chosen for study?
(5) Is there any special method of summarizing pertinent conclusions, and if so, what is it?

2. What is the phonetic value of the -*'s* inflection in the following words: *week's*, *day's*, *Jones's*, *Tom's*, *George's*, *Paul's*, *Jeff's*, *Arthur's*, *cat's*, *dog's?* Is there any difference in actual sound between the -*'s* inflection of the genitive singular and the regular inflection of the plural? Is there any distinction in pronunciation between the genitive plural and other forms of the plural? Would you conclude from this that the written form -*s'* as in *cats'* (plural) has a phonetic or a graphic function?

3. How do you form the genitive singular of those nouns which in connection with Question 2, Exercise XVII were found to have an irregular plural? Is the genitive of these nouns also irregular? What is the genitive singular inflection of the nouns considered in Questions 4 and 5, Exercise XVII? What is the genitive plural? Does the genitive or the plural inflection appear to admit of the greater number of irregularities? Which inflection would have the more frequent use? What does this suggest about the relationship between frequency of use and the maintenance of irregular forms?

4. What form does Webster's *New International Dictionary* (s.v. *possessive*) recommend for the genitive singular of nouns ending in *s*, as *Thomas*, *Bliss*, etc.? Refer this same problem to Leonard, *Current English Usage*, pp. 50–51. Do the Leonard findings agree with the Webster recommendations? Upon analyzing the Leonard report on this problem, do you find any one sphere or type of usage where the practice differs markedly from the others?

5. According to Webster, to what kinds of nouns is the inflected genitive generally restricted? Consult Hall,

English Usage, pp. 202–7, and Fries, *American English Grammar*, pp. 74–5, for their discussions of the same problem. What happens to the word order when an inflected genitive is transformed into a periphrastic genitive?

6. What is peculiar about such a construction as *a friend of my father's?* What name is frequently given to this construction? Is its final element usually an animate or an inanimate object? What part of speech other than a noun frequently appears as the final element of this construction? Does this type of genitive ever offer any advantage which could not be derived from the inflected or periphrastic genitive alone?

7. What would be the inflection of such a combination as *The Governor of Ohio* in the event that you wanted to speak of his administration? What name is sometimes given to this construction? Does it occur in situations other than that of a noun followed by a modifying phrase? If so, specify the types of situation. What is the genitive singular of *son-in-law?* How does it compare with the plural form?

8. What modification in idea is indicated by the genitive (inflected or periphrastic) in each of the following: *the officer's command*, *girls' school*, *the President's advisers*, *Mary's hat*, *garland of roses*, *a year's salary*, *the State of Indiana*, *rules of the game*, *Canada's tall pines*, *world's fair*, *stone's throw*, *St. Luke's Hospital*, *pail of milk*, *author of the book*. For suggestions as to possible classes or categories, see Webster, s.v. *genitive*, Fries, p. 77, Curme, *Syntax*, pp. 77–88. In which categories may both the inflected genitive and the periphrastic be used? Which categories are limited to one or the other of the two forms? What do you think of the appropriateness of the *possessive* for this case?

9. May the genitive relationship between the nouns *horse* and *hide* or between *goose* and *feathers* be expressed in any way other than by means of the inflected or peri-

phrastic genitive? In the light of this, do you think that the genitive is essentially of primary or secondary rank according to Jespersen's classification?

10. From the *Oxford English Dictionary* or any other source, find out all you can about the history of the apostrophe as a mark of the genitive case. From the discussion in Leonard, *Current English Usage*, pp. 51–4, what do you gather about present tendencies in respect to its use?

21. Nouns: Case (*Continued*)

From our analysis of the genitive, it is apparent that noun relationships in English are indicated by means of more than one language device, that inflection, word order, and the use of function words all play very important parts. Bearing in mind that the categories or divisions in any scheme of classification must rest upon a consistent and mutually exclusive set of criteria, we must now ask ourselves how many cases are to be recognized in Modern English.

In highly inflected languages, such as Latin or Greek, form can readily constitute the basis for a case system. Even in German, where there are few changes in the form of the noun, the inflections of the definite article provide a satisfactory basis for classification. In English, however, a classification solely on the basis of form gives us only the genitive case as distinct from the uninflected form common to all other uses in the singular of the noun, and no case distinction at all in the plural (except for the written apostrophe in the genitive plural, which of course cannot be heard). Such a division, although it is objectively accurate, contributes very little to our understanding of the mechanism of noun relationships because it ignores the phenomena of word order and the employment of function words.

If, on the other hand, we were to begin with meaning, or the actual ideas inherent in the various relationships, we should very likely have to recognize so many classes or categories that a classification would prove unworkable.

In an attempt to avoid these extremes, most school grammars recognize a case system somewhat similar to that which prevails in Latin or German. For English it is generally customary to recognize either three or four cases, although an occasional grammar will still insist upon five. This results, of course, in arbitrarily lumping a number of modifications in idea into a single case category, which, moreover, may possibly be expressed in more than one way. From the point of view of providing anyone with a set of concepts and a terminology which will be useful in his subsequent learning of foreign languages, there may be something to be said in favor of this procedure, but as an objective classification of the way the English language expresses noun relationships, there is little to recommend it.

The terminology for such a classification of cases also presents a problem. Those grammars which adhere to a four case system generally also use the traditional names of the Latin cases: nominative, genitive, dative, and accusative. Many grammars which recognize three cases employ the terms subjective, objective, and possessive.

We have already seen that the term *possessive* is scarcely broad enough to suggest satisfactorily the many functions of the genitive case. *Subjective* and *objective* possibly have the advantage of being more immediately meaningful than *nominative* and *accusative*, but very likely the term *nominative* will have to be learned anyway in connection with such constructions as the nominative of address and the nominative absolute.

Probably the most satisfactory solution is to give up the attempt at case classification altogether and to consider or recognize the various possible constructions only as case functions. Except for the fact that the same form of the personal pronoun is used as subject, as nominative absolute, and as predicate nominative, there is little usefulness in the assumption that these three constructions constitute a single case. From the standpoint of the nouns, there is none at all. That such a classification, when carried to its ultimate limits, will raise many troublesome questions we have already seen. If there is any potential virtue in case analysis, it comes from the recognition of the specific constructions as indirect object, cognate object, absolute, or what not. The final step, which must dubiously assume that three or four possible noun relationships have something essential in common, is well omitted.

One more factor which should not be allowed to mislead you is the supposed difficulty of the inflectional languages. Because our language does not make extensive use of inflectional endings, we are inclined to think of highly inflected languages like Latin as being difficult to learn and as having been difficult to speak. The latter, at least, was very likely not the case. It was conceivably no more difficult for the speaker of Latin to apply an *-am* inflection to the proper situation than it is for you to create such a word as *deplorable*, even though you may never have used it before. The verb *deplore* is an active part of your vocabulary; so is the suffix *-able*, which you recognize and customarily employ as a device for turning verbs into adjectives. When the occasion arises where you need such a word as *deplorable*, you create it from the materials which you have at hand. The speaker of a highly inflected language operates with inflectional suffixes in much the same way that we use derivative or word forming suffixes.

We must remember also that there is no essential difference in difficulty between adding suffixes at the end of a word and placing prepositions before a word. Our choice of *for* in 'I have been here for a year' seems no more reasonable to a foreigner whose own idiom demands *since* than the choice of an accusative inflectional ending for the same purpose appears to us. A glance at the number of definitions listed under the words *by* or *for* in any reputable dictionary may even suggest that our language is in its own way more complex, more flexible, and more capable of suggesting delicate differentiations in meaning than many which seem more difficult on the surface.

Additional Reading:

Curme, *Syntax*, pp. 3–5, Chapter vi.
Fries, *Grammar of American English*, Chapter vii, pp. 261–70.
Grattan and Gurrey, *Our Living Language*, Chapters xxviii, xxxi, xxxii.
Jespersen, *Essentials of English Grammar*, Chapter xi.
Modern English Grammar, iii, Chapters xi–xv.
Webster's *New International Dictionary*, s.v. *nominative case*, *nominative absolute*, *predicate nominative*, *accusative*, *object*, *objective*, *dative*, *ablative*.

Exercise XX

1. What is the etymology of the word *nominative?* In what sense is the word applicable to the grammatical function which the nominative ordinarily performs?

2. Is the subject of a verb usually distinguished by inflection, by position, or by use with a function word? In Milton's *Paradise Lost*, find two instances where, in a declarative statement, a noun in the nominative case occurs after the finite verb.

3. What, according to Webster, s.v. *nominative*, are the functions of the nominative case other than that of subject of a finite verb? Find illustrations for each of these other functions from any single copy of your daily newspaper. Does the nominative case represent one or more than one modification in idea?

4. What is the etymology of the word *accusative?* In what sense is the word applicable to the grammatical function which the accusative ordinarily performs?

5. Is the direct object of a verb ordinarily distinguished by inflection, by position, or by use with a function word? In Milton's *Paradise Lost* find two instances where, in a declarative statement, a direct object either precedes the finite verb or precedes the subject.

6. What, according to Webster, s.v. *object*, are the types of object other than the direct and indirect? Find illustrations of these other functions from any single copy of your daily newspaper. In classifying direct objects, Jespersen recognizes, besides the ordinary direct object, an instrumental object and an object of result. Which of the objects in the following sentences would be instrumental objects, which would be objects of result, which would be ordinary direct objects?

(1) John shovels coal.
(2) The baby weighed eight pounds.
(3) Clarence claps his hands.

(4) She nodded her head.
(5) The grocer weighed the sugar.
(6) Frank shovels a path to the door.

Does the accusative case or the direct object represent a single modification in idea?

7. What is the etymology of the word *dative?* In what sense is the word applicable to the grammatical function which the dative usually performs?

8. What, as regards the ACTOR — ACTION — GOAL or SUBJECT — VERB — OBJECT pattern, is the usual position of the indirect object when it is not indicated by a function word? How is this changed when a function word is used? What function word is ordinarily employed for this purpose? How else, in respect to the verb, might you classify the phrase introduced by such a function word? In answering this, observe the following:

I sent my friend a letter.
I sent a letter to my friend.
I sent a letter to New York.
I sent to the grocer for some sugar.

9. According to Curme, *Syntax*, pp. 106–8, how would you classify the following datives:

(1) He made his *son* a new toy.
(2) The hobby horse was far too large for *him*.
(3) But *me* no buts.
(4) Will you do *me* a favor?

Does the indirect object represent a single modification in idea?

10. According to Webster, what types of relationship were expressed in Latin by the ablative case? How are these relationships generally expressed in Modern English?

11. According to Fries, what are the nine function words used most frequently with nouns in Modern English? Classify these on the basis of the type of relationship they

normally indicate: place, time, state or condition, manner, agent, instrument. After you have assorted them, try to think of as many more function words as possible for each category.

12. What cases of the noun are demanded by a preposition in German and in Latin? How would you answer this question for Modern English?

22. Adjectives and Adverbs

The adjectives and adverbs occupy a unique position among the so-called full words (nouns, pronouns, verbs, adjectives, and adverbs) in that inflections for number, gender, case, or person are almost wholly lacking in English. There are very few languages which have entirely dispensed with such inflections on the adjective. In Greek and Latin the adjectives had as complicated an inflectional pattern as the noun. In German there is a forbidding array of three adjective declensions. Even the modern Romance languages, having gone farther than English in discarding noun inflections, retain adjective forms which are indicative of number and gender.

With a few exceptions, the adjective in English is inflected only to indicate degree. Formally, we may recognize three degrees of comparison:

positive	cold	agreeable	happy
comparative	colder	more agreeable	happier, more happy
superlative	coldest	most agreeable	happiest, most happy

Notice that in place of the *-er* and *-est* inflections attached to *cold*, the function words *more* and *most* are used when comparing the adjective *agreeable*. This is called *periphrastic comparison* (recall how *periphrastic* was used in connection with the genitive). In the exercise which follows, we shall try to come to some decision about the kinds of words demanding inflectional and periphrastic comparison, respectively.

In considering the modification in idea expressed by the comparative and superlative degrees, we must beware of the easy assumption frequently made, that these degrees signify merely a gradual increase in whatever quality is expressed by the adjective. It has been pointed out that the comparative and superlative forms may indicate the same degree of quality, only considered from different points of view. If, for instance, we are comparing the sweetness of three spices, we may say:

> Cinnamon is *sweeter than* the other spices. (nutmeg, cloves)
> Cinnamon is *the sweetest of* the three. (cinnamon, nutmeg, cloves)

The two sentences are saying essentially the same thing, but in the first, the comparative is self-exclusive from the general class and needs to be completed by reference to the other members of the class, whereas the superlative is self-inclusive. An interesting verification of this analysis of the ideas inherent in the comparative and superlative is to be found in Spanish, where the function word *más* is used for comparative and superlative alike, but with the connective *que* (than) for the comparative, but with *de* (of) for the superlative.

The range of ideas which may be indicated by the function of comparison is:

> *Superiority:* sweeter than, sweetest of
> *Equality, or comparison not specified:* as sweet as, sweet
> *Inferiority:* less sweet than, least sweet of

Notice that there are no inflectional endings to indicate the degree of inferiority, but that the idea may be suggested by the function words *less* and *least*. The comparisons with *less* are not so frequent, however, for it is often possible for us to use the antithesis of the adjective with the superior comparison: *less cold than* = *warmer than*. Naturally this analysis of comparison is equally valid for the adverbs.

Since adjectives have so completely lost their inflections, it is only natural that, as a compensating factor, their order in relation to the nouns they modify will be relatively fixed. In the modern Romance languages, the adjective may either precede or follow the noun it modifies, and in the classical languages, and even in Old English, the adjective could be separated from its noun by other intervening words.

Modern English, however, adheres to a basic MODIFIER — SUBSTANCE word order pattern, and there is for us a decided difference between the members of such pairs as: *pipe metal*, *metal pipe*; *flower garden*, *garden flower*; *swamp blueberry*, *blueberry swamp*; *house work*, *work house*; *a cleaner window*, *a window cleaner*. In addition to this presubstantive position, adjectives may also be predicative, separated from the nouns they modify by a linking or copulative verb: *The pipe is metal. The window seems clean.* As with the ACTOR — ACTION — GOAL pattern, certain departures from this set order will occur, either for stylistic or structural reasons.

According to Jespersen's system of ranks, adjectives are usually classified as secondaries or adjuncts. However, not all adjuncts are adjectives. We have already seen that genitive nouns were secondaries in reality, and we have also noted that the idea inherent in such a combination as *horse's hide* or *hide of the horse* might also be expressed in the compounded form *horse hide*. (Whether this is written as one word or as two makes little difference from the point of view of grammatical analysis.) We know also that one noun such as *walnut* can be used to qualify another noun as in *walnut desk*, even though the two might occur very infrequently in any type of genitive relationship. Such substantive modifiers are often classified as noun adjuncts, although the precise point at which the noun adjunct becomes an adjective, or at which the noun-adjunct–noun combination becomes a compound word requires careful analysis. Likewise, nouns in apposition also act as secondaries or adjuncts: Peter the Great; Bryant, the poet; my brother Harvey; the river Seine.

Additional Reading:

Curme, *Parts of Speech and Accidence*, Chapter xi.
Syntax, Chapters vii, xxv.

Fries, *American English Grammar*, pp. 255–61, 270–82.

Grattan and Gurrey, *Our Living Language*, Chapters xxiv, xxxiii.

Jespersen, *Essentials of English Grammar*, Chapter xxii.

Webster, *New International Dictionary*, s.v. *adjective*, *adjunct*, *apposition*, *comparative*, *compare*, v. trans. 3, *comparison*, *superlative*, *adverb*, *subjunct*.

Exercise XXI

1. What two devices does the English language employ for the comparison of adjectives? Sort out the words in the following list according to the way in which the comparative and superlative degrees are ordinarily formed,

being careful to distinguish between those which require one of the two types, and those which will permit either type of comparison.

fresh	severe	hot
suitable	general	certain
rabid	clever	high
narrow	red	difficult
divine	yellow	late
rustic	ingenious	cruel
sad	blessed	plain
near	diffident	honest
colored	hearty	gay
intricate	thrilling	rampant
dry	wasteful	rainy
stingy	pleasant	pale

On the basis of your observation, frame a series of general statements about the way in which the comparative and superlative degrees are formed.

2. How many adjectives can you think of that are compared irregularly (e.g. *good*, *better*, *best*)? What is the practice in comparing such compound adjectives as *good natured*, *warm hearted*, *level headed?* From a phonetic point of view, what is peculiar about the comparison of *strong*, *young*, *long?*

3. What are the normal positions of adjectives in respect to the nouns they modify? Compare the situation in English with that of any other languages you may know. From the point of view of position, what is peculiar about such adjectives as *former*, *latter*, *inner*, *outer*, *utter*, *upper?* About *alive*, *asleep*, *awake*, *afloat*, *alone*, *content?* About such expressions as *president elect*, *attorney general*, *time immemorial*, *snobs pure and simple*, *Poland proper?*

4. On what grounds is such an expression as: *Of two disputants*, *the warmest is generally in the wrong*, sometimes considered incorrect? What, according to Webster (s.v.

comparison) and to *Current English Usage*, is the present status of this construction? Consult also Jespersen, *Modern English Grammar*, II, p. 204, Hall, *English Usage*, pp. 279, 280, and Russell Thomas, 'The Use of the Superlative Degree for the Comparative,' *English Journal*, College Edition, 24 (1935), 821–9. On the basis of the evidence in these last three references, would you be inclined to agree with Webster and Leonard? Is this tendency to substitute the superlative for the comparative extended to all uses of the comparative? Do such comparisons represent inclusion in, or exclusion from the class as a whole?

5. What are the psychological factors which would account for such an expression as *more perfect union?* Do such expressions in reality violate a rule of grammar or of logic? What words other than *perfect* would be subject to this tendency? Look up any four that you can think of in the *Oxford English Dictionary* and find out if they are ever compared in actual usage.

6. Consult Webster, s.v. *comparative* and *superlative*, for the distinction between the relative and absolute comparatives and superlatives. Find illustrations of all four from any one novel you have been reading.

7. From the Webster definitions of *adjective* and *adjunct*, what do you gather to be the essential difference between the two? Why might *adjunct* be a convenient term for the first element in such combinations as *wood fence*, *iron kettle*, *ice cream*, *baby boy?* How do these combinations differ from *fountain pen*, *chain store*, *gold piece*, *cigar lighter?* How do stress and the liability to inflection enter into the situation?

8. Are adjectives ever used as nouns? Be able to illustrate your answer. What would you suggest as a criterion for distinguishing between an adjective used as a noun and an actual substantive? What do the answers to this and the preceding question suggest about the readi-

ness with which Modern English makes use of grammatical change as a functional device?

9. How are adverbs often classified according to meaning? What word-forming suffix is frequently associated with the adverbial function? Look up this suffix in Webster or in the *Oxford English Dictionary* (suffix 2 in the latter). To what parts of speech is it applied? What is meant by a *flat adverb?*

10. What parts of speech may an adverb modify? What is the usual position of the adverb in relation to each of these parts of speech when it modifies them? What difficulty frequently arises concerning the position of such adverbs as *only*, *nearly*, *scarcely*, *even*, *ever?* What sentence was used by *Current English Usage* as an illustration of this problem? What decision was reached there? Compare the *Current English Usage* findings with Hall's treatment of the same problem (*English Usage*, 187–93).

11. Which of the three ranks would you expect most adverbs to occupy?

12. What objection is often made to the use of *pretty*, *slow*, *quick*, *sure*, *bad*, *real*, and *good* as adverbs? Compare the status of these as given by Webster's *New International Dictionary* and by Leonard's *Current English Usage*. Consult the *Oxford English Dictionary* under *pretty* and *slow*. Do the citations show an adverbial use of these words? If so, is it recent or of long standing? Consult the same dictionary for the history of the adverbial development of *very*. Can you see any parallel between this and certain present-day tendencies toward the use of *real?*

23. Pronouns

The pronouns are divided into a number of different classes, based partly upon the nature of their antecedents, partly upon meaning, and partly upon the functions which they perform. Among the classes of pronouns generally recognized are: personal, possessive, relative, interrogative, demonstrative, indefinite, reflexive, and intensive or emphatic.

As with the other parts of speech, the pronouns by no means constitute a closed class. Webster's dictionary, for example, gives a separate part of speech entry for both *as* and *where* as pronouns, although we are more likely to think of these words as adverbs and conjunctions. At the same time, it is equally evident that certain words customarily recognized as pronouns may serve either in adjectival or connective functions.

One such question of classification arises with the pairs *your*, *yours*, *my*, *mine*, whose proper classification (pronoun or adjective) has given trouble to many grammarians.

a. This is *your* (*my*) book.
b. This book is *yours* (*mine*).

But the difficulty lies only on the surface and may easily be resolved by the application of the principle of adjective position discussed in the preceding section. Considered in this light, it is immediately clear that *my* and *your* used as in (*a*) above are pre-substantive modifiers, whereas *mine* and *yours* used as in (*b*) are predicate modifiers. The essential problem in classifying them is not whether they are pronouns or adjectives. Because our present system of classification into parts of speech admits of some overlapping, it happens that these words satisfy both the definition of a pronoun (they do 'stand for' a noun) and of an adjective (they do modify a noun). *Mine* and *yours* can, of course, also act as primaries (*Mine* is on the table), but when they are considered as secondaries, the essential difference between the possessive pronouns and the possessive adjectives is that of position.

It should be observed that the personal pronouns in English, as in many other languages, are notable for the retention of inflectional distinctions not found in other parts of speech. The English personal pronouns have distinctive forms for each of the three genders in the third person singular: *he*, *she*, *it*. Moreover, the form used for the various subject or nominative case functions is, with two exceptions (*you* and *it*), differentiated from that used for the various object functions: *I — me*, *he — him*, etc. In addition to the properties of case, number, and gender, already familiar to us by virtue of their manifestation in the nouns, we must also recognize that of *person*, indicating whether reference is being made to the speaker (I, we), the person spoken to (you), or some third person or thing (he, she, it, they). Finally, since the pronouns are very short words, often used in positions of little stress, they frequently have, as we have seen in our phonetic transcriptions, both a heavily and a lightly stressed form.

A curious feature of the English language is the lack of a wholly satisfactory impersonal pronoun corresponding to German *man* or French *on*. It is true that *one* may be and is often employed in this manner, but the problem of subsequent agreement and reference is troublesome. Should the writer or speaker say: *One rarely enjoys one's luncheon when one is tired*, or use the *one . . . his . . . he* construction? The difficulties in such a choice were admirably illustrated by the *Current English Usage* survey, where the *one . . . one* form, although rated as established, was severely criticized for its stilted and artificial quality, whereas the alternative *one* . . . *he* construction failed to receive the full approval of the judges.

Consequently several of the personal pronouns have been pressed into service as impersonals with varying degrees of acceptability:

> You had to have property to vote in the eighteenth century.
> They had many strikes in England in 1860.
> It says on the poster that tomorrow is election day.

Another result has been to throw many constructions, which in other languages might be expressed with an impersonal pronoun, into the passive voice: German: *Man sagte mir* . . .; English: *I was told* . . .

Additional Reading:

Curme, *Parts of Speech and Accidence*, Chapter x.
Fries, *American English Grammar*, pp. 78–96.
Grattan and Gurrey, *Our Living Language*, Chapter xxii.
Jespersen, *Essentials of English Grammar*, Chapters xvi, xvii.
Modern English Grammar, ii, Chapters xvi, xvii.
Sweet, *New English Grammar*, pp. 73–83.

Exercise XXII

1. Consult Webster or any of the suggested references for definitions of the following classes of pronouns: personal, relative, demonstrative, interrogative, reflexive, indefinite, reciprocal, intensive, or emphatic. On the basis of these definitions, decide whether function, nature of the antecedent, or meaning is the basis for each of the classes. Are there any pronouns which can be placed in more than one class?

2. Construct a paradigm in phonetic transcription of all three persons, both singular and plural, of the personal pronoun. Include also all three genders of the third person

singular. For each pronoun include at least two forms which will indicate the pronunciation in positions of heavy and light stress.

3. Consult Webster, Leonard, *Current English Usage*, pp. 108, 109, Hall, *English Usage*, pp. 153–7, and the *Oxford English Dictionary* to determine the present status of *it is me*. Which of the reasons given by Hall for the development of this form seems to you to be the most valid? In which persons of the pronoun would problems of this nature arise? Do the findings of *Current English Usage*, pp. 109–10, indicate any differences in the extent of this development in the various persons? See also Hall, *English Usage*, pp. 291–5.

4. Which persons, numbers, and genders of the personal pronoun maintain a distinction between the pre-substantive possessive (*my*, *your*) and the predicative possessive (*mine*, *yours*)? How many patterns seem to be apparent in the formation of these two classes? Can you account for the development of such a sub-standard form as *hisn?* How many similar sub-standard forms can you name? Does this suggest anything about the relationship of sub-standard English to the standard form?

5. Construct a paradigm of the demonstrative pronouns. In which of the ranks, according to Jespersen's scheme of classification, may these pronouns be placed? Which pronoun, belonging to another category in standard English, is often used as a demonstrative plural in sub-standard English? What is the unstressed form of the pronoun *that?* Is this unstressed form ever used as a demonstrative? If not, how does it function?

6. How many relative pronouns can you name? Which of the relative pronouns are declinable and which are not? Construct appropriate paradigms for those which may be declined. What ordinarily determines our choice of *who*, *which*, or *that* as relative pronouns? Is the situation the same for both written and spoken English?

7. Some authorities consider the following sentence incorrect on the grounds that *whose* can be used only as the genitive case of *who* and not of *which: Soon we came to a swamp on whose bank stood a hunter's cabin.* Use any source material you choose and find out what modern usage actually is in this matter. Do the same thing with the omitted relative construction as in: *This is the man I met last week.*

8. What, according to the *Oxford English Dictionary* and *Current English Usage* is the status of the interrogative and relative pronouns in the following sentences:

a. Who are you looking for?
b. Invite whoever you like to the party.

What grounds might there be for objecting to the forms of the pronouns used in these sentences? Can you explain the development of the nominative case forms here? How might the pressure of word order affect the occurrence of these forms? See also Jespersen's discussion of *who* and *whom* in his *Modern English Grammar*, III, 197–201. With what question is he chiefly concerned?

9. Construct a paradigm of the intensive and the reflexive pronouns. What elements go into the formation of these categories? Is the pattern of these pronouns consistent in its formation? How can you account for the appearance of such a form as *hisself* in certain varieties of sub-standard English? Do you know of any similar forms? Draw up a series of statements differentiating between the reflexive and intensive pronouns on the basis of stress and sentence position. With what question concerning the *-self* forms of the pronouns does *Current English Usage* appear to be concerned? Verify the *Current English Usage* findings by references to any other surveys of usage you may choose.

10. What attitude is often assumed toward the use of *none* with a plural verb? (*None of the books were on the*

shelf.) What do you find in Webster and the *Oxford English Dictionary* about the status of this construction in present usage and about its age? What other indefinite pronouns do Fries and Jespersen cite as being used with a plural verb? Consult *Current English Usage*, pp. 104, 105, for its treatment of number concord with *everyone* and *everybody*. In all these instances, does agreement of form or agreement of meaning seem to be the dominant factor?

24. Verbs, Formal Modifications

Person, number, tense, mood, and voice are the grammatical properties of the verb, and in many languages there is a distinct inflectional form for almost every possible combination of these qualities. In English, as with a good many other parts of speech, the verb has relatively fewer distinctive inflectional forms; person and number are specifically indicated only in the third person singular, present indicative, where there is the same distribution of the -*(e)s* [s, z, əz] inflection that occurs in the genitive singular and in the plural of the noun: *cuts*, *sings*, *pushes*. Consequently, the subject of the verb is usually expressed, even when it is pronominal, since there is not likely to be a distinct inflectional ending to suggest it: Latin, *canto;* English, *I sing*.

Nevertheless, it should be pointed out that in reality the properties of person and number are scarcely verbal qualities. They are characteristics of the subject rather than of the action or state which is indicated by the verb. Genuine verbal plurality would be the repetition of an action — not the performance of a single action by more than one person.

Next to the third singular, present indicative inflection,

the most commonly applied formal suffix is *-ed*, the so-called regular ending for the simple past tense and the past participle. The pronunciation of this inflection also varies according to phonetic considerations, as we may see from such forms as *pushed*, *pulled*, *baited*, *faded*. With the exception of possibly one hundred and thirty, all the verbs in the English language are inflected according to the regular pattern. About half the remaining verbs indicate changes in tense form by means of change in the stressed vowel, a phenomenon similar to that which we have already seen in connection with such nouns as *man* and *goose;* e.g. *sing*, *sang*, *sung; fall*, *fell*, *fallen; tear*, *tore*, *torn*. Note also that in certain of these verbs, the vowel of the past participle differs from that of the preterit. Other types of irregularity will be considered in detail in the exercise which follows.

So far we have dealt only with the declarative forms of the verb. But, in addition to making simple affirmative statements, our verb forms are also required to furnish us with a mechanism for asking questions, for expressing negation, and even for combining these two in negative-interrogative statements. Before we are ready to consider these mechanisms in detail, one more feature of the English verb formations must be observed.

As with the other parts of speech, function words and periphrastic constructions play an important role in doing much of the work which in other languages is relegated to the inflectional endings. In contrast to all the Romance languages, English has no inflectional form for the future, only a series of periphrastic formations. Even in the present tense, these periphrastic forms are extremely frequent in occurrence, for when we use the simple present tense, we rarely have reference to an action which is actually taking place here and now. Suppose one says:

I *eat* grapefruit in the morning.
Of course I *wear* a hat.
I *walk* from my home to the office in ten minutes.

It is obvious that I am neither eating nor walking as I speak or write, and although I may be wearing a hat, it is clear that my reference is to a much larger block of time than merely the present moment. If I were to refer to present action, I would be more likely to say:

I *am eating* grapefruit.
I *am wearing* a hat.
I *am walking* from my home to the office.

In other words, with many verbs the simple present tense is used to indicate eternal or habitual action without reference to any particular time. To express what is going on here and now, we ordinarily use a tense form which is expanded. This expanded present, composed of the present tense of the verb *to be* and the present participle of the verb in question, is usually called the *present progressive* because it refers to action progressing or going on (possibly the term *definite present*, used by Sweet is a more precise description of the idea which it communicates). Yet, with certain verbs of perception and some indicating mental attitudes (*hear*, *see*, *believe*, *think*, *doubt*), the simple present is used throughout. There is also the third possibility, *I do eat*, which, depending upon the context, may refer either to a specific action or to a habitual or an eternal one, but whose special contribution to meaning is that of emphasis. Observe also the corresponding past tense forms: *I walk*, *I was walking*, *I did walk*. When we turn from simple declarative statements to questions and denials, our practice is still different, and will be considered in detail in the questions which follow.

That the future tense is entirely periphrastic has already been indicated. In forming it the speaker or writer has to choose between two auxiliaries, *shall* and *will;* moreover, there appears to be a difference here between American and British English.

The most satisfactory brief statement of American practice is one which recognizes two kinds of future: the informal or simple future, and the formal or emphatic. The first is formed with the function word *will* for all three persons and represents the subject as an agent free from compulsion of any sort (*I*, *you*, *he will go*). The contracted forms *I'll*, *you'll*, *he'll*, etc., are more informal and less emphatic than the full forms.

The function word *shall* is used in all three persons to form the formal future, representing the subject as under constraint, especially in the second and third persons. It is used chiefly to express prophecy, legal enactments, judicial decisions, commands, determination or dominant authority on the part of the speaker — and to some extent, though not universally in American English, the first person is used to indicate simple futurity in formal writing.

We must not forget, however, that the present tense may convey future meaning in such a sentence as *I leave for New Orleans on Thursday*. Moreover the following periphrastic constructions are also commonly employed to indicate future time:

I *am going to go* to New Orleans on Thursday.
I *am to go* to New Orleans on Thursday.
I *am about to go* to New Orleans.

Additional Reading:

Curme, *Parts of Speech and Accidence*, pp. 242, 243, 252–61, 269–96, 304–19.
Syntax, pp. 49–60.
Fries, *American English Grammar*, pp. 59–61, 150–68.
Jespersen, *Modern English Grammar*, II, pp. 169–83; IV, Chapter XII.
Marckwardt, Walcott, *Facts About Current English Usage*, pp. 1–21.

Exercise XXIII

1. What is peculiar about the inflection of the verbs *must*, *can*, *may* in the present tense? How are these verbs ordinarily used? Are the expanded tense forms generally used with these verbs? How many other verbs can you name which behave in the same manner? What can you say about the verbs *dare* and *need* in connection with the foregoing questions?

2. Look up the word *strong*, definition 26, in Webster's *New International Dictionary*. What does it mean when applied to verbs? Look up the term *principal part* in Webster. In English what forms of the verb constitute thc principal parts?

3. Look up the principal parts of the following verbs in Webster's *New International Dictionary: spring*, *sing*, *awake*, *dive*, *beat*, *bite*, *get*, *show*, *light*. From the standpoint of the number of distinctive forms, what appears to be happening to the first two verbs listed? To what conjugation do the alternate endings for *awake* and *dive* belong? In which one of the principal parts does the conflict in the last five verbs appear to be centered?

4. Explain how each one of the following verbs deviates from the regular or weak verb pattern: *dream*, *put*, *do*, *bleed*, *shoe*, *build*, *mean*, *sell*, *teach*, *bring*, *cast*, *go*, *leave*, *hit*.

5. Which of the three forms of the present tense are employed in asking a question? Construct a diagram or paradigm which will show the relationship between the declarative and interrogative forms of the verb in the present tense. Will the same diagram or paradigm be equally applicable to the verbs *must* and *eat?* Explain. What fundamental alteration in the English word order pattern serves to indicate interrogation? Indicate this in the form which has been previously employed to set forth word order patterns. Compare the mechanism for interrogation in English with that of any other language you know.

6. Answer Question 5 in respect to the negative and to the negative interrogative forms of the verb.

7. What would appear to be the grammatical objection to *aren't I?* To *ain't I?* What other form of the first person negative interrogative is possible for the verb *to be?* Upon comparing this last form with the negative interrogative of other auxiliary verbs, can you see any reason why it is not entirely suitable for informal speech? What was the status of *ain't I* in *Current English Usage?* How did it differ from other uses of *ain't?* Can you suggest a reason for this?

8. It is generally assumed that in the English language the doubled negative is incorrect. The sentences below all contain types of double negation:

> I haven't hardly any money.
> He was not unkind.
> The team didn't win no games this year.
> The statement was not misunderstood.
> We haven't but a few left.

Which of these sentences are acceptable English? Revise the statement concerning the acceptability of the doubled negative in such a manner that it will be an accurate reflection of the situation in the English language.

9. Compare the results of Leonard, *Current English Usage* and Marckwardt-Walcott, *Facts About Current English Usage* in regard to the following sentences:

I will probably come a little late.
Will you be at the Brown's this evening?

Upon what kind of evidence is the Marckwardt-Walcott study based? What does Fries conclude about cultivated American practice in forming the future? What difference would stress make in your classification of the following as formal or informal future: [ɑɪl go; ɑɪ ˈwɪl go; ɑɪ wɪl ˈgo].

10. The following sentences illustrate a number of problems which arise about the agreement of subject and verb. On the basis of the assigned reading in Jespersen, Volume II, and in Curme, *Syntax*, and whatever information you can find in *Current English Usage*, select those forms which appear to you to be acceptable, and in each instance attempt to set forth the principle involved, in a single concise statement.

(1) A group of us (goes) (go) to the games regularly.
(2) Neither Duke nor Pitt (is) (are) likely to win the title.
(3) All that we can promise (is) (are) reasonably good results.
(4) My friend and colleague (does) (do) me great honor.
(5) There (has) (have) been many objections to his proposal.
(6) Three times four (is) (are) twelve.
(7) There (was) (were) a bed, a dresser, and two chairs in the room.
(8) Either the governor or his advisers (is) (are) responsible.
(9) At school every boy and girl (is) (are) taught to read.
(10) The captain with his soldiers (makes) (make) the charge.

25. Verbs: Tense, Aspect, and Mood

Thus far only the simple tense forms have been considered. Corresponding to the past, present, and future, the English language also has three compound tense forms: *I had looked*, *I have looked*, *I will* (*shall*) *have looked*. These are usually called the past perfect, present perfect, and future perfect, respectively. But before we discuss the functions of these expanded forms, we must understand something of the ideas related to the grammatical function of tense.

The category *tense* corresponds to the ideational concept of *time*. The tense system is divided into three categories: past, present, and future. Time, on the other hand, is capable of division into only two parts, past and future, with the present as a line of separation between the two. The present is therefore a point of division rather than a block of time, as we are likely to think of it when considering the tense categories. Moreover, from the point of view of idea, the notion *present* has no stability whatever, but is continually shifting from the past toward the future.

We must not forget, moreover, that a single tense may, on various occasions, represent quite different times of action. We have already seen that the simple present tense may represent either future or 'eternal' action; it may also be used, in the so-called historical present, to give a greater sense of reality to an event which has taken place in the past. Conversely, both present and future tenses, to say nothing of numerous other periphrastic constructions, may be used to indicate future time. In short, there is not a point by point correspondence between the functional category of tense and the ideational category of time.

When one time is being identified or discussed in reference to another, it becomes necessary to recognize certain other temporal divisions: a before past, a before present, and a before future:

> He had gone (*before past*) when I arrived (*past*).
> We shall have gone (*before future*) by the time you come (*future*).
> He has already gone (*before present*) before she notices his absence (*present*).

In general, the so-called perfect tenses are used to indicate these 'before' times, but even so, there is one particular difficulty here: because past time as well as 'before present' is anterior to the present, there is likely to be some complication in the use of the past and present perfect tenses. Notice that both *I ate the apple* and *I have eaten the apple* indicate action which has taken place in the past. Very likely, *I have eaten the apple* suggests a more immediate past, but observe that whenever a specific time is mentioned, the expanded form cannot be used: *I ate* (not *have eaten*) *the apple at ten o'clock.* However with an adverb indicating an immediate but not specific past, such as *just*, either form is permissible.

Yet the term *perfect*, which is commonly applied to these compound tenses, actually suggests nothing about time at all, but indicates another verbal property, that of *aspect.* Aspect is not customarily recognized in the conventional parsing of the English verb, but so long as we are attempting to understand something of the meaning and the assumptions resident in our grammatical terms, we must consider it. In the grammar of many languages the term aspect is used to indicate that property of the verb through which action or being is represented in terms of inception (action beginning), duration (action continuing), or completion. *Perfect* naturally implies a perfected or completed action, and in this connection it should be observed that certain languages, such as French, use the term *imperfect* for what we in English customarily call the past tense, and that Spanish recognizes as grammatical categories both a pluperfect and a past anterior, the latter term conveying a purely temporal implication.

We might naïvely assume, if our tense terminology means anything, that the perfect tense actually indicates completed action in opposition to incomplete action indicated by the past tense. But this is certainly not the case when we compare *I drank the milk* with *I have drunk the milk* where completed action is implied in both constructions. Moreover, in the light of the usual concept of the perfect as completed action, the name 'present perfect progressive' for such a construction as *I have been drinking milk* (*all day*) is actually a contradiction in terms, for the progressive construction suggests that the action has been continuous, and certainly nothing is implied as to a point or time of completion.

Similar complications exist with the use of the past and future perfect tenses, and these could all be discussed at great length. However, the main point for our purposes is to demonstrate that the names we give our tenses confuse the functions of tense and aspect, and that the classifications of time implied by our divisions into tenses do not permit a corresponding division of idea.

Mood (or *mode*, as it was called by earlier grammarians) is a designation of how an act is conceived, whether as a fact, a possibility, a desirability, or a command. The number of moods so recognized has varied from time to time; for the languages with which we are likely to be most familiar, the maximum number is four: infinitive, imperative, indicative, subjunctive.

The first of these will be considered later in connection with the nonfinite forms of the verb. The *imperative*, consisting of the uninflected present stem of the verb (*look!*), is conventionally analyzed as being in the second person, singular or plural (in terms of the person or persons addressed), and expresses a command, suggestion, request, or entreaty. There is in English no difference in form between a singular and a plural imperative.

As its name shows, the *indicative* mood refers to an action or state conceived of as fact; it indicates. It is the mood in which verbs most commonly occur, and to which belong all the verbal examples given so far.

The subjunctive mood is one of the most troublesome and elusive constructions of the English verbal system. Since the indicative has been called the 'fact mood,' it would be equally appropriate to call the subjunctive the hypothetical, the contrary-to-fact or the imaginative (in the sense of referring to an imaginary situation) mood. It is used to express the following attitudes:

Wish: If John *were* only here.
Exhortation: Heaven *forbid*.
Concession: *Be* it ever so humble, there's no place like home.
Condition contrary to fact: If it *were* later, I should expect them.

Condition possible in the future: We shall start, if the weather *permit*(*s*).

Improbability: If this report *be* (*is*) true, anything can happen.

In the last two sentences the possibility of a difference in usage has been recognized by placing the alternate form (indicative) in parentheses. This leads us to ask what the differences in form between the two moods really are.

For almost all English verbs there is no formal difference whatever between indicative and subjunctive in the past tense, and only one in the present conjugation. In the third person singular, present indicative, the distinctive inflection is *-s* (*looks*, *sings*, *rushes*), but the subjunctive here has no inflectional ending: *if he look*, *sing*, *rush*. The verb *to be* has the form *be* in all three persons and both numbers of the present subjunctive, making this conjugation wholly different from that of the indicative; in the past tense, *were* is the form for all persons and numbers, in contrast to *was* which is the form for the first and third persons singular, past indicative. There is little question that the pressure of identity between indicative and subjunctive at eleven of the twelve points of the simple conjugation of most verbs has been responsible for the intrusion of the indicative form in the circumstances noted.

It must also be recognized that almost all the verb forms which have been used to illustrate the subjunctive are interchangeable with periphrastic constructions, employing such function words as *may*, *might*, *can*, *could*, etc.

If John were only here — If John could only be here
Heaven forbid — May heaven forbid
If this report be true — If this report should be true

Moreover, the expressions of possibility, permission, power, or obligation to perform an action are not the same as expressing the action itself, and we must face the question of including as subjunctives such expressions as these:

I can believe	I could believe	I must believe
I may believe	I might believe	I should believe
	I ought to believe	

Observe that these modifications of attitude are expressed entirely by means of function words rather than by inflections. For this reason some grammarians have created a classification distinct from the subjunctive, and refer to expressions such as these as the *potential mood.*

All this illustrates a development in the verb which we have already observed in the noun and in the adjective. In the noun, the periphrastic genitive frequently conveys the same meaning as the inflected genitive, and in the adjective there is no functional difference between the periphrastic comparative or superlative (*more hearty*, *most hearty*) and the inflectional *heartier*, *heartiest*. So too, periphrastic verbal constructions perform many of the functions which in other languages or in older periods of the English language were the exclusive province of inflectional endings.

English has two voices, *active* and *passive*, which represent the subject either as acting or acted upon.

Active: John kicks the ball.
Passive: The ball is kicked by John.

The passive voice is formed by using the auxiliary *be* in combination with the past participle of the verb. In contrast to Latin, all the forms of the English passive are periphrastic in form. Note that *ball*, which functions as the direct object of the verb in the active voice becomes the subject in the passive construction, and that *John*, the subject of the verb in the active voice need not appear at all in the passive construction, or if it does, it is introduced by the preposition *by*, and is classified by some grammarians as the retained object.

Additional Reading:

Curme, *Syntax*, Chapters xviii–xxi.
Fries, *American English Grammar*, pp. 103–7, Chapter viii.
Grattan and Gurrey, *Our Living Language*, Chapters xxxv–xl.
Jespersen, *Essentials of English Grammar*, Chapters xxiii–xxvii.
Modern English Grammar, Vol. iv. The whole volume is devoted to an extended discussion of the questions which are touched on in this section.
Sweet, *New English Grammar*, pp. 98–114.
Webster's *New International Dictionary*, s.v. *aspect*, *subjunctive*, *tense*, *transitive*.

Exercise XXIV

1. What times of action are represented by the present tense in the following sentences:

(1) I hear the band playing as it marches down the street.
(2) He leaves for New Orleans tomorrow morning.
(3) The messenger comes up to me, hands me a letter, turns on his heel, and walks off — all this before I had a chance to recover from my surprise.

What do you conclude from this about the times of action which may be represented by a single tense?

2. How many simple and periphrastic constructions can you think of to indicate the future of the idea, 'John goes to New York'?

3. Conjugate the verbs *look* and *see* in the three perfect tenses (past, present, future perfect) of the active indicative.

4. Give the conjugation of all six tenses of the verbs *look* and *see* in the progressive form (*I am looking*, etc.).

5. What differences in meaning are indicated by the following constructions:

(1) I wrote the letter.
(2) I have written the letter.
(3) I was writing the letter.
(4) I have been writing the letter.

What logical distinction other than time enters into these verbal constructions? What is meant by a *point tense?*

6. Consult a Latin grammar and a French grammar and in each case make a list of those tense forms, in all voices and moods, which are constructed by the addition of an inflection only and not by the use of an auxiliary verb. Make a similar list for Modern English. How do your three lists compare in size? In which other parts of speech have you found an analogous situation?

7. Improve the following sentences by altering the verb tenses when necessary. Be able to justify the changes you make. Which of these sentences are included in Leonard, *Current English Usage?* What are the conclusions concerning them?

(1) The fairies want to surprise the old lady, and they proceeded to do so.
(2) As time rolls on and on, the government began to revise many of the outworn laws.
(3) She had no seeds to plant in the garden and must buy some immediately. (Keep this sentence in the past.)

(4) I wouldn't have said that if I thought it would have shocked her.
(5) If they had been born centuries ago under the same financial circumstances, they would still have been as unequal as they would be today.
(6) If the great scientists would have waited for inspirations, they would have accomplished little.
(7) Galileo discovered that the earth moved.

8. What can you conclude from Leonard, *Current English Usage* about the present status of inflected forms for the subjunctive mood? What particular uses of the subjunctive were included in this survey? Compare the Leonard findings with the treatment of the same problem in Fries, *American English Grammar.* Where, according to Fries, does the inflected subjunctive form persist most strongly?

9. What do you learn from Webster about the appropriateness of, or the justification for, the term *subjunctive?*

10. Sometimes the past tense form is used to indicate an assumption or an idea contrary to fact: If he *were* here, I should go home. If I *had* time, I would read the lesson. The actual time involved in these sentences is the present. How can you explain the mechanism of tense here taking the place of the mechanism of mood?

11. Conjugate the verbs *take* and *pull* in all six tenses of the passive voice. Give also the passive progressive forms for the three simple tenses.

12. From the definitions in Webster, what do you understand to be the difference between a transitive and an intransitive use of a verb? Not so long ago it was customary to refer to the verbs themselves as transitive or intransitive. Can you see any possible objections to such a procedure?

13. What is the distinction between such pairs of verbs as *lie* and *lay*, *sit* and *set?* From an examination of all

their possible forms, can you give any reasons why they are frequently confused?

ADDITIONAL READING:

Curme, *Syntax*, Chapters XXII–XXIV.
Fries, *Grammar of American English*, pp. 76–7, 130–46.
Jespersen, *Essentials of English Grammar*, Chapters XXXI, XXXII.
Modern English Grammar, IV, Chapter VII.
Sweet, *New English Grammar*, pp. 115–18.
Webster's *New International Dictionary*, s.v. *gerund*, *infinitive*, *participle*, *split infinitive*, *verbal*.

EXERCISE XXV

1. What, according to Webster, is the distinction between a *verb* and a *verbal?* What forms of the verb are considered to be verbals?

2. Does such a construction as *to come* tell you anything about who is coming? About how many are coming? About when the coming is to take place? In the light of your answers to these questions, what do you think is the relationship between the words *infinitive* and *infinite* or *infinity?*

3. What is the form of the perfect infinitive in English? What would be the perfect infinitive of the verb *see?* What is the form of the passive infinitive of the same verb? Of the perfect passive infinitive? Do you know any languages which have no passive infinitive construction?

4. What part-of-speech function does the infinitive usually perform? Illustrate, using infinitives both with and without an object.

5. Does the preposition *to* always appear with the infinitive? Consult Leonard, *Current English Usage*, for the treatment of the split infinitive. Read also the discussion of the split infinitive in Curme, in Fries, and in

Webster. What do you conclude about the present status of this construction? Upon examining the instances of the split infinitive which you do find, can you come to any conclusion about the kind of situation where a 'split' is difficult to avoid?

6. What inflectional ending is used to form the gerund and the present participle? What functional difference does there appear to be between the gerund and the present participle? Which of the following sentences contains a gerund and which contains a participle:

Imagine him dancing.
Imagine his dancing.

7. Grammarians used to insist that the subject of the gerund was in the genitive case. From your knowledge of the formation of the genitive, indicate under what circumstances such an inflection would not be apparent in the spoken language. Consult the treatment of this topic in Curme, in Fries, and in Webster, s.v. *gerund*. What is the inflection applied to phrases, clauses, and nouns in apposition acting as subject of the gerund? Is there any difference between nouns and pronouns?

8. What tense and voice combinations of the participle does Webster recognize? According to the treatment in Webster, under what circumstances is a participle classified as an adjective?

26. Sentence and Paragraph

Just as the various parts of speech may be considered from the points of view of meaning, function, or form, so the sentence may be approached from the standpoint of logic or meaning, of rhetoric or style, and of form or grammar.

In terms of meaning, the sentence is most frequently

defined as the expression of a complete thought. But completeness is highly relative, depending upon the purpose of the speaker or writer as well as upon context. It is difficult to see, for example, that the sentence which is quoted below expresses a thought either more or less complete than if it had been divided into two sentences at the semicolon:

> It is obvious that, with such scanty and unexciting materials, no biographer can say very much about what Sir Thomas Browne did; it is quite easy, however, to expatiate about what he wrote.

Obviously, meaning does not provide us with a sufficiently fixed or objective standard for sentence definition.

Whereas most definitions of a sentence from either a logical or a formal point of view are concerned with a minimum standard, insisting that a sentence must contain at least so much, rhetorical considerations more often affect the sentence maximum. It was very likely for rhetorical reasons that Lytton Strachey decided to include within the limits of a single sentence both of the independent clauses quoted in the preceding paragraph. Conversely, Henry Adams concludes a chapter in his best-known book with the two brief sentences: 'As yet he knew nothing. Education had not begun.' It might easily be argued that these are parts of a larger segment of thought, but quite possibly a desire for an emphatic conclusion led the author to this type of construction.

There is, of course, no such thing as a rhetorical definition of a sentence, but we must be constantly aware that the desire for emphatic and persuasive expression, the rhetorical purpose or impulse, will inevitably influence sentence construction, no matter how it may be defined or limited from other points of view.

Closest to a formal analysis is that definition or conception which considers the sentence as a group of words having a subject and a predicate. The chief difficulty here, however, is that *subject* and *predicate* are essentially logical rather than grammatical terms. That is, when we proceed to define the subject as 'the thing which is talked about' and the predicate as 'that which is said about the subject,' we are again defining in terms of meaning. Moreover, when we come to such pairs of sentences as: *Her work is her hobby* or *Her hobby is her work*, both of which say the same thing in effect, we are at a loss to apply our logical definitions and usually resort to the formal characteristic of word order to decide which of the sentence elements is the subject and which is predicate.

In fact, a definition of a sentence to which few or no exceptions can be taken has yet to be constructed. For this reason, description is preferable to definition, and possibly all that can be said is that the sentence consists of a number of standardized patterns that have been agreed upon by the users of a language, and that for English, a noun-verb or actor-action sequence such as *Dogs bark* is the simplest concrete form of such a pattern, liable to all sorts of extension and amplification.

Most definitions and analyses of the sentence have been made in terms of the written language. Yet, if we are to follow the basic linguistic procedure of considering the spoken language as fundamental, we must at least attempt to observe the characteristics which mark the spoken sentence.

The sentences which we employ in speaking are often simpler and more direct than those we write. This is partly because much of our ordinary conversation is directed toward the conduct of the everyday affairs of life: making purchases, giving simple directions, asking for food at the table, exchanging greetings and farewells. Another large part of our spoken language is simple narration. In addition to the bare words, our spoken language consists of volume, stress, and intonation, not to mention facial expressions and gestures. Moreover, if in speaking, we find ourselves in the middle of a sentence which we cannot or do not know how to finish, we can always break it off and start over again; yet even the fragmentary sentence that we have uttered has already conveyed something.

In writing, on the other hand, we frequently deal with ideas that are much more complicated than those which make up the bulk of our spoken utterance. When they write, millions of speakers for whom oral communication constitutes the major portion of their expression engage in subtleties and complexities of thought somewhat beyond their ordinary habit. Though their speaking may often be nothing more than thinking aloud, their writing must reflect the finished product of a thought process, set down in coherent and organized fashion. Moreover the writer has only words at his disposal to perform this task. Shouting, raising the voice pitch, the use of manual or facial gesture are not available for communication on paper. There is a limit to the usefulness of such devices as italic and bold face type and capital letters as substitutes for pitch, stress, and volume. This means that the written sentence must be put together with greater regard for form and logic in order to compensate for the absence of these speech auxiliaries.

Returning to the spoken sentence, however, we recognize it primarily in terms of the ending point, which is marked by a shift in voice pitch, either above or below that which has been maintained for the preceding few words, and by a brief pause before the speaker begins his next sentence. It is rarely necessary to make a grammatical analysis in order to discover whether or not a certain group of words constitutes a sentence. No matter how many subjects and accompanying verbs there may be, these are not primarily the factors which determine whether or not a sentence has been uttered. It is again a matter of pitch, stress, and pause. A series of pronouns, verbs, and objects, such as *I found it*, *I looked at it*, *I threw it away*, may be uttered as a single sentence or as three, irrespective of whatever formal analysis we may choose to make.

In attempting to comprehend the construction of the English language objectively, the student must be warned against another pitfall which often crops up in sentence analysis. This is the procedure of attempting to mold all sentences into a single pattern by 'understanding' non-existent parts of a sentence. For example, it is often insisted that the actual subject of an imperative verb (Come!) is a *you* 'understood,' and the final pronoun in such a sentence as *He is older than I* is rationalized on the grounds that it is the subject of an understood *am old*.

This is not scientific procedure, and furthermore, it opens the way to theories and arguments which may not be justified by the facts. First of all, every interpreter may not supply the same context, and second, this treatment gives rise to the mistaken notion that an elliptical construction or a sentence fragment does not or cannot convey a complete thought. The fallacy of this last assumption can be easily illustrated by the following reproduction of a not implausible dialogue:

'Where to?'
'Class.'
'Math?'
'No, Spanish.'
'In a hurry?'
'Rather.'
'What for?'
'Almost ten.'
'Well, so long. Call me up.'

The division of writing next larger than the sentence is the paragraph. Note that the paragraph belongs to the written language only. We speak in sentences as well as write in them but the paragraph has no actuality in speech. Paragraph length and content are extremely variable, depending not only upon the purpose and nature of the writing, but also upon such wholly mechanical factors as size of paper, width of column, whether the writing is hand- or typewritten. One purely formal use of the paragraph is that of the introduction of quoted material or responses from the different speakers in the portrayal of dialogue or conversation.

Additional Reading:

Aiken, *A New Plan of English Grammar*, Chapters II, III.
Curme, *Syntax*, pp. 1, 2.

Grattan and Gurrey, *Our Living Language*, Chapter XLI.
Jespersen, *Essentials of English Grammar*, pp. 95–106.
Philosophy of Grammar, Chapter XXII.
Kennedy, *Current English*, pp. 467–83.
Perrin, *Index to English*, pp. 538–52, 623–5.

Exercise XXVI

1. Is the definition of the sentence as given in Webster based upon form or meaning? Compare this with the definitions cited by Perrin. How many types of sentences (*i.e.* interrogative, declarative, etc.) are recognized in the Webster discussion? How many types are recognized by Jespersen and Curme? Can you see any reason for their not following the older classification?

2. In the sentence *John is reading a letter*, what differences in total meaning would be suggested by (*a*) heavy stress on the word *John;* (*b*) heavy stress on the word *reading;* (*c*) heavy stress on the word *letter?* What differences in interpretation would result from pronouncing the word *letter* with high and low pitch respectively? What interpretation would you make if there were high pitch and heavy stress on *John?*

3. Compare the discussions of Aiken, Jespersen, and Perrin concerning fragmentary sentences. What types of fragmentary sentence do they recognize as acceptable English?

4. Attempt a completion of all the sentences comprising the dialogue which is reproduced in Section 26. Compare your completions with those of your classmates. Are they alike in every respect?

5. Divide the selection below into what you consider suitable sentences and paragraphs. Compare your divisions with those of your classmates:

> what a world of foreign cares are merged in that absorbing consideration he has put on his strong armour of sickness

he is wrapped in the callous hide of suffering he keeps his sympathy like some curious vintage under trusty lock and key for his own use only he lies pitying himself honing and moaning to himself he yearns over himself his bowels are even melted within him to think what he suffers he is not ashamed to weep over himself he is forever plotting how to do some good to himself studying little stratagems and artificial alleviations he makes the most of himself dividing himself by an allowable fiction into as many distinct individuals as he has sore and sorrowing members sometimes he meditates as of a thing apart from him upon his poor aching head and that dull pain which dozing or waking lay in it all the past night like a log or palpable substance of pain not to be removed without opening the very skull as it seemed to take it thence or he pities his long clammy attenuated fingers he compassionates himself all over and his bed is a very discipline of humanity and tender heart he is his own sympathizer and instinctively feels that none can so well perform that office for him he cares for few spectators to his tragedy only that punctual face of the old nurse pleases him that announces his broths and his cordials he likes it because it is so unmoved and because he can pour forth his feverish calculations before it as unreservedly as to his bedpost

CHARLES LAMB

6. Consult the *Oxford English Dictionary* for the treatment of the word *paragraph.* What does the etymology of the word indicate? What was the earliest meaning of the word? Judging from the development of the meaning of the word, would you say that the paragraph was essentially a visual guide or a logical unit?

7. Examine the paragraphs in the editorial column of any one issue of your daily newspaper. What is the average number of sentences per paragraph? Of words per paragraph? Make the same computation for one nonfiction article in such a magazine as *Harpers* or the *Atlantic.*

Also for a comparable portion of a volume of critical or historical essays which your class may agree upon. How does paragraph length compare in the three types of published material?

8. Examine the same paragraphs for unity of content. Are they all devoted to the consideration of a single idea? Is there any difference in the three types of published material in this respect?

9. Select one novel and one magazine story for examination as to the use of paragraphing to introduce quotations, and to indicate change of speakers in dialogue. Is every quoted thought or statement indented? Are a question and response ever included in a single paragraph? Draw up a series of statements summarizing your findings.

27. Sentence Analysis; Clause and Phrase

In the preceding section, only the simplest type of sentence pattern was considered, the noun-verb sequence (*dogs bark*). Some grammarians speak of this predicative relation as *nexus*, in contrast to the quality-substance sequence which is termed *junction*.

Such a sequence or nexus may be amplified in a number of different ways:

Dogs *Simple Subject*	bark and play *Compound Predicate*
Dogs and cats *Compound Subject*	play *Simple Predicate*
Dogs and cats *Compound Subject*	run and play *Compound Predicate*
Brown dogs and gray cats from the village *Subject*	run through the streets and play in the fields *Predicate*

Yet none of these amplifications, even the long sentence given last, has fundamentally altered the basic subject-predicate pattern, the noun-verb sequence. These are all simple sentences, based upon a single nexus.

Observe also that we are accustomed to demand a finite verb as the core or basis of the predicate in the conventional sentence. This means that the participles and the infinitive, those verb forms which often function as other parts of speech, are not acceptable as independent predicate elements. Whether the words *barking dog* actually say less about the dog than *dog barks* is a problem of the nature of predication; as such it is a question for logicians and psychologists. The student of language is bound to observe that *barking* so used does not satisfy the conventional requirements for a second sentence element.

Nor in our discussion of the sentence elements must we overlook the fact that certain predicates require a third element to complete the thought and give meaning to the verb. (Tom was *a good athlete*. Father bought *a new automobile*. We considered this *a good plan*.) Such additional sentence elements are called complements. Note that *complement* and *complete* are etymologically related. The subjective complement refers to the subject and is ordinarily linked to it by a copulative verb. The direct object is the complement for a transitive verb, and the objective complement completes the meaning for the direct object when this is necessary.

The basic subject-verb pattern may be enlarged to include within the limits of a single sentence two or more subject-predicate sequences placed side by side.

Dogs	run	and	cats	play
Subject A	*Predicate A*	*Conjunction*	*Subject B*	*Predicate B*

Enlarging the pattern in this fashion gives us what is called a compound sentence. The elements of which it is formed could each constitute a satisfactory sentence by itself. Each of these subject-predicate sequences is therefore called an independent clause. Some grammarians distinguish between the compound sentence proper, where the clauses are joined by co-ordinating or equalizing conjunctions, and the sentence row or multiple sentence in which the separation or connection is effected by means of punctuation. (Dogs run; cats play.)

All clauses, though they may be parts of a single idea, are not necessarily of equal importance. We may, for example, wish to express the basic notion *dogs bark*, but we may also wish to include with it the idea *the dogs live on the hill*. This is accomplished in the following manner:

The dogs	who	live on the hill	bark
Subject A	*Subject B*	*Predicate B*	*Predicate A*

A further expansion may be illustrated by *The dogs who live on the hill bark when they hear a noise*, in which a final clause also amplifies the predicate element *bark*.

This type of sentence is called complex. It differs from the compound sentence in that only one of its subject-predicate sequences or clauses makes a satisfactory simple sentence. In the sentences which have just been illustrated, *dogs bark* alone satisfies the conventional demands for a simple sentence. *Who live(s) on the hill*, by itself, would also fulfill the requirements for a conventional sentence, but when this clause is inserted into the *dogs bark* sequence, the word *who* changes its character or function in such a way that it is no longer an independent subject. Likewise, *they hear a noise* also satisfies the conventional requirements for a sentence, but with the word *when* before it, it becomes dependent upon or subordinated to the *dogs bark* sequence. Such clauses are therefore classified as dependent or subordinate.

Much more complicated combinations of compound and complex sentences may be put together. (The dog barks, and the cat purrs when her fur is rubbed.) Although an elaborate terminology for these various types of sentences has been developed, it is of little importance here, and the term *compound-complex* is sufficient to serve as a single classification for them.

Dependent clauses are normally classified according to the part-of-speech function they perform. Thus we speak of noun clauses, adjective clauses, adverbial clauses. However it is also possible to employ the ranking system in respect to them, classifying them as primary, secondary, and tertiary. This latter has some advantage in that the clause is not always clearly a modifier of any single word (Though the hall was crowded, they managed to find a place) as is essentially implied when we use the noun-adjective-adverb terminology.

ADDITIONAL READING:

Aiken, *A New Plan of English Grammar*, Chapters v, vi.

Curme, *Syntax*, Chapters ix–xvi. (Pertinent selections from this large body of material may be chosen by the instructor.)

Grattan and Gurrey, *Our Living Language*, Chapter xlii.

Jespersen, *Essentials of English Grammar*, Chapters xxxiii–xxxv.
Modern English Grammar, ii, pp. 12–15; iii, Chapters i–x. (Pertinent selections from this large body of material may be chosen by the instructor.)
Philosophy of Grammar, pp. 102–7.

Exercise XXVII

1. Classify the sentences in the following selection as simple, compound, complex, or compound-complex. In each sentence underscore the independent clause once, the dependent clause twice:

> If I say, therefore, that Shakespeare is the greatest of intellects, I have said all concerning him. But there is more in Shakespeare's intellect than we have yet seen. It is what I call an unconscious intellect; there is more virtue in it than he himself is aware of. Novalis beautifully remarks of him, that those dramas of his are products of Nature too, deep as Nature herself. I find a great truth in this saying. Shakespeare's art is not artifice; the noblest worth of it is not there by plan or precontrivance. It grows up from the deeps of Nature, through this noble sincere soul, who is a voice of Nature. The latest generations of men will find new meanings in Shakespeare, new elucidations of their own human being; 'new harmonies with the infinite structure of the Universe; concurrences with later ideas, affinities with the higher powers and senses of man.' This well deserves meditating. It is Nature's highest reward to a true simple great soul, that he get thus to be a part of herself. Such a man's works, whatsoever he with utmost conscious exertion and forethought shall accomplish, grow up withal unconsciously, from the unknown deeps in him; — as the oak tree grows from the Earth's bosom, as the mountains and waters shape themselves; with a symmetry grounded on Nature's own

laws, conformable to all truth whatsoever. How much in Shakespeare lies hid; his sorrows, his silent struggles known to himself; much that was not known at all, not speakable at all: like roots, like sap and forces working underground! Speech is great; but Silence is greater.

CARLYLE.

2. Classify each of the dependent clauses in the preceding selection according to the part-of-speech function it performs. Do you find any clauses where such a classification is not wholly satisfactory, and where analysis on the basis of rank would give a truer picture of the clause function?

3. Some grammars and grammarians speak of the independent clause as the *principal* clause. On the basis of such sentences as *It is certain that they went to Chicago* and *I do not know if he has paid for the tickets*, can you see any objection to the term *principal* used in this manner? Justify your answer.

4. The conjunction *for* is usually classified with *and*, *but*, and *or* as a co-ordinating conjunction, and as such, would naturally introduce an independent clause. Yet *for* usually has the meaning of *because*, which is a subordinating conjunction and which normally introduces a dependent clause. Should we therefore change the classification of *for?* Can you find anything in Curme's *Syntax* which throws a further light on this problem?

5. Consult Leonard, *Current English Usage*, pp. 21–5, 148, 149, as to what is called the comma splice or comma blunder. In what sense is this a violation of the conventional sentence requirements? Does this type of construction appear to exist in actual usage? From the discussion in Leonard, what can you gather about the circumstances which might justify it?

6. Consult Webster's *New International Dictionary* s.v. *clause*. From the discussion here and in Aiken, would

you say that a clause necessarily demands a finite verb in the predicate? Explain and illustrate.

7. Consult Webster's *New International Dictionary* s.v. *phrase*. How does Webster classify phrases? What is the difference between the phonetic and grammatical concept of a phrase? Classify according to use or function all the phrases in the selection from Carlyle quoted in connection with Question 1.

28. Punctuation

Punctuation is in large part a system of conventions the function of which is to assist the written language in indicating those elements of speech which cannot be conveniently set down on paper: chiefly pause, pitch, and stress. It is relevant here that the words *period*, *colon*, and *comma* all signified a sentence, a portion of a sentence, or a pause, long before they came to be applied to the various points of punctuation. Such points as the question mark and the period are obvious substitutes or compensations for pitch modulation; the exclamation point suggests the element of stress or volume; frequently the comma and semicolon correspond to pauses in phonation.

Isolated words are usually not language in the functional sense of the term. Only upon rare occasions are they used to communicate meaning. Accordingly, the part played by punctuation in constructing visually unified groups, by putting certain words together and separating these words from other combinations, is vital to communication. To convince yourself of this, recall the unpunctuated passage given in Exercise XXVI, and how many re-readings of it were necessary before it began to make sense.

Not infrequently the placing of a comma or other point

may vitally affect the interpretation which is given to a sentence. Observe, as an example, the first sentence in Section 27, which reads: *In the preceding section, only the simplest type of sentence pattern was considered.* Note the change in meaning which would arise from placing the comma after *only* instead of before it, and the ambiguity which would result from not employing a comma here at all. A few years ago it was discovered that a carelessly inserted comma in a North Dakota law made it illegal for anyone to sleep in a hotel in that state.[17] A recent Michigan statute provided that, 'every railroad corporation shall provide a uniform, hat or cap and a distinguishing badge' for each conductor, brakeman, and other employees dealing with the public. Two English departments consulted about the meaning of the sentence came forth with quite different interpretations. The first maintained that the phrase 'must be understood grammatically as meaning *either* a uniform *or* hat *or* cap.' The other asserted that 'although the statement is slightly ambiguous it was intended . . . to indicate that the railroad corporation is to provide three things, viz.: (1) a uniform, (2) a hat or cap, (3) and a badge.' All these examples illustrate the familiar situation of the writer concerned with the idea he wishes to communicate and not realizing the possible other interpretations which may be given to his written statement of it.

Punctuation may at times also be put to a kind of symbolic use. At one stage in the history of Czechoslo-

[17] The text of the law read as follows: 'No hotel, restaurant, dining room, or kitchen shall be used as a sleeping or dressing room by an employee or other person.'

vakia, it was announced that the name of the country would henceforth appear as Czecho-Slovakia, to show the increased importance of the Slovaks in the reorganized republic. Possibly even more tenuous was the distinction made by a certain United States senator between the Federal Constitution and that of the Southern confederacy. 'The United States Constitution is by "We the People" *with no comma after "we"*; the Confederate is by "We, the People," and sets out each State is acting in its sovereign and independent character.' Whether such finely drawn distinctions are justified in terms of the functions which punctuation was originally designed to serve is doubtful. But such uses and interpretations of punctuation do exist and must be taken into account in any study of this system of conventions.

As with any other aspect of language, there is considerable division of usage in respect to punctuation. We shall examine certain of the moot points in the exercise which follows, but it is worth pointing out here that, as with the paragraph, much of the variation is a result of purely physical and mechanical factors. In general, newspaper punctuation is lighter, uses fewer points than book and magazine punctuation. The reason for this is apparent enough when we remember that newspaper sentences are frequently simpler in structure and shorter than those appearing in other types of published material. Moreover, the narrower newspaper columns and smaller type would not readily admit so many points as the more spacious format of books and magazines. A newspaper sentence bristling with commas and semicolons might be more of a hindrance and an eye strain than a help.

It is scarcely necessary to enumerate the various points which are employed, but it is useful to review the situations in which punctuation is used. These may be divided as follows: (1) end punctuation; (2) compounding punctuation; (3) punctuation to set off introductory material (phrases, clauses, or words); (4) punctuation to separate parenthetical material (including non-restrictive clauses and appositives) or subordinate material in final position; (5) series punctuation; (6) separation of contrasted elements; (7) indication of an interruption in thought. To these may be added the problems in mechanics which call for the use of quotation marks, the apostrophe, and for capital letters.

Additional Reading:

Leonard, *Current English Usage*, pp. 3–92.
Summey, *Modern Punctuation.*
Webster's *New International Dictionary*, s.v. *apostrophe, capital, colon, comma, exclamation point, interrogation point, period, punctuation, semicolon.*

Exercise XXVIII

1. Upon what sort of evidence is the punctuation survey in *Current English Usage* based? What is the significance of the critical ratio which is appended to each tabulation? Upon what kind of evidence did Summey draw for his work?

2. What end punctuation would you use in the following situations?

(*a*) A sentence declarative in form but interrogative in purpose
(*b*) An indirect question: *e.g. I asked him why he had come*

(*c*) A courtesy question: *e.g. Will you please send me two packages of nasturtium seeds*

(*d*) A question part declarative and part interrogative: *Take a look behind you — now you begin to recognize this country, don't you*
Now you begin to recognize this country, don't you — take a look behind you

3. Judging from the treatment in *Current English Usage*, pp. 12–17, under what circumstances may a compound sentence dispense with internal punctuation? When does a semicolon seem to be required? Which of the quasi- or adverbial conjunctions *so*, *yet*, *then*, *hence*, and *however* seem to require a semicolon before them; which may be used with a comma?

4. What factors determine whether or not an introductory clause or phrase is to be punctuated? Is there any perceptible difference in practice here among the various types of publication?

5. Be able to illustrate the difference between a restrictive and a non-restrictive clause. A restrictive and a non-restrictive phrase. A restrictive and a non-restrictive appositive. What is the justification for setting off the non-restrictive modifiers with punctuation? Find three examples of each of these constructions, both restrictive and non-restrictive, in whatever novel you happen to be reading at the present time. Is each punctuated according to the practices suggested by your references?

6. What division of usage do you find in respect to series punctuation? Include in your answer the practices adhered to by the various types of publication.

7. What is meant by saying that the colon is the mark of anticipation, and the apostrophe, of omission? From the point of view of present practice, is one of these statements more accurate than the other?

8. Webster's *New International Dictionary* gives twenty-

four uses for capitalization. Judging from *Current English Usage*, concerning which of these is there the greatest degree of uncertainty? Examine the results of the *Current English Usage* survey carefully. Do they point to any consistency in practice or philosophy? Are the newspapers as definitely committed to infrequent capitalization as to light punctuation?

9. Punctuate the following passage, maintaining paragraph indentation at the appropriate places:

> i know very little of that gentleman sir said neville to the minor canon as they turned back you know very little of your guardian the minor canon repeated almost nothing how came he to be my guardian ill tell you sir i suppose you know that we come my sister and i from ceylon indeed no i wonder at that we lived with a stepfather there our mother died there when we were little children we have had a wretched existence she made him our guardian and he was a miserly wretch who grudged us food to eat and clothes to wear at his death he passed us over to this man for no better reason that i know of than his being a friend or connection of his whose name was always in print and catching his attention that was lately i suppose quite lately sir this stepfather of ours was a cruel brute as well as a grinding one it is well he died when he did or i might have killed him mr crisparkle stopped short in the moonlight and looked at his hopeful pupil in consternation

❧ III ☙

English Vocabulary

29. Word Formation

Thus far we have considered only questions of phonetics and grammar. There is, however, still another important aspect of language to which some, if only brief, attention must be given. This consists of the words themselves: their meanings, their etymologies, the way in which they are formed through the use of derivational prefixes and suffixes. Needless to say, a speaker may possess flawless grammar and enunciation; yet if he is not keenly aware of word values, he will not be able to employ the language to its utmost capacity as an instrument of expression and communication.

Since word formation is a very active force in the operation of the English language, we study it first. In addition to the multitude of such simple root words as *cat*, *dog*, and *house*, we have in our language a large number of prefixes and suffixes which are usually not used as words by themselves, but which may be placed before or after independent words to alter or modify the meaning of those words and also to change their grammatical function.

To choose a very simple instance for our first illustration, we may convert the noun *cat* into the adjective *catty* by the addition of the *-y* suffix, which has the general sense of 'having the qualities of.' This suffix is extremely common, and, if we took the time, we could undoubtedly think of one or two hundred words in which it operates roughly in this fashion: *rainy*, *sleepy*, *messy*, *healthy*, etc.

A much more complicated analysis is afforded by the word *interventionist.* So far as English is concerned, our starting point is the verb *intervene*, which came from the Latin, but this too may be analyzed into its component parts, the preposition *inter* 'between' and the verb *venire* 'to come.' The next step was the addition of the suffix *-tion*, converting the verb into an abstract noun indicating state, result, or a concrete instance of the action indicated by the verb. (Incidentally, the Latin-French *-tion* is itself a compound suffix whose component parts may be discovered by consulting any good dictionary.) So far we have, then, the noun *intervention.* To this is finally added the suffix *-ist*, ultimately Greek in origin, which changes the abstract noun into what might be called an *agent noun*, signifying the performer of the action indicated by the noun *intervention.*

Another fertile word-forming element, especially in American English, is the prefix *anti-* 'against.' It was once remarked that the political history of this country could be written in terms of those opposition movements which employed this derivational element, ranging all the way from *anti-Federalist* to *anti-New Deal*. Early in 1938, when the State Department of the United States wanted a term to indicate the act of invoking the so-called 'escalator clause' in a naval treaty, the word *escalation* was coined. The economy of such a device is clearly apparent; by means of these prefixes and suffixes, we are often able to make a single word answer the purpose of a whole clause or phrase.

It must not be supposed, however, that whenever such a new word is coined, its inventor laboriously considers all the possible meanings of all the existing prefixes and suffixes in the English language. Although there are exceptions, the process of word formation is by and large quite as unconscious and automatic as the addition of the appropriate inflection to form the past tense of a regular verb, or the compounding of two nouns when the situation demands it.

The moment a word enters our active vocabulary it is no longer an isolated mental phenomenon; it is subject to all the inflectional and derivational patterns we normally employ. For example, suppose we have just become actively aware of the words *precocious* and *precocity*. If there should arise a situation in which more than one precocity was involved, it would not be necessary for us to have learned the plural *precocities* as a separate fact. We would automatically form the plural of this word by fitting it to the general pattern of all the regularly formed plurals that we already know.

But this tendency goes beyond mere inflection. If we know the adjective *precocious* and a particular context demands an adverb with this meaning, we again automatically apply the *-ly* adverb pattern to the adjective, thus creating what is for us a new word, *precociously*. It is true that some new combinations of word-forming elements are highly conscious and labored creations; especially those designed for new commercial products, and possibly many segments of the theatrical and sports vocabulary. But in the main the comparison of word formation with inflection and compounding is psychologically valid. Most languages employ all these devices to grow and to adapt themselves to new situations.

The extent to which word derivation (the combination of word-forming elements) has taken place in the English language is ably illustrated by A. G. Kennedy. From such a familiar root word as *bear*, he shows that at least thirty-six other words have been formed, ranging all the way from *barrow* to *birth* to *overburdensome*. The Latin root *ced*, 'go from,' with its participial form *cess-*, and the related French form *cease*, have been even more prolific, resulting in eighty modern English words.

There has been much written recently about the desirability and even the immediate profit of possessing a large vocabulary. Many of the schemes for increasing the size of one's vocabulary are highly fantastic and chimerical. Yet there is no doubt that a keen sense, on the part of the individual, of the value of these prefixes and suffixes operates in two ways to increase his verbal efficiency. In the first place it provides him with an effective tool for the analysis of unfamiliar words which he reads and hears. Secondly, it furnishes him with a mechanism which will give greater pliability and adaptability to the active vocabulary which he already possesses.

Additional Reading:

Greenough and Kittredge, *Words and Their Ways in English Speech*, Chapters XIII, XIV.
Kennedy, *Current English*, Chapter IX.
McKnight, *English Words and Their Background*, Chapter XII.

Exercise XXIX

1. Look up either in Webster or in the *Oxford English Dictionary* the meanings of the prefixes and suffixes here listed. Then form two words from each of them.

PREFIXES

ante-	dis-	omni-	super-
arch-	ex-	para-	trans-
com-	il-	pro-	ultra-
de-	ob-	semi-	vice-

SUFFIXES

-able	-ess	-itis	-ment
-age	-ism	-ive	-ous
-er	-ist	-ly	-ure

2. Examine the list of prefixes and suffixes below, and form all the words you can from each. What does each contribute to the meaning of the word to which it is affixed? Observe to what part or parts of speech each may be added, and what part of speech the result is. To illustrate, note the suffix *-ness* in such derivative formations as *redness*, *coldness*, *holiness*, *softness*. It appears that this suffix is added to adjectives, converting them into abstract nouns. It means 'state or condition of being'; *e.g. softness*, state or condition of being soft.

PREFIXES

amphi-	dia-	multi-	retro-
be-	for-	neo-	sur-
bene-	homo-	ob-	sym-
cath-	hyper-	pen-	under-
contra-	mal-	pseudo-	with-

SUFFIXES

-aceous	-fy	-let	-ster
-ard	-hood	-mony	-teria
-craft	-ish	-oon	-tude
-dom	-ile	-ory	-ward
-esce	-kin	-osis	-wise

3. By adding prefixes and suffixes, form as many derived words as you can from each of the following simple words or roots.

-*graph*, Greek, 'to write'	*lax*
dicta-, Latin, 'to say'	*broad*
ponder, Latin, 'to weigh'	*hand*
-*path*, Greek, 'suffering'	*say*
nomen, Latin, 'name'	*radi*(*us*), Latin, 'staff, rod, ray.'

4. Analyze all the derived forms occurring in any one selected editorial in your daily newspaper in the same fashion that the word *interventionist* was dealt with in the preceding section.

5. Improve the diction of the following sentences by selecting another word for the one italicized. Explain why each italicized word is open to criticism.

a. Doing things for yourself developes *independability*.
b. He did everything he could to bring about the *dissolvement* of the company.
c. The treatment of the prisoner indicates an *unjustness* in our social structure.
d. He looked at the alarm clock *disgustingly* when it rang.

e. Strikes are often caused by a small group who spread a feeling of *uncontentedness* among the employees.

30. Meaning and Changes in Meaning

It is a familiar experience, as we travel from one part of the country to another or meet someone from another portion of the English-speaking area, to find different names applied to the same thing or object. A tin vessel may be called a *pail* in one section of this country and a *bucket* in another; what I speak of as a city *block*, a friend hailing from elsewhere may call a *square*. Even within the relatively narrow limits of New England, a child's see-saw is known by six or eight different terms. When we make similar comparisons between American and British English, the differences are even more marked. What I should refer to as the *hood* of my automobile would be called a *bonnet* by my British acquaintances, and what they call the *hood* I usually speak of as the *top*.

Moreover, anyone from England would be shocked by seeing a sign which read 'No Solicitors Permitted,' for he could scarcely imagine any reason for expressly prohibiting lawyers from entering any house or its premises. Although I do not use the term *square* for what I call a *city block*, it, like the word *solicitor*, does exist in my vocabulary. But I apply both words to different sets of ideas and objects from those which have just been mentioned. In other words, the total meanings of the words *solicitor* and *square* are not the same for me as they are for certain other speakers of English. The converse of the proposition that the same thing may have different names is that the same word may be applied to different things by different speakers; when this is done, we say that such a word has more than one meaning or that it varies in meaning.

In addition to the variations in the meaning of a word which may exist at any one period, meanings differ from one century to another or even from one generation to another. Today we should not be able to use the verb *owe* in the sense in which Shakespeare employed it in a well known speech from *Othello:*

> Not poppy, nor mandragora,
> Nor all the drowsy syrups of the world,
> Shall euer medicine thee to that sweet sleepe
> Which thou ow'dst yesterday.

Moreover, unless the reader has had some particular knowledge of the English language, it is almost necessary for him to consult a glossary or a dictionary to find out just what Shakespeare meant. In the same passage, *medicine* is also used in a manner which we no longer employ, and even *drowsy*, though it still means 'soporific,' seems no longer to be applied to the herbs or medicines which induce sleep.

Or going back to a somewhat earlier period, we find that Chaucer speaks of the punishment which an official inflicted upon a certain group of criminals in these terms: 'With wilde hors he did hem drawe.' Here the auxiliary verb *did* deceptively suggests our past emphatic tense (he *did* draw them) but actually it meant 'Caused them to be drawn.' In the five and a half centuries separating us from Chaucer, the verb *do* has lost this important meaning of causation.

The whole problem of meaning and changes in meaning, to which the term semantics is often applied, has come into considerable prominence recently, especially through the writings of Ogden and Richards, Stuart Chase, and Count Koryzybski. Discussions of semantics often lead the student into the realms of logical speculation and psychological theory, for there is little agreement about the processes which are involved in this aspect of language. We shall confine ourselves, however, to a consideration of those types of change or development in meaning which over the centuries have affected a considerable portion of our vocabulary. Four of the most important of these types of change are: (*a*) specialization, (*b*) generalization, (*c*) pejoration, and (*d*) amelioration.

When Shakespeare speaks of 'rats and mice and such small deer,' he is using the word *deer* as its cognate *Tier* is still used in German, with the general meaning of 'an animal.' The word is now applied only to a single family of ruminant quadrupeds (*Cervidae*) which are distinguished by the possession of antlers. Because the term has thus become narrowed in the range of its application, we say that it has undergone specialization. Conversely, the first recorded meaning of the word *frock* is 'a coarse gown or habit worn by monks or friars.' Now it may be applied to any dress or gown. This illustrates the semantic process of generalization.

Again, certain words which, at the beginning of their history, denote thoroughly respectable ideas, in the course of time acquire somewhat disreputable meanings, and finally come to stand for an unpleasant or not wholly respectable thing or idea. When the word *villain* was taken into the English language it meant a farm laborer. Judged by feudal standards, farm laborers were people of ignoble birth and occupation. By gradual stages the central or core meaning of the word became fixed upon the aspect of ignobility, and then came to signify ignobility of character instead of occupation. Such a development is called *pejoration*. A change in the opposite direction is now often referred to as *amelioration*. The word *marshal* originally meant a groom or stable servant; today it may be used to denote an officer in a royal household or one of high rank in the army.

Linguistic scientists have not yet been able to give a complete account of all the causes of semantic change — or of any other type of language change, for that matter — but it will be helpful to consider some of the elements which play a part in it.

Possibly the most concrete reason for change in meaning may be found in the fact that things or objects themselves are subject to change. The invention and development of the automobile created a need for a host of new terms connected with its various parts and its operation. Some of these were naturally taken over from comparable things and situations having to do with horse-drawn transportation. When the automobile then came to replace the horse and buggy, the old meanings died out; the new ones remained.

That words do not stand for the same things to all who use them has already been remarked. This is partly because the total experience of no two persons is identical, and since experience is interpreted and communicated chiefly through the use of words, the words themselves will reflect the differences in experience. The immediate reaction of an author or scholar to the word *writing* would undoubtedly be that of composition; to a mechanic or gardener the word would very likely call up the idea of penmanship. *Basting* means one thing to a tailor and something quite different to a cook. Of course, the cook might ultimately be forced, by the context or the situation, to recognize that one particular use of the word *basting* meant sewing, but for him the set of experiences which are suggested or recalled by this word differs from the experiences and activities which it suggests to the tailor or to the housewife. Finally, for those who are neither cooks nor housewives, the word has a still different value, which is more or less a composite of the preceding two.

The result of this situation is that from the point of view of the language as a whole, many words, especially the most common, have one central or core meaning, and, extending from this, many marginal or peripheral meanings. A *head* of cabbage, the *head* of a river, the *head* of a class all employ one aspect of what might be considered the most common meaning of the word *head*. In this sense they are peripheral or marginal. A schoolmaster may *cane* a recalcitrant student; a gardener may speak of rose *canes;* in some parts of the country something or someone may be located as being down in the *cane*. These too are marginal in their use. Frequently, as in the case of the cook and the tailor, one person's core meaning is marginal for another, and it is this circumstance which is especially conducive to changes in meaning.

Moreover, we must not overlook the fact that the majority of words call up in any individual speaker, writer, hearer, or listener an emotional reaction as well as a purely intellectual concept. So common a word as *dog* will call up one mental picture and set of emotions in someone fond, say, of Irish terriers, whereas a person bitten as a child by a police dog, who has avoided dogs ever since, will have a quite different set of mental and emotional reactions to the word. It is scarcely conceivable that the use of the word *dog* as a derogatory term for a human being could have come from speakers of the first class. Because of the essential conservatism of many of us, the word *radical* arouses an intense emotional reaction, so that it has strayed far from its original meaning.

Additional Reading:

Bloomfield, *Language*, Chapters IX, XXIV.
Graff, *Language and Languages*, Chapter II.
Kennedy, *Current English*, Chapter XIII.
Robertson, *Development of Modern English*, Chapter XI.
Sturtevant, *Linguistic Change*, Chapter IV.

Exercise XXX

1. Trace the changes in meaning that have taken place in the following words, and in the case of each determine whether the development has been in the direction of generalization or specialization. Use either Webster's *New International Dictionary* or the *Oxford English Dictionary*. Both generally arrange the order of definitions to correspond with the historical order of the development of meanings for the treatment of each word. The *Oxford Dictionary* must be used, however, for *starve* and *quick*.

starve	undertaker	medium	ordeal
stool	worm	bereave	scissors
wade	discard	quarantine	butler
quick	walk (verb)	pipe (noun)	wretch
business	zest	propaganda	engine

2. In the case of *starve*, how long did the old meanings continue? How early is the present specialized meaning? What are the dates of the earliest occurrences of *die* and *perish* as verbs? How might the introduction of these words have influenced the status of *starve?*

3. What was the original meaning of *quick?* What are the dates of the earliest and latest citations for this meaning? What are the earliest dates of the generalized meanings? How great is the overlapping period, when both special and general meanings of the word are current?

4. Trace the changes in meaning that have taken place in the following words, and, in the case of each, determine whether the development has been in the direction of pejoration or of amelioration.

idiot	crafty	doom
luxury	minister	genius
seduce	boor	mischievous
conceit	regard	counterfeit
fame	steward	impertinent

5. Examine the citations for *impertinent* in the *Oxford English Dictionary*. Have the earlier meanings of the word died out? From the order in which the definitions are given, show how each stage in the development of this word arose from a peripheral, marginal, or implied meaning in the preceding stage.

6. In Webster's *New International Dictionary*, read § 53, p. lxxxviii. Be able to classify the change in meaning which has taken place in each of the words cited there.

7. Read *Midsummer Night's Dream*, Act II, scene i. Check the words in it which are no longer immediately familiar or idiomatic to a present-day native English speaker. Make two lists of the words you have checked: the first, of obsolete or archaic words; the second, of words still in present use whose meanings have changed. Then classify, in so far as possible, the words in the second list

according to the types of semantic change which have been considered in this exercise.

31. Etymology

The science of paleontology seeks to re-create the forms of life of past geological periods, and to show their relationship to present day organisms. That branch of language study which we know as *etymology* attempts to do somewhat the same thing for the individual words of a language. To trace words to their earliest ascertainable form in the language group to which they belong is the aim of the etymologist.

There are four important elements in the etymology of every word. First, the language from which it came must be determined. Because the English vocabulary is derived from a number of different sources, this is a basic problem. Many of our common words were in the Old English language, spoken by the invading Angles and Saxons who made their home on the island of Britain. For these, the etymologist attempts to find the earliest possible Teutonic form, common to all or almost all of the Germanic languages. But the English-speaking people have always been great word borrowers; consequently Latin, Greek, French, Scandinavian, Italian, German, Spanish, Dutch, and many other languages have contributed to our vocabulary.

When word borrowing has occurred, it is sometimes difficult to determine which language or group of languages has furnished the word, and which has been the borrower. For example, if we consult the *Oxford English Dictionary* for the etymology of *boast*, we discover that at one time it was supposed that it had been borrowed from Welsh or Gaelic. On the basis of later information it is now assumed that the borrowing was in the other direction. This is the kind of problem which frequently confronts the etymologist.

The second aim of the etymologist is to establish or determine the earliest form of a word in the language or family of languages to which it belongs. For instance, the *Oxford English Dictionary*, in its treatment of the verb *bow*, compares the Old English form of this word with what is to be found in Old High German, Old Saxon and Gothic; then it indicates the Old Teutonic form which was the ancestor of all these words. Finally there is a comparison with the related verbs in Latin, Greek, and Sanskrit. A word which came into English from one of the Romance languages, French let us say, is often compared to related words in Spanish, Italian, and Portuguese, so that its Latin forerunner may be determined, and the resulting Latin form may then be compared with other related words in Greek, Sanskrit, possibly even Slavic and Celtic.

Naturally, the etymologist is also interested in comparing the meaning of a word in its earliest known form with what it has become in the language he is studying. If such a word as *dwell*, for example, meant originally 'to lead or go astray' in English, but its cognate or corresponding forms in certain other related languages did mean 'to retard, delay, stop,' it would appear that the development of this word in English was influenced by the other languages in question. When we discover that *candidate* comes from a Latin word meaning 'to be clothed in white,' a knowledge of Roman political and social customs is required to tell us the whole story of this word. Upon learning that such words as *enormous*, *abnormal*, *eccentric* all meant at the outset 'away from the norm or center,' we see in their semantic development a reflection of certain aspects of the social psychology of the human race.

We have already learned in Section 29 that many words are formed of combinations of smaller units. It is the task of the etymologist to analyze such words into their component parts. He will show us, for example, that such a word as *energy* is derived from Late Latin *energia*, which in turn came from a Greek noun with the same form. The noun *energia* was a converted adjective *energos*, which in turn is composed of the prefix *en-* 'in' and the noun *ergon* 'work.'

Not infrequently two elements coming from different languages have combined to make a single English word. In the word *lovable*, the French suffix *-able* has been added to the native English verb *love*. *Beautiful* illustrates the opposite process, the addition of an English suffix to a French stem. Two foreign languages may furnish the elements for single English words, as in *bureaucracy*, a combination of French and Greek elements, and *asafetida*, in which Persian and Latin are joined. Words like these, composed of elements from different languages, are called *hybrids*.

It is sometimes assumed that the etymology of a word may serve as a guide to its proper use and meaning. There is some basis for the assumption that a knowledge of the origin and history of large sections of our vocabulary leads to nice discrimination in diction. However, the principle that the etymology constitutes the 'true' meaning of a word is frequently made the basis for ridiculous and extreme denials of what is unquestionably cultivated usage. In the last century one earnest reformer insisted that because *dilapidated* was from Latin *lapis*, 'stone,' it could be properly used only in reference to stone structures. Strictly speaking a wooden dwelling could not be dilapidated. A present-day writer tells us that *bureau* 'ought to mean' an office, the furniture of which included a table covered with red cloth, since the word comes from Latin *burrus*, 'dark red.'

To anyone already familiar with the phenomenon of semantic change, such arguments can have little plausibility. In matters of meaning, present usage is the only scientifically valid criterion. Yet a faith in the existence of some standard of propriety outside of usage itself is widespread and often crops up in totally unexpected places.

One other language phenomenon which must be considered here is that of popular or folk etymology. This is the name given to the transformation of a word so as to give it an apparent relationship to better known or better understood words. Historically our terms *crawfish* and *crayfish* have nothing to do with the word *fish*, but are conscious alterations of the Old French word *crevice*. Because these crustaceans lived in the water, it must have seemed to many speakers that the *-vice* portion of the word ought to be *fish*, hence the transformation. Similarly, *asparagus* is sometimes changed to *sparrow grass*, again in an attempt to resolve this word into familiar and meaningful elements. *Gooseberry* has nothing to do with a goose (Dutch *kruisebeer*), and *wormwood* (Old English *wermōd*) is wholly unrelated either to *worm* or to *wood;* the present form of both these words is due to the operation of folk etymology.

Exercise XXXI

1. Consult the *Oxford English Dictionary* for its etymological treatments of the words *hazel* and *harness* (noun). From the material which is given there, write a complete but simple report of the history of these two words which will demonstrate your ability to interpret this type of information.

2. Consult either the *Oxford English Dictionary* or Webster's *New International Dictionary* for the sources of each of the following words. Indicate both the ultimate and the immediate sources, as well as the intermediate, if there are any.

zebra	shako	taboo
mohair	balcony	squash
silk	gong	tulip
sloop	sash	fetish

3. What is peculiar about the origin of the following words? In what respect does group (*a*) differ from group (*b*)? What particularly characterizes group (*c*)?

(*a*)	(*b*)	(*c*)
bayonet	dunce	mentor
laconic	macadam	panic
milliner	silhouette	tantalize
copper	boycott	syringa
lumber (*noun*)	martinet	chimera

4. Explain the origin of the following in terms of the word-forming elements of which they are composed, and the languages from which these elements have been taken.

In the light of the last statement, how do groups (*a*), (*b*), and (*c*) differ from one another?

(*a*)	(*b*)	(*c*)
effort	breakage	interloper
ignore	foolish	television
diphthong	awkward	pacifist
perfect	falsehood	saxophone
estuary	martyrdom	peajacket

4. In each of the following words point out the deviations from the original or etymological meaning which have taken place in their subsequent use.

bonfire	curfew	supercilious
bedlam	dandelion	dicker
fee	nice	transpire
hussy	pedigree	provoke

5. What language process is illustrated by the following words? Be able to give an account of the development of each.

penthouse	Welsh rabbit	cutlet
belfry	reindeer	salt cellar

32. Loan Words: Latin and Greek

The most complete dictionaries of Modern English record about a half-million words. Of these, the vast majority have been borrowed from a large number of languages with which English speakers and writers have come into contact during the last fifteen hundred years.

We must not, however, allow ourselves to be deceived by gross figures. Only a small proportion of these five hundred thousand words are in the vocabulary of any one speaker. But the vocabulary of the individual speaker will show a considerably greater proportion of words descended from the native Old English vocabulary than will the total word stock of the English language.

There is also the question of frequency to be considered. Allowing ourselves for the moment the easy generalization that the native words from Old English stock are the familiar, homely type, and that many of the borrowed words are somewhat more erudite and artificial, the ratio of native to foreign words based upon actual use would be considerably higher than a ratio giving an equal value to every word in the English vocabulary no matter how often or how little it might be used. The articles *a*, *an*, and *the*, most of our pronouns, prepositions and conjunctions, the verbs *do*, *be*, and *have*, such nouns as *man*, *woman*, *child*, *father*, *mother*, *brother*, *sister*, *week*, *day*, *month*, *year*, *house*, *farm*, all native English, are virtually indispensable and naturally are used more often than the borrowed element of the vocabulary. In general, the more colloquial the language situation, the greater is the proportion of native words.

Yet the whole question of word borrowing is very interesting and we can learn much from an analysis of some of the strata of loan words in the English language. We may best begin by asking why, and under what circumstances, words are borrowed, and as usual when we deal with language problems, we find that there are several answers to the question.

A lexical problem arises whenever we need to name certain objects, ideas, concepts, and operations for which the English language has not already provided. Thus the development of science and invention, or any other widening of the intellectual and cultural horizon, poses a problem in providing an adequate terminology. Such a problem might be solved in one of two ways. The needed terms could be created out of elements already within the language, or they could be taken over from some language where they are in actual or potential existence.

In circumstances of this nature, the English language has preferred to borrow rather than to employ resources already within the language. Comparing the technical grammatical vocabulary of German with that of English furnishes an interesting illustration of how differently the two languages operated when the need for a terminology of language elements made itself felt. German has the native compounds *Hauptwort* (head word) *Fürwort*, *Zeitwort* (time word) where English has *noun*, *preposition*, *verb* all derived from Latin. German has *Fall* and *Geschlecht* where English has the Latin loan words *case* and *gender*. *Hauptsatz*, *Nebensatz*, and *Satz* are the German equivalents, again composed of native elements, for *principal clause*, *subordinate clause*, and *sentence*. A comparison of these two languages in respect to chemical or medical terminology would point to the same general conclusion.

The extensive use of foreign, chiefly Latin and Greek, elements to fulfill this particular need of the English language has come about in part because, up until the present, men of science and learning were generally familiar with the classical languages. A further advantage of employing Latin and Greek elements in the scientific and philosophical vocabularies arose from the fact that an understanding of them might well extend beyond the limits of the English language proper. Moreover, when we go back to the earlier periods of our language, we find the extensions of our mental and cultural life generally bound up with an interest in and a revival of the literature and thought of classical antiquity. This was true of the Renaissance, of which Humanism was so essential a part. It was equally true of the later Middle Ages, when Scholasticism was the dominant intellectual force.

In dealing with any single group of loan words, we shall generally want to know when they were borrowed, and what classes of ideas and realms of human activity are reflected in the borrowings. From the answers to these questions, we can learn much about the nature of the cultural impact of the language we are concerned with upon English thought and life as well as upon the English language.

In the case of Latin, our borrowings from this language extend over a period of some two thousand years, beginning even before the migration to Britain, when the ancestors of the Angles and Saxons were still in continental Europe. In the present exercise, however, we shall be chiefly concerned with the Latin borrowings of the fifteenth and sixteenth centuries, when the intellectual stimulation of the Renaissance is reflected by a period of extensive word borrowing.

Additional Reading:

Baugh, *History of the English Language*, pp. 262–89.
Emerson, *History of the English Language*, pp. 125–35.
Jespersen, *Growth and Structure of the English Language*, Chapter VI.
Robertson, *Development of Modern English*, pp. 310–7.
Webster's *New International Dictionary*, § 39, p. lxxxvi.

Exercise XXXII

1. Consult the *Oxford English Dictionary* for the derivation of the following pairs of words: *frail*, *fragile*; *blame*, *blaspheme*; *reason*, *ration*; *sever*, *separate*; *assoil*, *absolve*. Of each pair, which word comes directly from the Latin and which does not? What is the ultimate source of the words which did not come directly from the Latin? In each instance, observe which of the two words was introduced first. How can you explain the difference in the spelling of the stressed vowels in *example* and *exemplary?* Can you suggest a reason for the difference in the pronunciation of *ch* in *machine* and *machinate?*

2. In connection with the same problem which was considered in the previous question, what can you discover about the derivation of *gravity*, *consolation*, *natural*, *figure*, *motive?* How different are the possible Latin and French antecedents of these words?

3. Consult the *Oxford English Dictionary* to discover earlier forms and spellings of the following: *describe*, *verdict*, *adventure*, *doubt*, *victuals*. In each instance be able to account for the change of form or spelling in Modern English.

4. Consult the *Oxford English Dictionary* for the derivation of *folio*, *affidavit*, *interim*, *innuendo*, *alibi*, *minimum*, *quorum*, *omnibus*. What inflectional forms in Latin do these words represent? What can you conclude as to the form of a Latin word which would constitute the basis for its transmission into English? From this, can you derive any principle governing this aspect of linguistic borrowing?

5. Consult the *Oxford English Dictionary* to discover the meaning of each of the following words at the time they were taken into the English language: *ponder*, *recipe*, *item*, *climax*, *nostrum*. Was the significance in each case the same as at present? If not, try to account for or to trace the shift in meaning, pointing out in each instance the specific semantic processes which are involved.

6. Consult the *Oxford English Dictionary* for the pronunciation of the following words: *acclimate*, *arbutus*, *abdomen*, *inquiry*, *oleomargarine*. Next, consult the second edition of Webster's *New International Dictionary* for the pronunciation of the same words. Put into phonetic notation *all* the pronunciations recorded by each dictionary. What differences do you find? With which dictionary does your own pronunciation agree? Can you discover a general principle behind the pronunciations as given in the *Oxford Dictionary?* Is there a general tendency or principle to be seen in the deviations from the *Oxford Dictionary?*

7. Determine the derivation of the following words and the dates of their first appearance in the English language:

(*a*)	(*b*)	(*c*)
deliberately	starvation	scientist
eventful	witticism	fatalistic
copiousness	tidal	fratricidal
motionless	refill	transcontinental

How do these three groups of words differ as to derivation? Which of the two linguistic processes illustrated by groups (*a*) and (*b*) would you imagine to be the more common? What is indicated by the fact that both of them are present in English? Compare the dates of the earliest citations for the words in each group. Which group is earliest and which is latest? Can you account for this?

8. Read the speeches of Holofernes in *Love's Labour's Lost*, IV. ii and V. i. What was Shakespeare satirizing in this character? Consult the *Oxford English Dictionary*, s.v. *inkhorn* to find out what was meant by an *inkhorn term*. Are there any examples given? What derivatives of this word are recorded by the *Oxford Dictionary?* Read the poem in Jonson's *Poetaster*, V. iii, 299–316. What seems to be the point of the satire here?

9. Make a list of twenty-five words belonging to the basic vocabulary of any one of the sciences or of philosophy. What proportion of the words are of Latin and Greek derivation?

10. From what you know of the Renaissance, what languages other than Latin and Greek would you expect to have furnished a considerable number of words to the English vocabulary? In what fields?

33. French Loan Words

Although of great importance, the Latin influence discussed in the preceding section was essentially literary in character. The borrowed words were in the main 'book words' and the borrowers often quite as familiar with the languages of the ancients as with their own tongue.

More often linguistic borrowing takes place as the result of contact between two spoken languages, between two peoples speaking what are at first mutually unintelligible tongues. This was true, for example, when the English, French, and Spanish explorers and colonists first came to mingle with the Indians on the shores of America. And inevitably some Indian words passed into all three languages — especially into English, where the contact was maintained over a longer period.

The impact of American Indian upon English, however, was that of a wholly dissimilar language and civilization and the resulting loan words, though interesting and revealing, are not numerous. A quite different situation was that represented by the mixture of English and French after the Battle of Hastings in 1066, when the Norman French became for the time masters of England. Unlike the Indians, who constantly receded before the advance of the American colonists, the English had no wilderness behind them in which they could take up new lands and establish new homes. English and French lived together in the little island; government, commerce, and agriculture all had to go on. Small wonder then that English words should filter into the language of the conquerors, and French words into the language of the conquered.

The types of words which found their way into English bear eloquent witness to the relationship between the two peoples at this period. Terms of government and law, words pertaining to the church, and to the army and navy point to the fact that the administration of the country was in French hands. Terms pertaining to art, learning, and medicine testify to the temporary dominance of the French in cultural and scientific matters. Finally, then as now, there was extensive borrowing of terms having to do with food, dress, and sports, pointing to French leadership in the world of fashion and good living. Observe that here the borrowings are not always for the purpose of filling a gap in the English vocabulary. Frequently a French loan displaced an already established native word.

It is necessary also to distinguish between the borrowings from the Norman French and those from Parisian French. The earliest borrowings into English were almost all in the dialect spoken by William the Conqueror and his followers, that of Normandy in the north of France. After the reign of King John, when the continental French possessions of the English crown were lost, new streams of influence came into England from the south of France, chiefly from Poitou and Provence. Moreover, by the thirteenth century, the dialect of the Isle de France, where Paris is situated, had gained great influence throughout the French-speaking world, and wherever differences between the two dialects are perceptible, the later borrowings are seen to be Parisian French.

Before leaving this topic, it is necessary to caution the student against one misconception, namely that there was any considerable influence of French upon the structure of English. It is quite true that coincidental with the period of French domination, the English language was undergoing certain radical changes in its inflections and syntax. Nevertheless, there is every reason to believe that these changes were wholly indigenous, although they may have been hastened by the linguistic confusion into which the country was thrown. But aside from the adoption of a few idiomatic expressions, the French influence was strictly limited to matters of vocabulary.

ADDITIONAL READING:

Baugh, *History of the English Language*, pp. 205–31.
Emerson, *History of the English Language*, pp. 52–78.
Jespersen, *Growth and Structure of the English Language*, Chapter v.
Robertson, *Development of Modern English*, pp. 317–26.
Webster's *New International Dictionary*, §§ 30, 35, pp. lxxxiv–v.

EXERCISE XXXIII

1. The two members of each of the following four pairs of words are virtually the same in meaning. Would you be likely to find them used interchangeably or with equal frequency? How do the two groups differ in derivation? Does this suggest any conclusion about the subsequent

history of borrowed French words or the sphere of use in which they are likely to be found?

truth	veracity
fat	corpulent
help	assistance
friendship	amity

2. Apply the questions asked in (1) above to the following pairs of words. Do the conclusions you reached in connection with the previous group apply here? Notice particularly the date of adoption of the French loan word in each pair. Is it relatively early or late?

travel	fare
people	folk
prophet	soothsayer
valley	dale

3. Determine the derivation of each of the following words and explain the relationship between the members of each pair. In each instance, notice also which of the two words was borrowed first.

guardian	warden
chase (*verb*)	catch (*verb*)
real	royal

In this same connection, how do you explain the discrepancy between our pronunciation of *qu* in *question* and its value of *k* which is sometimes heard in the word *questionnaire?*

4. At what time may the French influence upon English be said to have begun? Was there any contact between French and English prior to the Norman Conquest? In what centuries was the French influence upon the English vocabulary most marked? Be able to describe in detail the method employed by Jespersen and Baugh to determine the extent of borrowing from the French

throughout the history of the English language. Does such borrowing appear to have ceased at the end of the Middle Ages?

5. How do you explain the form of the English verbs *finish*, *flourish*, *nourish*, *punish*, in view of the fact that the French infinitive is *finir*, *nourrir*, etc.? By a comparison of the etymology of *dace* and *dart*, can you learn anything about the inflectional form of a French noun which usually constituted the basis for its transmission into English?

6. Consult the *Oxford English Dictionary* to determine the meaning of each of the following words at the time it was taken into the English language: *curious*, *quaint*, *engage*, *cheat*, *danger*, *tweezer*. Was the significance in each case the same as at present? If not, try to account for or to trace the shift in meaning, pointing out in each instance the specific semantic processes which are involved.

7. Consult the *Oxford English Dictionary* for the derivation and original meaning of the following: *forehead*, *front*, *churl*, *villain; seethe*, *boil*. Describe and account for the shifts in meaning which have taken place in one or both of the members of each pair.

8. Compare the French and popular English pronunciations of the following words: *liqueur*, *lingerie*, *puree*, *menagerie*, *bonbon*. Account for the development of the English pronunciation in each instance. From the evidence here, can you formulate a principle of the treatment of loan words in popular pronunciation? Why do we adopt the French pronunciation of the diphthong in *coiffure* but not that of the simple vowel? Why is the vowel *a* in *demitasse* sometimes pronounced [ɑ] in English and sometimes [æ]?

9. Determine the derivation of the following words and the dates of their first appearance in the English language:

(*a*) bountiful	(*b*) shepherdess	(*c*) duty
falseness	lovable	dalliance
governorship	wondrous	reliable
gentleman	laughable	

How do these three groups of words differ in derivation? Which of the linguistic processes illustrated by groups (*a*) and (*b*) would you imagine to be the more common? What is indicated by the fact that both of them are present in English? Is there any pronounced difference between the earliest appearances of the words in groups (*a*) and (*b*)? How do the words in group (*c*) differ in derivation from those in the other two? What do you learn from the *Oxford Dictionary* about the past attitude toward the word *reliable?* Can you explain it?

10. Select a short editorial from your daily newspaper and list the words in it which are of French derivation. Compute the proportion of such words to the total number in the passage, first counting each word only once, and then counting each word every time it occurs.

34. Scandinavian Influence

The Scandinavian influence on the English language is not so widely recognized as the Latin or French, but nevertheless it is of considerable importance. In a sense the contact between these two peoples was even more intimate than that between the Norman French and English, for the Scandinavians were more like the English in culture and in language. Even though the Norse first appeared as heathen raiders, when they finally did settle down in the country and eventually came to found a dynasty, they became absorbed into English life and culture rather than dominating it as the French did after 1066.

We are also likely to forget how long the Norse and the English lived side by side before the advent of the Norman French. The first permanent Scandinavian settlements on English soil were made shortly after the middle of the ninth century. During most of the tenth century, after the establishment of the Danelaw by the treaty of Wedmore in 878, the Scandinavians pursued a peaceful life and remained upon friendly terms with the English. Aside from a brief struggle just before the accession of Cnut in 1016, these friendly relations were maintained until the time of the Conquest. Thus we have a little more than two centuries of contact between the two peoples, a century and a half of which was essentially tranquil and peaceful.

Old Norse, the language of the Scandinavian invaders, belonged to the Teutonic branch of the Indo-European family. It had many words in common with English, not to mention such important structural characteristics as a twofold declension of the adjective, weak and strong verb conjugations, and customarily heavy stress on the root syllable. Often the corresponding words in the two languages are identical or nearly so, making it difficult to determine whether or not the presence of the word in Scandinavian was a force in maintaining the native English word in the language. As we shall see in the exercise which follows, the Old Norse word sometimes imposed its meaning upon the English cognate — in fact, one instance of this has already been considered, the word *dwell* which was discussed in Section 31.

Although the Scandinavian loan words do not permit so neat a classification into categories reflecting spheres of activity and fields of interest as do the French, certain groups are clearly discernible. All the Scandinavians were great sailors, and a number of the words which the English borrowed from them have to do with types of ships and naval operations. There are as well certain terms pertaining to the army and to land fighting. The majority of these borrowings, however, were not of a permanent character, and were replaced later by French loan words. Somewhat more enduring were the borrowings having to do with law and political organization, another aspect of life in which these peoples were exceedingly able. The word *law* itself is a Scandinavian loan word, as are *husting*, *bylaw*, *outlaw*, *wrong*, *riding*, and *wapentake*.

We are naturally led to wonder whether two languages so similar in structure might not have influenced each other grammatically as well as lexically. In considering questions of this nature it is the present tendency of linguistic scholarship to place the burden of proof upon the foreign influence: that is, not to admit the assumption of foreign influence unless all the possibilities of explaining any particular structural change as a purely native development have been exhausted or proved unlikely. Accordingly, the question of possible Scandinavian influence upon English inflections and syntax becomes very complicated, and in many instances it seems that certain Norse inflectional patterns and syntactical constructions served chiefly to reinforce similar already existing but by no means predominant patterns and constructions in English.

We shall have to content ourselves, therefore, with listing those matters of inflections and syntax which *may* have been influenced or strengthened by similar constructions in the Scandinavian, but it should be understood that not all these are to be interpreted as *borrowings* from that language. Nevertheless Scandinavian influence has contributed in some degree to the following morphological and syntactic features of present-day English:

(1) *Both* and *same* as pronouns.
(2) *Fro* and *till* as prepositions.
(3) *Are* as the present plural indicative of the verb *to be*.
(4) *-s* as the third person singular, present indicative inflection of verbs.
(5) *They*, *their*, and *them* as plural personal pronouns.
(6) The omitted relative construction.
(7) Certain uses of *will*, *shall*, and *should* as function words.
(8) Present practice of omitting or retaining the conjunction *that*.

In a number of instances, particularly the use of the third person singular verbal inflection and the plural personal pronouns, the presumption of Scandinavian influence is strengthened by the circumstance that these forms were first established in the Northern and North Midland dialects, and were only gradually adopted into standard English. It was, of course, precisely in those regions where the Scandinavians had settled.

This suggests also another important effect of Scandinavian upon the English language: that which appears in the regional dialects in the north and north central counties of England. A glance at Wright's *English Dialect Dictionary* will indicate how numerous are these Scandinavian borrowings which did not become a part of, or remain in, the standard language. One scholar has compiled a list of over a hundred Norse borrowings, not standard English, in the dialect of one Lancashire village alone. Thus by nature of its very intimacy and pervasiveness, the Scandinavian element in English often seems less important than it really is, and we are all too likely to remain unaware of it.

ADDITIONAL READING:

Baugh, *History of the English Language*, pp. 110–29.

Jespersen, *Growth and Structure of the English Language*, Chapter IV.

Serjeantson, *History of Foreign Words in English*, Chapter IV.

Webster, *New International Dictionary*, § 29, p. lxxxiv.

EXERCISE XXXIV

1. Consult the *Oxford English Dictionary* for the etymology and date of adoption of the following: *die*, *hit*, *take*, *call*, *sky*, *wrong* (adjective and adverb), *window*, *blend* 'mix.' During which centuries does the Scandinavian influence upon English seem to have been most pronounced? Do the Scandinavian borrowings comprise a learned and artificial or a familiar part of our vocabulary? In connection with this last question, consult the dictionary for the etymology and earliest appearance of the adverb *nay*. How would the fact of the borrowing of an adverb of negation and the possible borrowing of certain personal pronouns affect your answer to this question?

2. The earliest citation given by the *Oxford English Dictionary* for *till* (preposition) is *ante* 800, yet this is frequently classified as a Scandinavian loan word. From the etymological discussions in the *Oxford Dictionary* and in Webster, and by an examination of the *Oxford* citations, attempt to clear up this apparent contradiction.

3. Consult the *Oxford English Dictionary* for the etymology and meaning of the suffixes *-by*, *-thorpe*, *-thwaite*,

-dale, *-beck*, *-holm*, and *-toft*. In what important class of words do these suffixes frequently appear?

4. Be able to trace the historical development of the meaning of each of the following: *bloom*, *dream*, *gift*, *plow*. Note particularly the differences in meaning between the Scandinavian and native English forms of the same word at the time of adoption. Trace the development of the meaning of the word *fellow* from the time of its adoption to the present, and indicate the semantic processes which it illustrates.

5. Consult the *Oxford English Dictionary* for the difference in derivation between the following pairs of words:

shirt	skirt
rear	raise
shriek	screech
edge (verb)	egg (verb, 'to incite')

What reason is there for having arranged these words in pairs? Account for the differentiation in form and explain the distinction in meaning which has developed within each pair of words.

6. Consult Wright's *English Dialect Dictionary* and compile a list of twenty words of Scandinavian origin which are still extant in one or more of the English dialects but are not a part of standard English.

35. Celtic Borrowings

When the invading Angles, Saxons, and Jutes settled in the island of Britain in the late fifth and early sixth centuries, they found it inhabited by a Celtic-speaking people. It is true that Britain had been a Roman colony for approximately four centuries, the legions having been withdrawn in 410, but at the time of the Anglo-Saxon invasion it is reasonably certain that the bulk of the

Celtic inhabitants felt little of the Roman influence, either in their language or culture.

The Anglo Saxon conquest of the island of Britain was chiefly in the nature of a colonization. These Teutonic peoples came to settle permanently, and, in doing so, drove the Celts to the north and west, into Ireland, Wales, and Northern Scotland (regions where Celtic continued to be spoken for centuries and is still spoken). Unlike the later Norman French conquest, here was a situation comparable to the white colonization of North America, with the same result so far as linguistic influence was concerned — few Celtic loan words were taken into the English language.

We must remember also that here alone, of all the situations where English culture and language came into close contact with that of another people, the force of circumstances made English the dominant language and culture. The Norman French and even the Scandinavians, though to a less marked degree, came in as invaders and conquerors, and for the time being the English occupied the position of the underdog.

In a situation of this nature, it is the language of the conquered, the language of the political and social inferiors, which shows the greatest effect of such a mixture or contact. The language of the dominant group is much less likely to be influenced. In other words, it was to the advantage of the conquered Celt to be able to speak to his Anglo-Saxon superior. In attempting to do so, he learned Anglo-Saxon, with the result that his Celtic, if we had any traces of it, would undoubtedly show many borrowings from Old English. At the same time, the language of the Anglo-Saxons shows little effect of contact with the Celts; the conquerors needed to trouble themselves little with the language of the conquered.

This whole situation is roughly analogous to that of the foreign language groups in the United States. German, Swedish, Polish, Italian, Finnish, in fact almost all foreign languages spoken by immigrant groups, have made extensive borrowings from English, and in many instances, even the structure of these languages as spoken in America has been influenced by English. At the same time, American English has been scarcely touched by these languages, for it is to the interest of the immigrant to learn to speak English as soon as possible, and if he does not himself succeed in the task, the speech of his American-born children will very likely be indistinguishable from that of third or fourth generation Americans. Remember that it is not the superiority of one language over another as a means of communication which concerns us here; it is solely a matter of the political, economic, and intellectual prestige which circumstances have thrust upon one of the languages in the conflict. When such a situation occurs, it is the language lacking this circumstantial prestige which will show the influence of the more favored language.

The few Celtic words (possibly not more than a dozen) which were borrowed during this early period were chiefly names of everyday things, natural objects, and animals. Most of them have dropped out of the language completely or are no longer in common use. Possibly the most widespread influence of Celtic which remains in the language is to be found in place names. River names such as *Avon*, *Stour*, *Dee*, *Cam*, the town and city names of *London*,

Carlisle, *Reculver*, *Catterick*, the elements *-combe* and *-tor*, are all of Celtic origin. Here again the parallel between Celtic and American Indian influence may be pointed out. Like Celtic, the Amerindian languages left few traces on the vocabulary as a whole, but, from Tallahassee to Kalamazoo, the United States is dotted with place names of Indian origin.

36. Early Latin Borrowings

We must recognize three strata of early Latin loan words in English. The first group consists of those which were borrowed while the Angles, Saxons, and Jutes were still on the continent of Europe, before their invasion of Britain. These were, of course, incidental to the Roman conquest of the territory of many of the Teutonic tribes, and to commercial relationships even with those who remained outside the boundaries of the Roman Empire. Possibly between fifty and one hundred words came into the language in this fashion. Included among these early borrowings are military and legal terms, terms of measures, coins, metals, and other articles used in trade, words for garments and textiles, terms connected with food, drink, cooking, some words for towns, houses, and buildings, some plant and animal names. In contrast to the later Latin borrowings of the Renaissance, these were generally words connected with everyday life and its simple necessities. They came into English from the spoken rather than the written language.

A second group of Latin words found its way into English immediately after the invasion of Britain. The Celts had borrowed some words from the Latin, and a few of these eventually passed into English. Most of the words borrowed during this period were topographic terms, which became elements in place names, although some plant names and terms for household objects were taken over as well. Again the terms are simple in character and came through the spoken language.

These words were borrowed during the first century and a half after the invasion. However, since very few texts have come down to us from these early centuries, we must rely upon presumptive evidence to distinguish the insular from the earlier continental borrowings. The simplest way to do this is to notice whether there are cognate forms in several of the other Teutonic languages. If a word such as *camp*, for example, is found to occur in High German, Dutch, Low German, and the Scandinavian languages, it is preferable to assume that it was borrowed at a period prior to the breakup of early Teutonic into its several related languages, than to suppose that each language borrowed it independently. When we find, on the other hand, that Modern English *cockle* is derived from Latin, that it appears in our earliest records, but does not appear in any other Teutonic language, we then conclude that it was adopted *after* the Anglo-Saxon invasion of the island.

The factor which led to the most considerable borrowing from Latin during this early period was the introduction of Christianity, which began at the very end of the sixth century. Along with the adoption of the new religion came the need for a host of new words: terms for the church hierarchy, for ritualistic practices, for parts of church buildings, for new concepts and a whole new philosophy. This was the first real challenge which the English language had faced, and it was met in a manner prophetic of its great adaptability in centuries to come.

Since Latin was the language of the church, there were, of course, many direct borrowings. Of these, *disciple*, *minister*, *mass*, and *martyr* may be named as typical illustrations. In addition, however, many existing native words were so modified in meaning as to express the new Christian ideas: *Easter*, for example, was the name for an old pagan festival of spring. *God*, *heaven*, *sin*, and *hell* are all instances of this same type of word conversion.

Finally, a good many compound and derived Latin words were analyzed into their component elements, and the equivalent combinations of native words were substituted in their stead. Thus patriarch (*patri* + *arch*) was rendered by Old English *hēahfæder* (high father) and *viaticum* by a compound which had the Old English form of the word *way* (= Latin *via*) as its first element. In addition, all these words, borrowings and new combinations alike, were subject to all the word-forming patterns already in the language, so that a word like priest soon gave rise to *priestly*, *priesthood*, *priestlaw*, *priestshire*, and *priestrule*.

This final stratum of Latin loans came primarily from the written language, and as the influence of the church grew and produced such theologians and divines as Aelfric, Wulfstan, and Dunstan, the borrowings became more and more learned in character. It is estimated that possibly three hundred words came into the language at this period.

ADDITIONAL READING:

Baugh, *History of the English Language*, pp. 86–110.
Jespersen, *Growth and Structure of the English Language*, pp. 29–46.

Serjeantson, *History of Foreign Words in English*, Chapter III, Appendix A.

Webster's *New International Dictionary*, §§ 27, 28, p. lxxxiv.

Exercise XXXV

1. What are some of the theories concerning the language spoken in England at the time of the Anglo-Saxon invasion?

2. Consult the *Oxford English Dictionary* for the derivation and time of adoption of the following: *bannock*, *bog*, *stock*, *brat*, *brogue*, *crag*, *dun* (adjective) *shamrock*, *slogan*, *whiskey*. Which of these represent the earliest stratum of Celtic loan words in English? What is your conclusion as to the range of time when Celtic had some influence on the English language?

3. In view of the extensive influence of Scandinavian, French, and Latin upon English, how do you explain the comparatively few Celtic borrowings?

4. Consult the *Oxford English Dictionary* for the derivation of the following words: *chalk*, *chester*, *cup*, *kettle*, *mile*, *mint*, *mount*, *pit*, *port*, *short*, *street*. Which of these words have cognate forms in other Teutonic languages? What does that indicate about the time of their adoption? When do the remaining words seem to have been taken into the language?

5. List the classes of ideas and spheres of human activity which were reflected in the pre-Christian ideas from the Latin and illustrate each class with at least two words.

6. What linguistic need arose in England in connection with the introduction of Christianity? How extensive was the verbal borrowing that occurred to meet this need? Through what means other than borrowing did the English language meet this situation?

7. Determine the derivation and early meaning of the following words and use them as appropriate illustrations for your answer to the last question under (6).

holy	gospel	bishopdom
noon	pope	housel
abbott	psalm	Lord
fiend	heathen	gossip

8. What is the ultimate source of the following words? When and through what immediate source were they taken into English: *angel*, *devil*, *church*, *priest*.

IV

Early Modern English

37. Historical Grammar

So far our attention has been devoted almost entirely to present-day English. We have been concerned with what was earlier defined as *descriptive* grammar. We are ready now for an examination of the language of some of the early periods of English.

It is customary to recognize three divisions of the English language prior to the modern period. The language which was spoken from the time of the Anglo-Saxon invasion (about 450) until 1050 is known as Old English. The English language between 1050, or just before the Norman Conquest, and the approximate date of the beginning of printing (1450) is called Middle English. The period from 1450 to 1700, during which the language developed many of the features which characterize it today, is known as Early Modern English. After 1700 the modern period is considered to have begun. In the remainder of the text, the abbreviations OE, ME, EMnE, and MnE will be used for Old English, Middle English, Early Modern English, and Modern English respectively.

Instead of commencing with the earliest period and proceeding chronologically to the present, we shall begin our examination of earlier English with the period most like our own, Early Modern English, following which, we shall deal in turn with Middle English and with Old English. This procedure has been chosen so that we may grasp more readily the continuity of development from one period to another, an advantage which might be lost if we jumped back a thousand years before beginning to build up to Modern English.

We shall choose the language of Shakespeare as representative of the Early Modern period, first of all because we are generally familiar with his work, and secondly, since it consists chiefly of drama, we have the advantage of dealing with something fairly close to the spoken language. Specimen selections from Shakespeare's plays, carefully chosen to represent the speech of various social levels, will be found on pp. 228–38.

Although we have shifted our field of observation, the method to be employed in dealing with this new material is essentially that which was pursued in our treatment of Modern English, namely observation, classification, and generalization. (See pp. 3 and 83.) The student of the language of former centuries and eras is a scientist in the same sense as is the grammarian of Modern English.

At this point, we may well ask ourselves what the purpose is of such a grammatical analysis of the language of earlier periods as we propose to make. First of all, as students of English, it is important that we be able to read earlier writings and authors with the fullest comprehension. We can succeed in this only through an accurate knowledge of the grammar of these earlier periods. If Shakespeare, for example, has one of his characters refer to another as *thou*, whereas the second always addresses the first as *you*, we must be able to interpret this in the light of the language practices which were current at the time. We must understand Chaucer's use of the auxiliary verbs, not according to their present-day meaning, but in terms of what they meant to him and his contemporaries. An important clue to the attitude of a writer toward what he is saying may be found at times in so minor a feature as the choice of a subjunctive verb instead of one in the indicative mood.

Moreover, a study of the sounds, inflections, and syntax of the earlier periods of the language may succeed in throwing much light upon the structure of present-day English. When seen in the light of the constantly increasing use of function words, beginning at a period even prior to Old English, the virtual disappearance of the inflected subjunctive seems less like a radical upheaval or a complete breakdown of formal distinction than when we look at it solely from the point of view of the present-day language. The development of *have got* in the sense of 'to be obliged to' (I have got to go at once) takes on a new significance when we see that the verb *owe* (past tense *ought*) underwent precisely the same semantic development some centuries ago.

Moreover, many apparent irregularities and inconsistencies in the present-day language acquire a semblance of reason and system through a study of historical grammar. At the present time most of our frequently used auxiliary verbs, *can*, *may*, *shall*, etc., seem to be irregular in that they do not have the *-s* inflection in the third person singular, present indicative. From examination of Old English grammar we learn that these verbs belong to the preteritive present conjugation; they are, in reality, the past tenses of certain verbs whose present tense forms had disappeared from the language at an earlier period. Even in Old English they were used with present time significance, but maintained the form of the past tense conjugation, which was without inflection in the third person singular. From a purely descriptive point of view, they are, of course, still irregular, but what appears at first glance to be nothing but wanton misbehavior is seen, after such analysis, to have a historical reason behind it. If we can assume that a knowledge of the history of any organism, social or biological, gives us a better understanding of it and makes us the better able to interpret its present form and behavior, we must grant the same advantage to an understanding of the history of our language.

For the remainder of this text, as we deal with the language of each period, we shall consider in turn the sounds, and the inflections and syntax of the various parts of speech. Since we have already touched briefly upon the history of the English vocabulary, it shall concern us only incidentally in our present analysis.

38. Early Modern English Sounds

Most of us are aware that the English language, as it was spoken five hundred and fifty years ago, during the lifetime of Chaucer, differed considerably from our own, in sound as well as in inflections and vocabulary. When we take a course in Chaucer, or even when in our high school English classes we memorize the first portion of the Prologue to the *Canterbury Tales*, we are obliged to learn how to pronounce this strange, archaic English almost as if it were a foreign language. Curiously enough, we read Shakespeare in Modern English, scarcely ever troubling ourselves with the question of pronunciation, yet Shakespeare's birth was scarcely more than a century and a half after Chaucer's death, and it is hardly conceivable that the English language could have acquired all its present-day characteristics between 1400 and 1564. In fact, it did not; Shakespeare's pronunciation, were we to hear it today, would sound quite foreign to our ears.

By dint of careful study and painstaking research, scholars have succeeded in determining, more or less exactly, what the sounds of English were throughout the earlier periods of our language. Selection A, pp. 228–31, illustrates for us their conception of how Hamlet's first soliloquy would have sounded, and in connection with the exercise which follows you will be asked to make a careful examination of this transcription. Before going on to such an analysis, there are certain concepts or postulates fundamental to the historical study of language which must be pointed out. These have to do with the regularity of sound change.

If the sounds of English, say at 1400, differ from the sounds of English in 1940, it is obvious that between the two dates a multitude of changes must have taken place. On the one hand it is possible that such changes were thoroughly chaotic in nature; that each word in the language underwent, quite independently of other or similar words, some sort of alteration in sound at some time during the intervening five centuries, with the result that our language is what it is today. Another point of view would assume a kind or degree of regularity in this process. We might take the point of view that all the words that Shakespeare pronounced with the vowel [e], such as *feat* [fet], *steal* [stel], *mean* [men] are today pronounced as [i]: [fit, stil, min]. This might be reduced to the single formula: EMnE [e] > MnE [i].

In truth, language historians do make the latter assumption, namely that there is a fundamental orderliness about the whole process of sound change, and they sometimes go so far as to call the type of change illustrated by the equation in the foregoing paragraph a *phonetic law.* This term is somewhat dangerous, perhaps, for it may lead us to approach the whole problem in too mechanical a fashion, but nevertheless we do assume that when a sound change such as that of [e] to [i] has occurred, all the words which contain that particular sound will eventually participate in the change, unless prevented from doing so by a particular set of conditions or combination of circumstances leading either to resistance of this particular change, or to a development of another kind.

Sound changes of this nature are sometimes termed *isolative* in contrast to another type of sound change which we shall call *combinative.* Recall that in studying Modern English fricatives and affricates, we learned that EMnE [z] followed by [j], as in *vision* became [ʒ], and that medial [t] followed by [j] as in *feature* became (tʃ). Not every [z], not even every medial [z], changed to [ʒ]. The sound [ʒ] developed *only* when medial [z] was followed by [j] in words of a certain stress pattern. In other words, a peculiar combination of conditions was required to produce the change in question. Moreover, combinative sound changes can generally be explained or understood in terms of the movements of configuration of the vocal organs producing the sounds in question, as [ʒ] and [tʃ] were explained on pp. 33, 40.

Linguistic science has been less successful in satisfactorily accounting for the phenomenon of isolative sound changes, and we are not even wholly certain about the physiological mechanism of such changes. For the present, at least, our chief concern is to discover whatever relationship may exist between the sounds of Shakespeare's English and English spoken in our day, hoping to throw some light upon certain of the variations and seeming vagaries in the latter. We shall find it advantageous, for the time being, to relegate the difficult questions of ultimate and immediate causation of linguistic change to the physiologists, psychologists, and philosophers, all of whom will have to attack the problem in close co-operation with students of language, if a satisfactory solution is ever to be discovered.

Additional Reading:

Graff, *Language and Languages*, pp. 215–37.
Sturtevant, *Linguistic Change*, Chapter III.
Wyld, *Short History of English*, Chapter IV.
Webster's *New International Dictionary*, § 1, p. xxiii, §§ 31, 32, pp. lxxxiv–v.

Exercise XXXVI

1. Examine carefully the phonetic transcription of Selection A, pp. 228–31. Read it aloud several times in order to familiarize yourself with the context and the new combinations of sounds.

2. Determine the relationship of Shakespeare's stressed vowel sounds to those of Modern English. This may be done most easily by drawing sixteen columns on a sheet of paper, one for each of the stressed vowel sounds and the diphthongs of Modern English. Next, place each fully stressed word from Selection A in the column headed with the symbol which represents the present pronunciation of its stressed vowel. Observe the illustration below, which carries out the above instructions in respect to line 142 of the text. To facilitate future reference it is advisable to put the appropriate line number after each word.

MnE	i	ɪ	e	ɛ	æ	u	ʊ	o	ɔ	ɝ	ʌ	ɑ	ɑɪ	ɑʊ	ɔɪ	ɪu
		vɪzɪt	fæːs	hɛvn		tuː				ɛrθ	rʊflɪ					

Observe that *face* [fæːs] has been placed in the [e] column because its MnE pronunciation is [fes]; likewise *earth* [ɛrθ] has been placed in the [ɝ] column because it has this vowel in MnE. The words *her* and *and* have been omitted because of their light sentence stress. Always copy the symbols for vowel length as they appear in the transcription.

3. Make a list of the stressed vowel sounds and diphthongs which occurred in EMnE. What are the stressed vowel sounds and diphthongs which are found in MnE but which did not occur in EMnE? What are the stressed

vowels and diphthongs which were present in EMnE but which do not occur in MnE?

4. What instances do you find of EMnE vowels, similar in quality but different in quantity, having had a different subsequent development?

5. Which two EMnE vowel sounds are the sources of MnE [i]? What do you notice about the MnE spelling of those words which are pronounced with [i] in MnE but which in EMnE were pronounced [e]. Do you know of any present-day dialects in which standard English [i] is sometimes pronounced as [e]? What does this suggest about a possible relationship between dialect pronunciation and the chronological development of sounds?

6. Which two EMnE vowel sounds are the sources of MnE [e]? What do you notice about the MnE spelling of the words in both groups?

7. What appears to have been the development of EMnE [e] followed by *r?* How does it differ from the development of the same vowel in other phonetic environments? Judging from the evidence before you, what do you conclude about the general tendency of EMnE back vowels before *r?* From what you know of the way in which [r] is produced, can you see any phonetic reason for the development of these vowels?[18] See also, Wyld, *Short History of English*, §§ 238, 241, 247.

8. Explain in terms of the configuration of the vocal organs the difference between the development of EMnE [ɔ] and [ɔː]. What are the two sources for MnE [ɑ]? How do they differ in spelling? Can you see any phonetic reason why EMnE *was*, *what*, *father*, and *want* should not have had a development similar to other words with a stressed

[18] Note that the consonant symbol [r] rather than the unstressed vowel [ɚ] is used in the EMnE transcription of final and post-vocalic *r*. Because of the uncertainty of the precise nature of the *r* sound at this time, it seemed desirable to conventionalize the transcription in this fashion.

[æ] sound? For an explanation of *garden* and *are*, see Wyld, *Short History of English*, § 222.

9. According to your evidence, which EMnE vowels seem to have developed into MnE [ɝ]? Did these same vowels under other circumstances remain unchanged or develop into other sounds? Would you then conclude that MnE [ɝ] developed as the result of isolative or combinative sound change? See also Wyld, *Short History of English*, §§ 228, 239, 252, and 256.

10. Put your conclusions concerning the relationship between EMnE and MnE vowel sounds into a single table. What, in general, has been the direction of vowel development during the last three hundred and fifty years: that is, have high vowels become low, or vice versa? Which have shown the greater tendency to change, the diphthongs, the vowels which are often popularly but incorrectly termed 'long,' or those which are often similarly called 'short'? Which show the least tendency to change?

11. Examine all the illustrative selections for this period, pp. 228–38, to determine the phonetic values of the letters *u* and *v*. How did the orthographical practice of this period differ from that of MnE in respect to these letters?

12. What is the spelling of *mistress* in the first line of Selection C? In Selection C *cousin* is spelled twice as *cosen* and the same word appears in Selection D as *cosin*. What do these spellings suggest about the pronunciation of the unstressed vowel in this and similar words? What are you able to learn about pronunciation from the form *then* which occurs in C 94 and D 10, and *a* which is to be found in D 5?

13. Note the spelling *doombe* for *doom*, Selection C, line 85. Consult the *Oxford English Dictionary* to discover if this word had a final [b] sound in earlier stages of the language. What does such a spelling suggest about the EMnE pronunciation of such words as *comb* and *lamb* in which the final *b* was pronounced prior to 1450?

14. Put Shakespeare's second sonnet into phonetic transcription indicating the pronunciation of the EMnE period.

39. Noun and Pronoun Inflections

In approaching the question of Early Modern English inflections, our first task is to read through the illustrative selections and note whatever differences or deviations from Modern English forms are to be found. In doing so, we immediately notice that many words not so spelled in Modern English are to be found here with final *e: selfe*, A 130, *grosse*, A 136, *possesse*, A 137, *toole*, B 38. This immediately raises certain questions for the linguistic scientist. On what parts of speech do these final *e*'s occur? Were they pronounced? Are they to be considered as regular inflections?

Our first question may be answered in part by the four words cited above. Included among them are an adjective, a verb, a noun, and the second element of a reflexive pronoun. Clearly the final *e*'s seem not to be confined to any single part of speech. Therefore, we must consider the questions of pronunciation and regularity of occurrence in respect to each of the parts of speech on which they are found.

We are aided considerably in solving the problem of pronunciation by those portions of Shakespeare's works which are written according to a definite metrical pattern. This includes not merely the sonnets and other poems, but the many blank verse passages in his plays as well. Of the specimen passages which have been reproduced on pages 228–38, Selections A and C, those from *Hamlet* and *As You Like It*, and the last seven lines of Selection B, from

Romeo and Juliet, are in blank verse, unrhymed iambic pentameter.

The *Hamlet* selection contains no instances of nouns with final *e* other than those which have them in Modern English as well. In Selection C, however, we find *highnesse*, 54, 62; *soverayne*, 69; *doombe*, 85; *foole*, 89; *greatnesse*, 91, and *girle*, 100. Our next task is to scan these lines, to determine if they will permit the assumption of a syllabic value for the final *e*'s. Observe, for example, lines 62 and 89:

> So wás I when your híghness*e* bánisht hím
>
> Yóu are a fóol*e*: you neíce províde your sélf*e*

Certainly these two lines contain no justification for any assumption that the final letter could have been pronounced, and a similar reading of the others would lead us to the same conclusion. Therefore, because it appears that the *e* in these words was not pronounced, we no longer need to trouble with the question of a possible inflectional significance.

One other factor could also be taken into consideration here. Observe that the word *highness* occurs three times in Selection C: once, line 61, with its present-day spelling, and as *highnesse* in lines 54 and 62. Moreover, the construction of the word in line 61, where it is spelled *highness*, is absolutely identical with its construction in line 62, where it appears as *highnesse*. In both instances it is the subject of a dependent clause. Therefore, even if we had not the evidence of metre to help solve the question of pronunciation, the fact that two different forms of the word are serving an identical grammatical function, whereas one of the two forms is also found in a quite different construction (direct object, line 54) would again suggest that very likely there was little consistency or pattern in the addition of this letter.

This problem has been treated in so detailed a fashion chiefly to illustrate the way in which the historical grammarian must work to reach his conclusions. It should serve as a model for the consideration of some of the questions which will be taken up in the exercise which follows.

Exercise XXXVII

1. The following spellings of noun plurals in Selections A, B, and C differ from the corresponding MnE forms: *windes*, A 141, *teares*, A 149, 154; *hindes*, B 74; *daies*, C 45. Using the method employed in the foregoing discussion, determine whether the *-es* inflection had a syllabic pronunciation. How do the rhymes to be found in *Venus and Adonis*, 119–20, and in *Rape of Lucrece*, 933–6, 674–6 bear upon this question? How is the last of these references important as evidence for the vocal quality (voiced or voiceless) of the plural inflection? Are there, in Selection C, any instances of the plural inflection without the intervening vowel?

2. Under what circumstances does the MnE plural inflection have a syllabic value? Review the conclusions reached in connection with Question 7, Exercise VII, p. 38. What noun plurals in *Venus and Adonis*, 632–4, *Rape of Lucrece*, 909–10, and Sonnet 17 might be used to determine the corresponding values for EMnE? Put your conclusions concerning the formation and pronunciation of the regular plural inflection in EMnE into a single definitive statement.

3. What genitive singular nouns do you find in Selections A and C? Does the inflection have syllabic value? Verify your impression on this point by listing all the genitives in Sonnets 25–30 and scanning the lines in which they occur.

4. Judging from the nouns in Selections A and C, do you believe that the apostrophe was used to indicate the genitive in EMnE? List the words in Selections C and D in which the apostrophe is employed. Draw up a series of statements summarizing its functions.

5. From the evidence offered by the illustrative selections, construct a paradigm of the personal pronoun in EMnE. You will find it useful to record line references. The following will prove a convenient form of arrangement. Include under the genitive, both the so-called 'possessive pronouns' and the 'possessive adjectives' but keep them separate within the category. These selections are without forms for the neuter genitive singular and the object pronoun for the second person plural. You may assume the MnE form for the latter; the former is dealt with in Question 7.

PERSON	NUMBER	GENDER	SUBJECT	OBJECT	GENITIVE
1	singular		——	——	——
2	singular		——	——	——
3	singular	masculine	——	——	——
3	singular	feminine	——	——	——
3	singular	neuter	——	——	——
1	plural		——	——	——
2	plural		——	——	——
3	plural		——	——	——

6. What pronouns do you find for the second person singular? Consult the *Oxford English Dictionary* or Webster's *New International Dictionary* s.v. *thou* to determine which forms were originally used in the singular.

7. For instances of the third person neuter genitive singular see: *Lear*, I. iv. 236; *Hamlet*, I. ii. 216, V. i. 244; *Wint. Tale*, I. ii. 151, 152, 157; III. ii. 101; *As You Like It*, II. vii. 163; *Merch. Ven.*, IV. i. 72, V. i. 90. Was Shakespeare consistent in respect to his use of the neuter genitive singular? Which is the older form? Consult the *Oxford English Dictionary* s.v. *its*.

8. What forms do you find for the so-called 'possessive adjective'? Are *mine* and *thine* ever used in this function? When they are, what is the nature of the following sound? In addition to the examples in the four selections in this book, collect the instances of these pronouns to be found in *Merry Wives of Windsor*, II. ii. 1–30, II. iii. 24–31, IV. V. Frame a statement or series of statements summarizing Shakespeare's practice regarding these pronouns.

9. Observe the reflexive pronouns in C 43, 44, D 8, 10. Does EMnE appear to be consistent in the formation of the reflexive?

40. Analogy: Noun and Pronoun Syntax

The process which resulted in the creation of the form *its* illustrates one of the most important factors in the operation and development of language: that of *analogy*.

Analogy may be defined as the creation of a new linguistic form or structure, or the modification of an already existing one, in conformity with some established language pattern. When, for example, a small child uses the form *tooths* as the plural of *tooth*, instead of the established plural *teeth*, such a plural has been created according to the pattern of the so-called 'regular' English plural form. A past tense form such as sub-standard or dialect *brang* for *brought* may arise from conformity to the pattern of such verbs as *sing*, *ring*, *begin*. Many students of language use a proportional equation as a graphic means of describing what has taken place:

bring : sing :: *brang* : sang

Analogy operates not merely in the speech of children and in the sub-standard sector, but over the language as a whole. The noun *book*, like the noun *tooth* once formed its plural by means of vowel change instead of the addition of an inflectional suffix, but it has come to conform to the plural pattern of the majority of English nouns. The verb *help* once had as past tense and past participle the forms *holp* and *holpen;* it now has forms which are in conformity with the regular weak verb pattern.

Analogy is likely to operate in situations where an already existing pattern has been weakened or disrupted by some other linguistic factor or process; in many instances sound change provides the disrupting force. Analogy also frequently takes place when an existing pattern is not very strongly embedded in the consciousness of the speakers of a language. There never were, for example, more than twenty-five nouns which underwent internal vowel change to indicate plurality; during the last thousand years, this group has dwindled to a mere half dozen. The regular weak conjugation has also grown steadily at the expense of the strong verb groups. Nor does analogy operate solely within the sphere of inflection. The folk etymologies which we observed in Section 31 were essentially the result of an analogical process, as are the creation of such hybrid derivatives as *beautiful* and *dukedom*. One of the major tasks of linguistic science is to determine the relative parts played by the forces of analogy and sound change in bringing about alterations in the structure of the language from one century or one period to another.

With this introductory sketch in mind, let us return to the form *its*. We know from the dictionary discussions that *his* was originally the genitive of *it* as well as of the masculine pronoun *he*. But this situation went back to the days when the English language, like Latin and German, had a system of grammatical gender, in contrast to the logical gender which prevails in Modern English and which had developed three or four centuries before Shakespeare. Along with the development of logical gender, there was a sweeping loss of inflectional endings on the noun and adjective, resulting in the assignment of a new importance to the personal pronouns as gender tags or indicators for the noun.

Thus *his* came to be definitely associated with the masculine gender, and accordingly must have been felt somewhat unsatisfactory as a neuter form, although it still does appear in some of Shakespeare's earlier plays. The first attempt to improve on this situation seems to have resulted in the form *it*, which we see, for example, in the citations from *Lear* and *Hamlet*. This may have been formed on the pattern of the feminine pronoun *she*, in which there is identity of form between objective *her* and genitive *her*. In the case of *it*, however, the subject pronoun was already identical with the objective, resulting in an undifferentiated form for all three case functions. This was also contrary to the general features of the English pronoun declension, which preserves a diversity of forms for the various case functions to a greater extent than any other part of speech.

Finally the form *its* was created, very likely on the pattern of the noun genitive, as such other forms as *hers*, *ours*, *yours*, and *theirs* had been formed during the past century for pronouns used in absolute rather than secondary function. However, since there is rarely any occasion to use the neuter genitive in a primary or pure pronominal function, the lack of a distinctive form here has caused no particular difficulty. Here, then, is an illustration of the way in which analogy may operate in the course of the development of a language. Moreover, as we go back into the more remote periods of the English language, we shall find that it plays a very important part in the creation of many of the forms which are now in everyday use.

In the examination of Early Modern English noun and pronoun inflections, made in connection with the previous exercise, we found relatively few variations in actual form from those which prevail at the present time. Yet there is a considerable difference between the language of Shakespeare and that, let us say, of Galsworthy or Hardy. This difference presumably lies not so much in the forms themselves as in the way in which they were used; in other words it is a matter of syntax rather than inflection. In the exercise which follows we must attempt to define as accurately as possible the precise nature of these syntactical differences.

ADDITIONAL READING:

Bloomfield, *Language*, Chapter XXIII.
Graff, *Language and Languages*, pp. 251–7.
Sapir, *Language*, pp. 200–4.
Sturtevant, *Linguistic Change*, pp. 38–44.

Exercise XXXVIII

1. Read *As You Like It*, I. i. 1–20, and rewrite the passage as you would normally speak it. List all the nouns and pronouns which in your MnE version occupy a different position in relation to the verb than do those of the original, and summarize what changes in noun position are indicated.

2. Make a similar comparison of Acts iii. 1–10, in either the Goodspeed or Moffatt modernizations of the Bible, with the King James version. In addition to listing changes in noun and pronoun position, note also all constructions which in MnE employ a substantive for what in EMnE is expressed through some other part of speech, and vice versa.

3. Observe the genitive constructions in *Richard III*, I. iii. 264; *Julius Caesar*, I. ii. 61; *Titus Andronicus*, II. i. 70; *Love's Labour's Lost*, V. ii. 354; *Hamlet*, III. iv. 193. Would the same constructions be employed in MnE in every case?

4. Consider the following questions, having in mind the purpose of determining the particular conditions under which *thou* and its related forms are used in the second person singular, and those under which *ye* or *you* and its related forms appear:

a. In Selection C, which pronoun do Rosalind and Celia use in speaking to each other? Compare this with the pronoun Rosalind uses in speaking to the Duke. What does the Duke use in addressing Rosalind? Is it the same one which he generally uses in speaking to Celia?

b. Make a similar analysis of Selection D.

c. In Selection B, to whom do Gregory and Sampson use *thou* and to whom do they use *you?* To which social class do they belong?

d. What pronoun is used by Tybalt and Benvolio in addressing each other? To which social class do they belong? What is the emotional tone of their interchange?

e. In some one of the historical plays, observe the pronoun used in addressing royalty, and note also the pronoun employed by the king in speaking to his subjects.

f. Observe also Benedict's use of the pronoun in *Much Ado*, IV. i. 257–340, and the practice of Hotspur and Lady Percy in *1 Henry IV*, II. iii. 38–120.

g. In the light of your observations, set forth your conclusions about the social and emotional factors governing the distribution of *thou* and *you* forms in EMnE.

h. Do you know of any analogous situation in modern foreign languages?

5. What form of the second personal pronoun do you find in *Troilus and Cressida*, I. ii. 230, 301; *Tempest*, V. i. 33–41; *King John*, V. ii. 88–91; *Henry VIII*, III. i. 102–111? Does Shakespeare use *ye* or *you* the more frequently as a subject pronoun? Does he ever use *ye* as an object pronoun? Consult the *Oxford English Dictionary* for the original function of *ye*.

6. Compare the King James version of the Bible with Shakespeare for its use of the second personal pronoun. You will find *Romans* i and ii useful for reference in this connection. Which do you suppose was closer to the spoken English of the time?

7. What is the construction of *me* in C 44? What would be the attitude of some grammarians as to the 'correctness' of this construction? See also the forms of the personal pronouns in *Romeo and Juliet*, III. v. 84; *Macbeth*, V. viii. 34; *Merchant of Venice*, III. ii. 321; *Antony and Cleopatra*, III. iii. 14, III. xiii. 98. Can any of these constructions be accounted for by the pressure of word order?

8. Examine Selection D for the forms of the relative pronoun. Are the various relatives used in about the same proportion that you might expect to find in MnE? If not,

would you say that the distribution more nearly approximated that of present-day spoken or written English? Are there any instances of the omitted relative construction?

Exercise XXXIX

Adjective and Verb Inflections

1. Examine Selections A and C for examples of adjectives ending in a final *e* which is no longer present in MnE. Using the method employed in Exercise xxxvii, determine whether or not these final *e*'s were pronounced.

2. Make a list of the comparative and superlative adjective forms which occur in Selections C and D. In addition read *II Henry IV*, iii. ii and iv. i, or *As You Like It*, i. ii, also excerpting the comparatives and superlatives. How does Shakespeare's usual practice compare with MnE? Observe also the adjective inflections in the following: *Cymbeline*, iv. ii. 331; *Taming of the Shrew*, iii. ii. 156; *Coriolanus*, ii. i. 91; *As You Like It*, iii. v. 51, iv. i. 162; *All's Well*, iii. v. 77, 82, 83; *Macbeth*, i. v. 2, iii. iv. 126. Do these forms differ from MnE usage? If so, how? Would it appear that MnE was tending toward a greater use of inflections or function words in this respect?

3. List the adjective constructions in *Antony and Cleopatra*, iii. vi. 76; *Merchant of Venice*, iv. i. 251; *Tempest*, i. ii. 19; *As You Like It*, iii. ii. 62, iii. iii. 59; *Julius Caesar*, iii. i. 121, iii. ii. 187; *King Lear*, ii. iii. 7. Would these constructions be permissible in MnE? From what tendency or desire do they arise?

4. Observe the adverbs in *Timon of Athens*, i. ii. 136; *Antony and Cleopatra*, ii. ii. 98; *Twelfth Night*, iii. i. 42, iii. iii. 37, v. i. 86. What is the nature of the development which seems to have occurred here? Have we considered any instances of the same tendency in certain adverbs in MnE?

5. Examine Selections A, C, and the last seven lines of B for examples of verb forms ending in a final *e* which is no longer present in MnE. Using the method employed in Exercise XXXVII, determine whether or not these final *e*'s were pronounced. Make a list of the forms of the verb which you found to appear with this final *e*.

6. Examine Selections C and D for examples of the third person singular, present indicative. What inflectional forms do you find? Which verb has the *-th* inflection most frequently? Would this verb be likely to occur frequently or infrequently in daily use? How might this fact help you to explain the occurrence of the *-th* form in it?

7. What spellings do you find to indicate the *-s* inflection of the verb in the third person singular, present indicative? What is your conclusion about the pronunciation of these forms, and how do you reach it? Sonnets 56–65 will furnish additional examples for analysis.

8. Examine Selections B and C for examples of the second person singular, present indicative. What variations do you find in the form of the inflection? What relationship is there between the inflectional form and the pronoun which serves as the subject? Does the *-st* inflection appear to have syllabic value? Examine also Sonnets 1–10 in the light of this question.

9. Compare the King James version of the Bible with Shakespeare in respect to the inflectional forms of the verb in the present indicative singular. Which do you think more accurately represents the spoken language of the time?

10. Examine Selection C for instances of the past tense and the past participle inflections of regular verbs. From the spellings and meter, what can you conclude about the pronunciation of this inflection?

11. Examine the following references for the past tense and past participle forms of strong verbs which are contained there: *Comedy of Errors*, I. i. 6, I. ii. 45, V. i. 388;

King John, v. vii. 12; *II Henry VI*, III. ii. 84. Explain how analogy might have operated to produce these forms.

Exercise XL

Syntax of the Verb

1. Extract from the four illustrative selections all the verbal constructions employed to indicate negation. Beside each put the form which would be used in conversational MnE. Review the conclusions which were reached in Exercise XXIII, p. 130, concerning negation in MnE. Put into one or two general statements the differences and similarities between MnE and EMnE in this respect.

2. Extract from Selections B, C, and D all the interrogative forms of the verb. Repeat the instructions for the preceding question in respect to verbal interrogation.

3. Observe the simple present tense constructions in *Macbeth*, II. ii. 49–64. If the material in this passage were being retold in MnE prose, which verbs would very likely be used in the progressive instead of the simple present tense? What might you conclude from this about the relative frequency of the simple and progressive constructions at this time? Can you see any relation between this and your answer to the two preceding questions?

4. Make a list of those verbal constructions in Selections B and C which employ some form of the auxiliary *do* in a simple declarative statement. Study each one carefully, attempting to determine the precise force of the auxiliary in every instance. In how many cases would the same construction be used in MnE? What constructions would be used in the remaining instances? See the *Oxford English Dictionary*, s.v. *be*, 14 c. How common does such a passive progressive construction as 'is being explained' appear to have been at this time?

5. As far as possible, classify the verbal constructions with *shall*, *will*, and *'ll* in Selections B, C, and D, according to the ideas which they convey or imply: futurity, deter-

mination, prophecy, desire, habitual action or custom, etc. Are there any categories which employ only the one auxiliary? What are they? Are there any categories in which both *shall* and *will* are used as auxiliaries? Is there within those categories any definite distribution of the auxiliaries according to person?

6. Do you feel that any of the constructions with *shall* or *will* that you have collected would in MnE be more likely to be expressed with the *am to* or *going to* constructions? In which category do these occur? Do you find in the three selections any instances of a present tense used to convey a future meaning?

7. From Selections B, C, and D, select those verbal constructions which express condition contrary to fact, condition possible in the future, exhortation, wish or desire, concession, improbability, supposition. In each instance put beside it the form which would be used in informal, present-day speech. Assuming the EMnE subjunctive to be like the MnE, do you find any instances where the subjunctive form in EMnE would be replaced in MnE by a periphrastic construction? By the simple indicative? Do you find any instances in which Shakespeare uses an indicative form to convey a subjunctive idea?

8. What is peculiar about the construction in C 99? Would it be considered 'correct' in MnE? Explain. Can you account for it upon any linguistic or psychological grounds? Answer the same questions for *As You Like It*, I. ii. 125, 126, V. i. 66; *Two Gentlemen of Verona*, I. iii. 39–41; *Henry V*, V. ii. 18, 19.

9. What is peculiar about the verbal constructions in *As You Like It*, II. iv. 9–10, I. ii. 29–31? Would they be considered 'correct' in MnE? From what impulse or desire did this type of construction very likely arise? Consult the *Oxford English Dictionary* s.v. *not*, adverb, I. 5. b. How long does this construction seem to have prevailed in standard English?

Illustrative Selections from
EARLY MODERN ENGLISH

Selection A

Hamlet i. ii, iii

As the first specimen of the language of this period, Hamlet's first soliloquy (i. ii. 129–56), as well as the first ten lines of the third scene, are reproduced in the spelling of the 1623 Folio. Accompanying the original is a phonetic transcription which represents the speech of Shakespeare as, according to modern scholarship, it would have sounded during the lifetime of the author.

In the phonetic transcription, two dots [ː] following a vowel character indicates that the vowel is long. Remember, however, that length is a measure of quantity, not quality. That is to say, there is no difference in sound between [ɔ] and [ɔː], the only distinction being in the actual length of time consumed by the sound. If you are not clear on this point, review Section 11, p. 54.

The spelling, punctuation, and line arrangement of all the selections reproduce that of the First Folio, and the line numbers follow the Globe and Cambridge editions. There has been little attempt at textual emendation; self-evident corrections are enclosed in parentheses.

i. ii. 129–56

Oh that this too too solid Flesh, would melt,
oː ðæt ðis tuː tuː sɔlɪd flɛʃ wuːld mɛlt

Thaw, and resolue it selfe into a Dew:
*θ*ɔː ænd rɪzɔlv ɪtsɛlf intuː ə dɪu

Or that the Euerlasting had not fixt
ɔr ðæt ðɪ ɛvərlæstɪŋ hæd nɔt fɪkst

His Cannon 'gainst Selfe-slaughter. O God, O God!
hɪz kænən gæɪnst sɛlf slɔːtr oː gɔd oː gɔd

How weary, stale, flat, and vnprofitable
həʊ weːrɪ stæːl flæt ənd ʊnprɔfɪtæːbl

Seemes to me all the vses of this world?
siːmz tə miː ɔːl ðə jusɪz əv ðɪs wɔrld

Fie on't? Oh fie, fie, 'tis an vnweeded Garden
fəɪ ɔnt oː fəɪ fəɪ tɪz ən ʊnwiːdɪd gærdn

That growes to Seed: Things rank, and grosse in Nature
ðæt groːz tə siːd θɪŋz ræŋk ənd groːs ɪn næːtjər

Possesse it meerely. That it should come to this:
pəzɛs ɪt miːrlɪ ðæt ɪt ʃuːld kʊm tə ðɪs

But two months dead: Nay, not so much; not two,
bʊt tuː mʊnθs dɛd næɪ nɔt soː mʊtʃ nɔt tuː

So excellent a King, that was to this
soː ɛksəlɛnt ə kɪŋ ðət wæz tə ðɪs

Hiperion to a Satyre: so louing to my Mother
hɔɪpeːrjən tuː ə sæːtɪr soː lʊvɪŋ tə məɪ mʊðr

That he might not beteeme the windes of heauen
ðæt i məɪt nɔt bɪtiːm ðə wɪndz əv hɛvn

Visit her face too roughly. Heauen and Earth
vɪzɪt ər fæːs tuː rʊflɪ hɛvn ənd ɛrθ

Must I remember: why she would hang on him,
mʊst əɪ rɪmɛmbr ʍəi ʃi wuːld hæŋ ɔn ɪm

As if encrease of Appetite had growne
əz ɪf ɪnkreːs əv æpətəɪt həd groːn

By what it fed on; and yet within a month?
bəɪ ʍæt ɪt fɛd ɔn ənd jɛt wɪðɪn ə mʊnθ

Let me not thinke on't: Frailty, thy name is woman.
lɛt mi nɔt θɪŋk ɔnt fræɪltɪ ðəɪ næːm ɪz wumən

A little Month, or ere those shooes were old,
ə lɪtl munθ ɔr ɛr ðoːz ʃuːz weːr oːld

With which she followed my poore Fathers body
wɪð ʍɪtʃ ʃi fɔloːd məɪ puːr fæðərz bɔdɪ

Like *Niobe*, all teares. Why she, euen she.
ləɪk nəɪobɪ ɔːl teːrz ʍəɪ ʃiː iːvn ʃiː

(O Heauen! A beast that wants discourse of Reason
oː hɛvn ə beːst ðət wænts diskuːrs əv reːzn

Would haue mourn'd longer) married with mine Vnkle,
wuːld əv muːrnd lɔːŋgər mærɪd wɪð məɪn uŋkəl

My Fathers Brother: but no more like my Father,
məɪ fæðərz bruðər bət noː moːr ləɪk məɪ fæðər

Then I to *Hercules*. Within a Moneth?
ðən əɪ tə hɛrkɪuliz wɪðɪn ə munθ

Ere yet the salt of most vnrighteous Teares
ɛr jɛt ðə sɔːlt əv moːst unrəɪtjəs teːrz

Had left the flushing of her gauled eyes,
əd lɛft ðə fluʃɪŋ əv ər gɔːləd əɪz

She married . . .
ʃi mærɪd

II. iii. 1–9

Laer. My necessaries are imbark't; Farewell:
məɪ nɛsəsærɪz ær ɪmbærkt færwɛl

And Sister, as the Winds giue Benefit,
ænd sɪstər æz ðə wɪndz gɪv bɛnəfɪt

And Conuoy is assistant; doe not sleepe,
ənd kɔnvɔɪ ɪz əsɪstənt duː nɔt sliːp

But let me heare from you.
bət lɛt mi heɪr frəm juː

Ophel. Doe you doubt that?
duː juː dəut ðæt

Laer. For Hamlet and the trifling of his fauours,
fɔr hæmlət ænd ðə trəɪflɪŋ əv ɪz fæːvrz

Hold it a fashion and a toy in Bloud;
hoːld ɪt ə fæʃən ænd ə tɔɪ ɪn blud

A Violet in the youth of Primy Nature;
ə vəɪələt ɪn ðə juːθ əv prəɪmɪ næːtjər

Froward, not permanent; sweet not lasting
froːwərd nɔt pɛrmənɛnt swiːt nɔt læstɪŋ

The (perfume and) suppliance of a minute?
ðə pɛrfɪum ənd suplɪəns əv ə mɪnət

Selection B

Romeo and Juliet, I. i. 35–79

Samp. Me they shall feele while I am able to stand:
And 'tis knowne I am a pretty peece of flesh.
Greg. 'Tis well thou art not Fish: If thou hadst thou
had'st beene poore Iohn. Draw thy Toole,
here comes (two) of the House of the *Mountagues.*

Enter two other Seruingmen.

Sam. My naked weapon is out: quarrel, I wil back thee.
Gre. How? Turne thy backe, and run.
Sam. Feare me not.
Gre. No marry: I feare thee.

Sam. Let vs take the Law of our sides: let them begin.

Gr. I wil frown as I passe by, & let the(m) take it as they list.

Sam. Nay, as they dare. I wil bite my Thumb at them, which is a disgrace to them, if they beare it.

Abra. Do you bite your Thumbe at vs sir?

Samp. I do bite my Thumbe, sir.

Abra. Do you bite your Thumbe at vs, sir?

Sam. Is the Law of our side, if I say I? *Gre.* No.

Sam. No sir, I do not bite my Thumbe at you sir: but I bite my Thumbe sir.

Greg. Do you quarrell sir?

Abra. Quarrell sir? no sir.

Sam. If you do sir, I am for you, I serue as good a man as you.

Abra. No better? *Samp.* Well sir.

Enter Benuolio.

Gr. Say better: here comes one of my masters kinsmen.

Samp. Yes, better.

Abra. You Lye.

Samp. Draw if you be men. *Gregory*, remember thy (s)washing blow. *They fight.*

Ben. Part Fooles, put vp your Swords, you know not what you do.

Enter Tibalt.

Tyb. What are thou drawne, among these heartlesse Hindes? Turne thee Benuolio, looke vpon thy death.

Ben. I do but keepe the peace, put vp thy Sword,
Or manage it to part these men with me.

Tyb. What draw, and talke of peace? I hate the word
As I hate hell, all *Mountagues*, and thee:
Haue at thee Coward. *Fight.*

Selection C

As You Like It, I. iii. 43–105

Duk. Mistris, dispatch you with your fastest haste,
And get you from our Court.

Ros. Me Vncle.
Duk. You Cosen,
Within these ten daies if that thou beest found
So neere our publike Court as twentie miles,
Thou diest for it.
Ros. I doe beseech your Grace
Let me the knowledge of my fault beare with me:
If with my selfe I hold intelligence,
Or haue acquaintance with mine owne desires,
If that I doe not dreame, or be not franticke,
(As I doe trust I am not) then deere Vncle,
Neuer so much as in a thought vnborne,
Did I offend your highnesse.
Duk. Thus doe all Traitors,
If their purgation did consist in words,
They are as innocent as grace itselfe;
Let it suffice thee that I trust thee not.
Ros. Yet your mistrust cannot make me a Traitor;
Tell me whereon the likelihoods depends?
Duk. Thou art thy Fathers daughter, there's enough.
Ros. So was I when your highness took his Dukdome,
So was I when your highnesse banisht him;
Treason is not inherited my Lord,
Or if we did deriue it from our friends,
What's that to me, my Father was no Traitor,
Then good my Leige, mistake me not so much,
To thinke my pouertie is treacherous.
Cel. Deere Soueraigne heare me speake.
Duk. I Celia, we staid her for your sake,
Else had she with her Father rang'd along.
Cel. I did not then intreat to haue her stay,
It was your pleasure, and your owne remorse,
I was too yong that time to value her,
But now I know her: if she be a Traitor,
Why so am I: we still haue slept together
Rose at an instant, learn'd, plaid, eate together,

And wheresoere we went, like *Iunos* Swans,
Still we went coupled and inseperable.
Duk. She is too subtile for thee, and her smoothness;
Her verie silence, and (h)er patience,
Speake to the people, and they pittie her:
Thou art a foole, she robs thee of thy name,
And thou wilt show more bright, & seem more vertuous
When she is gone: then open not thy lips
Firme, and irreuocable is my doombe,
Which I haue past vpon her, she is banish'd.
Cel. Pronounce that sentence then on me my Leige,
I cannot liue out of her companie.
Duk. You are a foole: you Neice prouide your selfe,
If you out-stay the time, vpon mine honor,
And in the greatnesse of my word you die.
Exit Duke, etc.
Cel. O my poore *Rosaline*, whether wilt thou goe?
Wilt thou change Fathers? I will giue thee mine:
I charge thee be not thou more grieu'd then I am.
Ros. I haue more cause.
Cel. Thou hast not Cosen,
Prethee be cheereful; know'st thou not the Duke
Hath banish'd me his daughter?
Ros. That he hath not.
Cel. No, hath not? Rosaline lacks then the loue
Which teacheth thee that thou and I am one,
Shall we be sundred? shall we part sweete girle?
No, let my Father seeke another heire:
Therefore deuise with me how we may flie
Whether to goe, and what to beare with vs,
And doe not seeke to take your change vpon you,
To beare your griefes your selfe, and leaue me out:
For by this heauen, now at our sorrowes pale;
Say what thou canst, Ile goe along with thee.

Selection D

Twelfth Night, I. iii. 1–125

Enter Sir Toby, and Maria

Sir To. What a plague meanes my Neece to take the death of her brother thus? I am sure care's an enemie to life.

Mar. By my troth sir *Toby*, you must come in earlyer a nights: your Cosin, my Lady, takes great exceptions to your ill houres.

To. Why let her except, before excepted.

Ma. I, but you must confine your selfe within the modest limits of order.

To. Confine? Ile confine my selfe no finer then I am: these cloathes are good enough to drinke in, and so bee these boots too: and they be not, let them hang themselues in their owne straps.

Ma. That quaffing and drinking will vndoe you: I heard my Lady talke of it yesterday: and of a foolish knight that you brought in one night here, to be hir woer.

To. Who, Sir *Andrew Ague-cheeke?*

Ma. I he.

To. He's as tall a man as any's in Illyria.

Ma. What's that to th' purpose?

To. Why he ha's three thousand ducates a yeare.

Ma. I, but hee'l haue but a yeare in all these ducates: He's a very foole, and a prodigall.

To. Fie, that you'l say so: he playes o'th Viol-de-gamboys, and speaks three or four languages word for word without booke, & hath all the good gifts of nature.

Ma. He hath indeed, almost naturall: for besides that he's a foole, he's a great quarreller: and but that hee hath the gift of a Coward, to allay the gust he hath in quarrelling, 'tis thought among the prudent, he would quickly haue the gift of a graue.

Tob. By this hand they are scoundrels and substractors that say so of him. Who are they?

Ma. They that adde moreour, hee's drunke nightly in your company.

To. With drinking healths to my Neece: Ile drinke to her as long as there is a passage in my throat, & drinke in Illyria: he's a Coward and a Coystrill that will not drinke to my Neece till his braines turne o'th toe, like a parish top. What wench? *Castiliano vulgo:* for here coms Sir *Andrew Agueface.*

Enter Sir Andrew.

And. Sir *Toby Belch.* How now sir *Toby Belch?*

To. Sweet sir *Andrew.*

And. Bless you faire Shrew.

Mar. And you too sir.

Tob. Accost Sir Andrew, accost.

And. What's that?

To. My Neeces Chamber-maid.

(*And*). Good Mistris accost, I desire better acquaintance.

Ma. My name is *Mary*, sir.

And. Good mistris *Mary*, accost

To. You mistake knight: Accost, is front her, boord her, woe her, assayle her.

And. By my troth I would not vndertake her in this company. Is that the meaning of Accost?

Ma. Far you well Gentlemen.

To. And thou let part so Sir *Andrew*, would thou mightst neuer draw sword agen.

And. And you part so mistris, I would I might neuer draw sword agen: Faire Lady, doe you thinke you haue fooles in hand?

Ma. Sir, I haue not you by 'th hand.

And. Marry but you shall haue, and heeres my hand.

Ma. Now sir, thought is free: I pray you bring your hand to'th Buttry barre, and let it drinke.

An. Wherefore (sweet-heart?) What's your Metaphor?

Ma. It's dry sir.

And. Why I thinke so: I am not such an asse, but I can keepe my hand dry. But what's your iest?

Ma. A dry iest Sir.

And. Are you full of them?

Ma. I Sir, I haue them at my fingers ends: marry now I let go your hand, I am barren. *Exit Maria*

To. O knight, thou lack'st a cup of Canarie: when did I see thee so put downe?

And. Neuer in your life I thinke, vnless you see Canarie put me downe: mee thinkes sometimes I haue no more wit than a Christian, or an ordinary man ha's: but I am a great eater of beefe, and I beleeue that does harme to my wit.

To. No question.

An. And I thought that, I'de forsweare it. Ile ride home to morrow sir *Toby*.

To. *Pur-quoy* my deere knight?

An. What is *purquoy?* Do, or not do? I would I had bestowed that time in the tongues, that I haue in fencing dancing, and beare-bayting: O had I but followed the Arts.

To. Then hadst thou had an excellent head of haire.

An. Why, would that haue mended my haire?

To. Past question, for thou seest it will not (curle by) nature.

An. But it becoms (me) wel enough, dost not?

To. Excellent, it hangs like a flax on a distaffe: & I hope to see a huswife take thee between her legs, & spin it off.

An. Faith Ile home to morrow sir Toby, your niece will not be seene, or if she be it's four to one, she'l none of me: the Count himselfe here hard by, wooes her.

To. Shee'l none o'th Count, she'l not match aboue hir degree, neither in estate, yeares, nor wit: I haue heard her swear't. Tut there's life in't man.

An. Ile stay a moneth longer. I am a fellow o'th strangest minde i'th world: I delight in Maskes and Reuels sometimes altogether.

To. Art thou good at these kicke-chawses Knight?

And. As any man in Illyria, whatsoeuer he be, vnder the degree of my betters, & yet I will not compare with an old man.

V

Middle English

41. The Rise of a National Language

The English language between the year 1050 and 1450 has already been characterized as Middle English. We shall examine, as representative of this period, the language of Chaucer. Since Chaucer died in 1400, only a half century before the end of this period, his language might be very appropriately called Late Middle English, but nevertheless it still contains the essential characteristics of Middle English as opposed to Early Modern. Earlier specimens of Middle English may be seen in Webster's *New International Dictionary*, §§ 67–70, p. lxxxix.

Another reason for choosing Chaucer as the representative of Middle English is that he wrote in the London dialect which was the ancestor of our present-day standard English, both literary and colloquial. Even as early as Shakespeare, those of his contemporaries who were carrying on the affairs of the English-speaking world, with a few notable exceptions, spoke and wrote a relatively standardized English. This was not the case with Chaucer and his contemporaries, as we can readily see by comparing the specimens of the several Middle English dialects given in Webster's *New International Dictionary*, §§ 71–5, p. xc.

In the confusion attending the Norman Conquest, the English language had temporarily lost much of its preeminence as a means of communication in the political, social, and economic, as well as the cultural, spheres of life. At the same time, it was undergoing certain fundamental changes in structure, and these changes progressed more rapidly in certain portions of England than in others. When in the second half of the thirteenth century the language again emerged from its temporary obscurity, no one dialect immediately acquired a position of dominant authority. Important literature was written in all four dialects, Northern and Southern, Kentish and Midland, and each dialect, of course, was the medium of intercourse in its own area.

This situation continued well into the fourteenth century. In the meantime, London was growing in importance as a center of government, business, and culture, and gradually the speech of this East Midland center established its authority over the other regional types of English. In addition to the pre-eminence it achieved through being the language of the capital, it was also favored because it constituted a kind of mean between the extremes of the Northern and Southern dialects; it was probably intelligible to more speakers of fourteenth-century English than any other single dialect.

Finally the circumstance that it was the native dialect

and the form of English used by the greatest literary figure of the time, Geoffrey Chaucer, settled without further question this conflict of regional forms of English. This is not to say that Chaucer made the London dialect into a literary standard. Had he been born elsewhere, he would still very likely have written in the London dialect or something approximating it, as did his contemporaries Wycliffe, who was born in the north of England, and Gower, who hailed from Kent. Chaucer found the dialect of his native city already in a position of superiority, but by using it as a vehicle for his own work he gave it added prestige.

Nor does this account of the rise of the London dialect differ essentially from what was happening in the countries of continental Europe at the time. The language of the Isle de France gained pre-eminence over other French dialects because it was the speech of Paris. Tuscan Italian and Castillian Spanish similarly became the standard forms of those languages, partly because of such writers as Dante and Cervantes and partly because of the social and economic domination of those sections of Italy and Spain.

In our analysis of Middle English we shall follow the same general procedure that was established for Modern and Early Modern English. Several specimens of Chaucer's works will be reproduced. These will form the bulk of the material to be examined and analyzed. We shall deal first with the sounds and then with the inflections and syntax of the individual parts of speech. At this stage, however, a new difficulty arises. Early Modern English is sufficiently like the language of our own time that it gives rise to few difficulties of comprehension through obsolete words or constructions. Middle English is not always so easy to understand, and you should make a practice of first reading over the specimen passages assigned in connection with each exercise, making certain they are wholly clear in meaning. For interpreting difficult words and passages, consult the aids mentioned on p. 264.

ADDITIONAL REFERENCES:

Baugh, *History of the English Language*, pp. 236–41.
Emerson, *History of the English Language*, pp. 78–83.
Webster's *New International Dictionary*, § 34, p. lxxxv, § 36, p. lxxxvi, § 71–9, p. xc.

EXERCISE XLI

Middle English Stressed Vowels

1. Examine carefully the phonetic transcription of Selection E. Read it aloud several times so that you may familiarize yourself with the context and the new combinations of sound.

2. Determine the relationship of Chaucer's stressed vowel sounds to those of Modern English. Use the same sixteen-column arrangement which was suggested in Exercise XXXVI, and again place the words in their Middle English transcription in the column headed by the present pronunciation of the stressed vowel or diphthong. This time, however, use as evidence only those words which are italicized in the original version of Selection *E*. The reason for restricting the evidence in this fashion is that this particular analysis is directed at determining the isolative sound changes which have taken place since

Chaucer's time. As we go farther back, we find that more and more words have been influenced by combinative changes of one sort or another, but to include these among the words that have undergone a wholly regular isolative change would only confuse the problem. The word *entuned*, 123, should be classified as MnE [ɪu]; *ferthing*, 134, and *yerde*, 149, should be considered as MnE *farthing* and *yard*.

3. Make a list of the stressed vowel sounds and diphthongs which occurred in ME. What are the stressed vowels and diphthongs which are found in MnE but which did not occur in ME? What are the stressed vowels and diphthongs which were present in ME but not in MnE? Are there any sounds present both in ME and MnE but not in EMnE?

4. What instances do you find of ME vowels identical in quality but different in quantity, having a different subsequent development?

5. Which EMnE sounds developed into MnE [i]? Which ME sounds became MnE [i]? What do you notice about the MnE spelling of those words which are pronounced as [i] in MnE, but which in ME were pronounced [æː]? What did ME [æː] become in EMnE?

6. Which two ME sounds developed into MnE [e]? What do you notice about the MnE spelling of these words? What were the EMnE equivalents of MnE [e]? Frame a complete statement of the history of MnE [e], connecting its EMnE antecedents with those in ME.

7. What are the ME sources for MnE [u] and [o]? What had the ME sounds become in EMnE? What is the phonetic direction of these changes? Is it the same as that indicated by the changes which took place in the front vowels?

8. List the three stages in the development of MnE [ɑɪ] and [ɑʊ]. What has been the phonetic direction of these developments? Are they in accord with the general direc-

tion in the development of simple vowels between the ME and MnE periods?

9. Expand the table you made in connection with Question 10, Exercise XXXVI, to include the ME equivalents for MnE [i, ɪ, e, ɛ, æ, u, o, ʌ, ɑɪ, ɑʊ, ɔɪ].

Exercise XLII

Middle English Stressed Vowels (continued)

1. List the ME sources for MnE [ɔ]. Compare them with the EMnE sources. At what period did most of the changes which produced this sound take place? Would you say that this vowel in MnE is primarily the result of isolative or combinative change?

2. What is the phonetic direction of the development of [ʊ] to [ʌ], particularly with reference to tongue and lip position? Can you explain why ME [fʊt], [wʊlf], did not follow the general tendency of this sound in MnE?

3. What do such spellings as *good*, *took*, and *hood* suggest about an additional source for MnE [ʊ]? See Wyld, *Short History of English*, § 236. Can you point to any MnE variant pronunciations which suggest that the change was never completed, or is not wholly complete at the present time? How do the Scotch pronunciations of *good* and *book* enter into the situation?

4. Would the development of EMnE [guːd] into MnE [gʊd] have taken place before or after the change of [ʊ] to [ʌ]? In the light of your answer, can you explain our present pronunciation of *blood* and *flood?* Do you know of any dialect pronunciations of *soot* or *took* that might be relevant here? Can you explain them?

5. What was Chaucer's pronunciation of *e* before *r*? What have Chaucer's [fɛr] and [smɛrtə] become in MnE? Consult Shakespeare's *Sonnets*, Nos. 11, 14, 48, 72, to see if you can determine through the rhymes Shakespeare's

pronunciation of similar words. What is the Modern British English pronunciation of *clerk*, *Berkley*, *Derby?* Chaucer's Shipman was from Dartmouth. Turn to the description of this character in the *Prologue* to discover how Chaucer spelled this place name. Where did *Hartford*, Connecticut, get its name? Consult a county map of England if you are not familiar with English county names. See Wyld, *Short History of English*, §§ 222, 228.

6. In view of what you know about the EMnE sources for MnE [ɑ], what would you conclude about the phonetic direction of the EMnE development of ME [ɛ] before [r]? Do you recall if *r* influenced any other vowels similarly? See Question 7, Exercise XXXVI. In the light of these facts, account for the dialect forms *sartin*, *varmint*, and the term *'varsity*.

7. Complete the table which you began in connection with Question 9 of the preceding exercise.

8. What would have been the pronunciation in ME of *grace*, *ease*, *flower*, *course?* Compare the MnE pronunciation of these words with that of the cognate words in Modern French. Compare the ME cognates with Mn French. Do loan words appear to participate in the general sound changes of a language after they become parts of it?

42. Middle English Spelling

So far we have been concerned solely with the relationship of Middle English and Modern English sounds, and have paid no attention to the way the Middle English sounds were spelled. Although it is true that the spelling of the fourteenth century was almost as chaotic as our own, nevertheless it often serves as a kind of negative help in determining the phonetic values of individual words. For example, if we know that the spelling *au* had only one value in Middle English, that of [ɑu], we must conclude that such a word as *daunce* was pronounced with this particular stressed vowel, and we see in addition that the pronunciation suggested by Chaucer's spelling could not have been the direct forerunner of MnE [dæns]. If we find the ME equivalent of our word *deaf* [dɛf] spelled with two *e*'s, and we know that a doubled symbol always represented a long vowel, we realize again that the dialect pronunciation [dif] rather than the standard English [dɛf] is the direct descendant of the Middle English pronunciation.

The following table shows the presumable phonetic values in stressed vowels of the various letters of the alphabet for Chaucer's period and dialect. Observe that a doubled letter always indicates a long vowel, but that a single letter may indicate either a long or a short vowel. When a single spelling may represent more than one pronunciation, the only way to determine its value is by reference to its phonetic value in Modern English. Therefore the Modern English development of the sound is given in the third column.

To illustrate how the table may be used, let us suppose we come upon the spelling *sooty*. We find from the first column in the table that *oo* could represent either ME [ɔː] or ME [oː]. But Middle English [ɔː] had become MnE [o]; ME [oː] has become MnE [u] or [ʊ]. The last of these developments rather than the first represents the word *sooty;* therefore its ME pronunciation must have been [soːtɪ].

ME Spelling		ME Pronunciation	MnE Pronunciation
a	*thank*	[ɑ] [θɑŋk]	[æ] [θæŋk]
	shave	[ɑː] [ʃɑːvə]	[e] [ʃev]
aa	*caas*	[ɑː] [kɑːs]	[e] [kes]
e	*leg*	[ɛ] [lɛg]	[ɛ] [lɛg]
	shepe	[eː] [ʃeːpə]	[i] [ʃip]
	bete	[æː] [bæːtə]	[i] [bit] [19]
ee	*preest*	[eː] [preːst]	[i] [prist]
	heeth	[æː] [hæːθ]	[i] [hiθ]
i, y	*bin* or *byn*	[ɪ] [bɪn]	[ɪ] [bɪn]
	like or *lyke*	[iː] [liːk]	[ɑɪ] [lɑɪk]

[19] Because ME [æ:] and [e:] both developed into MnE [i], the present pronunciation of such words as *sheep* and *beat* is of no help in determining their ME value. This has to be done principally by determining their Old English pronunciation. Old English words with *ē* and *ēo* as their stressed vowels became ME [eː]. Old English words with *ǣ*, *ēa*, and *e* in an open syllable as their stressed vowels became ME [æː]. In general, words with ME [æ:] acquired the *ea* spelling in MnE: compare *beat*, *heath* with *sheep*, *deep*. ME [eː] is represented in MnE by *ee*, *e*, *ei*, and *ie* spellings.

It should be pointed out, also, that for what is usually called 'long open *e*' in such a word as *heeth*, MnE *heath*, the transcription [ɛː] is more frequent than the value [æː] which is assigned it here. My reasons for employing the [æː] transcription are twofold. First, I have never succeeded in getting Chaucer students with a General American speech background to pronounce what to my ear is a satisfactory *long* mid front vowel. Second, most scholars who assign the value [ɛː] to ME long open *e* generally equate this symbol with such words as MnE *air*, *bare*, *Mary*, where the vowel occurs before *r* and in many forms of MnE is considerably lowered from the [ɛ] position. That is, they have in mind something raised above [æ] in *hat* but lower than [ɛ] in *net*.

A considerable portion of the speakers of General American, however, make no distinction between the vowels of *air* and *e'er*, *fairy* and

ME Spelling		ME Pronunciation	MnE Pronunciation

ii or *ij*. Rarely used in Chaucer but these do appear in some Middle English texts with the value of [i], which developed into MnE [ɑɪ].

o	*top*	[ɔ] [tɔp]	[ɑ, ɔ] [tɑp, tɔp]
	bot, *bole*	[ʊ] [bʊt, bʊlə]	[ʌ] [bʌt]
			[ʊ] [bʊl]
	cote	[ɔː] [kɔːtə]	[o] [kot]
	to, *gode*	[oː] [toː, goːd]	[u] [tu]
			[ʊ] [gʊd]
oo	*boon*	[ɔː] [bɔːn]	[o] [bon]
	food, *hood*	[oː] [foːd, hoːd]	[u] [fud]
			[ʊ] [hʊd]
U	*buk*, *ful*	[ʊ] [bʊk, fʊl]	[ʌ] [bʌk]
			[ʊ] [fʊl]
	tune	[ɪu] [tɪun]	[ɪu, u] [tɪun, tun]
y	see *i*		

ferry, *Mary*, *marry*, and *merry*, and in order to suggest a lower vowel to students who normally speak this dialect, it becomes virtually necessary to use the [æ] symbol.

This transcription suggests, of course, that the vowel in question was not raised between the OE and ME periods. This is scarcely a difficulty, however, for many of the authorities who suggest [ɛː] as the value for ME open *e*, also assign the same value to OE ǣ. Joseph Wright, for example, says flatly: 'This change of [OE] ǣ . . . was not a sound change, but merely an orthographical change.' (*Elementary Middle English Grammar*, p. 26.) Nor is it generally assumed that any of the other OE vowels were raised between 900 and 1400. The greatest difficulty resulting from the [æː] transcription arises in connection with the lengthening of OE *e* in open syllables (see Exercise L, Question 4), where the [æː] value suggests a lowering as well as a lengthening. The disadvantage of this minor inconsistency is, I believe, far outweighed by the advantages of [æː] transcription for speakers of General American.

ME Spelling		ME Pronunciation	MnE Pronunciation
ai, ay	*gain, gayn*	[æɪ] [gæɪn]	[e] [gen]
au, aw	*sauce, sawce*	[aʊ] [sɑʊsə]	[ɔ] [sɔs]
ei, ey	*grein, greyn*	[æɪ] [græɪn]	[e] [gren]
eu, ew	*leued, lewed*	[ɪu] [lɪuəd]	[ɪu, u] [lɪud, lud]
iu, iw	*niue, niwe*	[ɪu] [nɪuə]	[ɪu, u] [nɪu, nu]
ou, ow	*doun, down*	[uː] [duːn]	[ɑʊ] [dɑʊn]
	oune, owne	[ɔːʊ] [ɔːʊnə]	[o] [on]
	brought	[ɔʊ] [brɔʊxt]	[ɔ] [brɔt]
oy, oi	*coy*	[ɔɪ] [kɔɪ]	[ɔɪ] [kɔɪ]
ir, er	*bird, herd,*	[ɪr, ɛr, [bɪrd, hɛrd	[ɜ] [bɝd, hɝd,
or, ur	*word, turn*	ɔr, ʊr] wɔrd, tʊrn]	wɝd, tɝn]

Before going on to some of the analyses required in connection with the following exercise, it must be pointed out that modern scholarship assumes that Chaucer wrote in iambic pentameter comparable to that of modern poetry. Therefore a reading of Chaucer which will allow the normal stress pattern to assert itself will, as with Shakespeare, help us to determine much about the pronunciation of final *e* and about the stress pattern of his plurisyllabic words. In preparation for Exercise XLIII you should re-read Selection E aloud, observing the syllables upon which the stress naturally falls, and noting the relationship between final *e* in the spelling of the original and its presence in the phonetic transcription.

Additional Reading:

Webster's *New International Dictionary*, Guide to Pronunciation, pp. xxiii–xxv.

Exercise XLIII

Middle English Unstressed Vowels and Consonants

1. Make a list of those words in Selection E in which the stress in ME is perceptibly different from that of MnE. In each case observe the direction in which the stress has shifted, or from which of two or more syllables it has disappeared. Can you put your observations into one or two general statements? Are the words which participated in this shift for the most part of native or of foreign origin? What has happened to the vowel quality of those syllables which were accented in Chaucer's time but have become unstressed in MnE?

2. What does the position of the stress in the following words suggest about the probable date of their adoption into English: *bagatelle*, *cadet*, *caprice*, *ballet*, *fiancee*, *technique?* Verify your conclusion by securing the date of the earliest *Oxford English Dictionary* citation for each of them.

3. Examine the transcription of Selection E to determine whether or not spelled final *e* is consistently pronounced. Do the transcriptions of *nonne*, 118, *simple*, 119, *gretteste*, 120, *faire*, 124, *scole*, 125, *carie*, 130, *fille*, 131, *digne*, 141, *charitable*, 143, *wepe*, *sawe*, 144, *trappe*, 145, *conscience*, 150, lead you to any conclusion about the pronunciation of final *e* and the nature of the following sound? Consider in this connection also the words *wette*, 129, *muche*, 132, and *hadde*, 135. Do these essentially modify your previous conclusion? Explain. What can you say about the pronunciation of final *e* at the end of a line of poetry?

4. Review your conclusions about the pronunciation of final *e* in EMnE. Between what dates must the total disappearance of final *e* have taken place? What can you learn from Shakespeare's spelling in this respect about the readiness with which orthographical systems reflect changes in pronunciation?

5. What do you observe about the pronunciation of initial *h* in Selection E? In what kinds of words or parts of speech is initial *h* not always pronounced? Scan the verses in which words of this nature occur. Is there any connection between stress and pronunciation of the initial *h*? Compare the situation with that which prevails in MnE.

6. Compare the MnE pronunciation of *hour*, *honor*, *host*, *horrible*, *hostler*, *humor*. Consult Webster for the recorded pronunciation of the last two words. Judging from the early spellings recorded in the *Oxford English Dictionary*, how were these words pronounced at the time of their adoption into English? Account for the differences in their pronunciation in MnE. See also Webster, Guide to Pronunciation, § 3, p. xxv.

7. What was the pronunciation of final *ng* in Chaucer's speech? What was it in Shakespeare's? State your conclusion as to the development of this sound.

8. What do you observe about the pronunciation of initial *th* in Chaucer? How does the speech of Shakespeare differ in this particular? For the most part, what kinds of words are affected by this difference? Are they normally stressed or unstressed? State the difference between the pronunciations in phonetic terms. Can you account for it?

9. How was the sound [x] spelled in ME? Does this sound occur in MnE? Does the spelling occur? What do you conclude from this concerning the flexibility of orthographic systems?

10. Put the first nine lines of Selection G into phonetic transcription showing the pronunciation of Chaucer's time. The word *slee* (MnE *slay*) has developed irregularly and should be transcribed [slæːɪ].

43. Noun and Adjective Inflections

As with the language of Shakespeare, we are again faced with the problem of interpreting the final *e*'s which are found on a good many nouns. In Early Modern English, we concluded that they were not pronounced, so it was possible to dismiss them from further consideration. We have seen, however, from the phonetic transcription of Selection E, that in Middle English the final *e* is often represented in the pronunciation by the sound [ə]. The problem is not quite so simple, therefore, as in Early Modern English and deserves a careful analysis.

We may best begin by examining all the nouns in Selection F which are spelled with final *e*. There are fifteen in all: *reve*, 587, *binne*, 593, *droghte*, 595, *dayerye*, 597, *pultrye*, 598, *age*, 601, *arrerage*, 602, *herde*, 603, *hyne*, 603, *sleighte*, 604, *covyne*, 604, *place*, 607, *cote*, 612, *youthe*, 613, and *wrighte*, 613.

Next, we must scan all the lines in which these nouns occur to determine in which of these words the final *e* is actually pronounced. Observe, for example, line 595, in which the final *e* of *droghte* is clearly without value in pronunciation:

W̆el wíst*e* hĕ, bý thĕ dróght*e* ănd bý the réyn

Scanning the remaining lines, we find that in the nouns *herde*, 603, *sleighte*, 604, *cote*, 612, *youthe*, 613, and *wrighte*, 614, the final vowel is similarly syncopated. If we were to make an extensive study of this problem, it would be desirable to consult a Chaucer concordance or glossary for other examples of these same words, to determine if they ever appear without the final *e*, or, if it is always present in the spelling, to see how consistently it is present or absent in pronunciation. For our immediate purpose, however, we may dispense with this step and turn our attention to the remaining nine nouns: *reve*, *binne*, *dayerye*, *pultrye*, *age*, *arrerage*, *hyne*, *covyne*, *place*.

It is immediately apparent that the greater portion of these nouns are of French origin. Among them are *age*, *arrerage*, *covyne*, *place*, and *pultrye*. Moreover, *dayerye* is a hybrid word, consisting of a native stem and the French suffix *-erye*. In these French borrowings the final *e* is to be considered etymological rather than inflectional. That is, its presence in Middle English is not dependent upon any particular construction of the noun. It was present in these words when they were taken into the language, and it did not disappear until some time after 1450, when final *e* was generally lost.

The remaining words, *binne*, *hyne*, and *reve* are native, and have as their Old English forms *binne* [bɪnːə], *hīne* [hiːnə] and *ġerēfa* [jɛreːvɑ]. Observe that the original forms of these words did end in a vowel which, early in the Middle English period, had become unstressed and centralized, thus acquiring the value of [ə]. As with the French words, the final *e*'s in those of native origin are to be accounted for in the main on the grounds of their presence in an earlier form of the word rather than as a specific indication of any particular construction or function.

It is very likely true that many words, such as *cote*, in which the final syllable is not pronounced in Selection F but which in Selection H occurs with final *e* at the end of a line, would by this time have lost the final vowel in ordinary daily speech. Chaucer was writing poetry, and it is conceivable that if two forms of a word existed, one in general use and the other a slightly more archaic form, he would choose whichever one fitted his purpose at the time. To this extent we may suspect that the poetry of Chaucer, or of anyone else during this period, is a step behind the colloquial language. Nevertheless, by dint of careful analysis we are enabled to see in it the language processes which were taking place during his lifetime.

Exercise XLIV

1. Using Section 43 as a model, make a similar analysis of the nouns with final *e* in lines 4011–44 of Selection H. Use Webster and the *Oxford English Dictionary* to determine the etymology of those words which have been preserved in MnE. Stratmann's *Middle English Dictionary* (edited by H. Bradley) will be useful for those words which are no longer current.

2. How many ways of forming the plural are you able to find in Selections F, G, and H? Note also the plural forms in lines A 323, 2607, B 1674, 4063, 4370, 4383, and 4446 of the *Canterbury Tales*. List all the nouns which have changed their manner of forming the plural since Chaucer's time. Which inflection have they adopted? Do you find among these any noun which formed its plural in two different ways. Consult the *Oxford English Dictionary* to determine which inflection it originally had.

3. Consult the transcription of Selection E, and scan the lines in Selections F, G, and H, to determine how frequently the *-es* inflection had syllabic value.

4. Note the plural form *staves*, Selection G, 3088. Find in Selection F the singular form of this same noun. Is it the same as in MnE? Can you think of any similar instances in MnE of such a relationship between singular and plural forms? What kinds of consonants are involved in this problem?

5. What is the regular ending of the genitive singular

as evidenced by the nouns in Selections E–H? For instances of genitives formed in other than the regular manner, see *Canterbury Tales*, A 88, 781, 1051, 3084. What is your impression concerning the comparative regularity of the genitive and the plural, both in ME and in MnE? What is the MnE genitive singular of *wife?* What form do you find in Selection G? What linguistic process has operated to produce the MnE form?

6. List the periphrastic genitives in Selections F–H. What type of relationship is indicated by each of these constructions?

7. Using the evidence offered by Selections F and G, try to determine whether there is any inflectional significance in the final *e*'s on the adjectives. List the adjectives with and without final *e* (not including pronominal and participial adjectives). Note which final *e*'s are pronounced and which are not. Classify the adjectives into singular and plural, according to the number of the noun modified. Are there any singular adjectives in which final *e* is present and pronounced? Are there any plural adjectives without final *e?* Could any of the final *e*'s on the singular adjectives be considered etymological? Summarize your conclusions about the inflectional pattern of the adjective in ME.

8. Do you find any instances of periphrastic comparison in Selections F–H? Consult the *Oxford English Dictionary*, s.v. *more*, C. 1. b and *most*, adverb, B. 1. b to determine how early this construction appears.

44. Development of the [əs] Inflection

We have seen that in Middle English the regular plural inflection of the noun still had the full syllabic value of [əs]. By Shakespeare's time the present-day distribution of these inflections as [s, z, əz], depending upon the nature of the preceding sound, had already taken place. Therefore the change must have come about in the fifteenth or early sixteenth century. It is of some interest to trace the successive steps in this development.

First, the final *s* of the inflectional syllable became voiced, very likely because of light stress. (For the relationship between stress and vocal quality see Section 7, p. 35. Recall also what happened to the initial consonant of the definite article between the periods of Chaucer and Shakespeare.) As a result of this change, the following forms would have arisen:

ME [rɔːzəs] > EMnE [roːzəz] *roses*
ME [kneːəs] > EMnE [niːəz] *knees*
ME [dɔgəs] > EMnE [dɔgəz] *dogs*
ME [boːkəs] > EMnE [buːkəz] *books*

Notice that so far as the noun *rose*, or in fact any other noun ending in one of the sibilants [s, z, ʃ, tʃ, dʒ], is concerned, this one change was sufficient to produce the form which has prevailed in Modern English.

The next change affecting the remaining nouns was the syncopation or disappearance of the vowel [ə]. This resulted in the forms:

ME [dɔgəs] > EMnE [dɔgəz] > EMnE [dɔgz]
ME [kneːəs] > EMnE [niːəz] > EMnE [niːz]

In those words ending in a vowel or a voiced consonant, this second change resulted in the present-day forms of the plural, *dogs* and *knees*. In the noun *books*, however, this change would have produced the difficult sound combination [kz], so for those nouns ending in a voiceless consonant, the further development of assimilation was required to produce the modern plural:

ME [boːkəs] > EMnE [buːkəz] > EMnE [bʊkz] > EMnE [bʊks].

The genitive inflection developed in precisely the same way to produce the present-day form.

Exercise XLV

Pronoun Inflections and Syntax

1. Construct a paradigm of the personal pronoun in ME from the evidence offered in Selections E–I, supplemented by Sections 5 and 9 of the *Tale of Melibeus*, B 2165–75, 2197–2200, and the Prologue to the *Pardoner's Tale*, C 454–62. These selections contain no instances of the neuter genitive singular, which we already know to have been *his* at this time. Arrange the paradigm as suggested in Question 5, Exercise XXXVII.

2. What are Chaucer's forms for the third person plural? What are the MnE forms? Consult the *Oxford English Dictionary*, s.v. *they*, *their*, *them*. What was the source of these forms? How early were they adopted into the English language? Does Chaucer's use of these pronouns indicate that all three forms were adopted into Standard English at the same time?

3. Throughout the development of the English language, what has frequently happened to initial *h* in pronouns? In view of this development, what might be concluded about the antecedent of the lightly stressed MnE *'em?* Do you see in Chaucer any form which might be considered its original? Consult the *Oxford Dictionary* or Webster, s.v. *'em* to verify your conclusion.

4. Compare Chaucer's use of the second singular personal pronoun in Selections G and I. What is the relationship between the speakers in each instance? Compare

the pronouns used by the Host in addressing the Monk (A 3118) and the Miller (A 3135). Which of these latter characters would be more nearly the Host's social equal? In the *Knight's Tale*, observe how Palamon and Arcite address one another (A 1080–1186). How does Palamon address Emelye (A 2765–97)? How does Emelye address the goddess Diana (A 2297–2330)? What pronoun is used by the Prioress in her Prologue, in addressing God and the Virgin Mary (B 1625–42)? Look through the *Tale of Melibeus*, Sections 13–15, for the forms of address between husband and wife. Draw up a series of statements summarizing Chaucer's use of the *thou* and *ye* forms. Do you find any instances of *you* in the nominative?

5. Do you find any instances of the absolute forms *ours* and *yours* in Chaucer? Consult the *Oxford English Dictionary* to determine at what time they were first used. Does either form appear to have occurred in Chaucer at all? In what part of England were these forms first used?

6. What determines whether the forms *my* or *mine*, *thy* or *thine* are to be used? Lines A 1095–1110, 1130–65 contain sufficient illustrative material for this question. How does Chaucer's practice compare with Shakespeare's in this respect? Where in MnE is the same type of phonetic distinction maintained? How can you explain the form *an*, Selection F, line 606?

7. Make a collection of the relative pronouns which you are able to find in Selections F–I. How does the situation here compare with MnE in respect to the choice of pronoun? With EMnE?

8. From the evidence offered by lines B 4014, 4141, 4266, E 1251 of the Canterbury Tales, construct a paradigm of the demonstrative pronoun in ME. Which form present in MnE does not seem to be present in ME? Consult the *Oxford English Dictionary* to determine when this MnE form first became common. What linguistic process could have given rise to it?

EXERCISE XLVI

Verb Inflections

1. Classify according to person, number, tense, and mood all the present and past tense forms of the verb in Selection J. Then, to find forms for those categories which do not occur in this selection, or occur only once or twice, read in the *Tale of Melibeus* until your conjugations are completed. Try also to get a complete conjugation for the present and past tenses of the verb *to be*.

2. What ending do you find for the first person singular, present indicative? Is it consistently present? If not, what might you be led to suspect concerning its pronunciation? Verify this by scanning the lines in Selection I containing forms in the first person.

3. What variations do you find in the form of the second person singular, present indicative? If the evidence for this question does not seem sufficiently complete, amplify it with the references given in connection with Question 4, Exercise XLV. Upon what factor does the choice of inflectional ending seem to depend? What verbs have merely a *-t* inflection in this construction? What is the usual function of these verbs?

4. How does the inflection of the third person singular, present indicative, compare with that found in Shakespeare? What does this suggest about the date of the adoption of the *-es* inflection in standard English? Observe the inflection for verbs in this construction in the selection from the *Cursor Mundi* given in § 71, p. xc of Webster's *New International Dictionary*. In what part of England was this poem written? What does this suggest concerning the origin of our present third person singular inflection?

5. Is the vowel of the *-eth* inflection always pronounced? Examine Selection G for evidence on this point.

6. What forms do you find for the present plural

inflection? Judging from the spellings, what do you conclude about the pronunciation of the present plural form? Examine lines A 747–860 of the *Canterbury Tales* to verify your conclusion.

7. What form do you find for the present plural of the verb *to be?* What form occurred in Shakespeare? What does this suggest about the date of adoption of the present form?

8. Does Wycliffe's spelling of the weak past inflection differ from Chaucer's? If so, how? What conclusions might you draw from the difference? Examine Selections F and H for evidence concerning the pronunciation of the regular past inflection. Is a final *-e* always present in spelling? Is it always pronounced when it is present? What verbs do you find with a *-t(e)* inflection?

9. Do the regular past tense and past participle inflections in Selection F have the value of a full syllable? Using the discussion in Section 44 as a model, explain how the present-day inflectional pattern arose from the [əd] inflection in ME. Would you suppose this change to have taken place by Shakespeare's time?

10. Do you find in Selection J any strong verb past tense or past participle forms that differ from MnE? Try to determine the MnE pronunciation in each instance. Consult the *Oxford English Dictionary* and discover, if possible, the reasons for the deviation from the MnE form. What do you learn from Selection F about the forms of the past participle and their pronunciation?

11. What are the forms of the present participle and the infinitive in Middle English? Examine Selections F–H carefully for the evidence they have to offer concerning the pronunciation of these inflections.

12. Would you conclude that the final *-e*'s in the verb forms we have studied are to be considered as inflectional or etymological? How does this compare with the situation in respect to the nouns and adjectives?

13. What is the construction of the verb *reste* in Selection J, verse 20? Of *be*, in verse 13?

Exercise XLVII

Syntax of the Verb

1. Extract from Selections E, J, and K all the verbal constructions employed to indicate negation. At the side of each put the form which would be used in conversational MnE. Review the conclusions which were reached in Question 1, Exercise XL. Put into one or two general statements the differences between ME and EMnE in this respect.

2. Look up *ne*, adverb A. 1, in the *Oxford English Dictionary*. How long does it seem to have been current as a negative particle? Do you think that the last of the illustrative citations should be given serious consideration in answering this question? Why?

3. What is peculiar about the verbal construction in Selection E, line 131? See also *Canterbury Tales*, A 70–71. How many negatives do you find in this last reference?

4. Extract from Chaucer's *Boethius*, Book III, Prose III, all the interrogative forms of the verb. Apply the instructions for Question 1 to the problem of verbal interrogation.

5. Observe the simple present tense constructions in the Prologue to the *Canterbury Tales*, A 747–809. Are there any which in MnE would very likely be put into the progressive form? From the reading you have done, what is your impression of the frequency of the progressive in Chaucer?

6. In this same passage, observe the use of the verb *do* in lines A 766, 768, 776. What is its force or meaning in these constructions? Is there any construction in this passage which in MnE would use the past perfect, but which here uses some other form of the verb?

7. Observe the verbal constructions in lines A 756, 777, and 785 in this same passage. What case form of the pronoun precedes the verb? Judging from the inflection of the verb in A 777, what person is the subject? Consult the *Oxford Dictionary* concerning these verbs, with a view to determining how long the constructions exemplified by Chaucer's use remained current, and when the modern construction first arose.

8. As far as possible, classify the verbal constructions with *shall* and *will* in Selections J and K according to the ideas which they convey or imply: futurity, determination, prophecy, desire, habitual action or custom, etc. Are there any categories which employ only the one auxiliary? Which are they? Are the auxiliaries in Selection J always the same as those used in the corresponding passage of the King James version of the Bible? How does the use of these auxiliaries in ME compare with their use in EMnE?

9. From Selections J and K, select those verbal constructions which express condition contrary to fact, condition probable in the future, exhortation, wish or desire, concession, improbability, supposition. In each instance put the form which would be used in informal present day speech alongside the form which was used in ME. Are the forms in Selection J always the same as those which are used in the King James version of the Bible? How does the ME use of the subjunctive compare with the EMnE use?

10. Do you find any instances where the subjunctive form in ME would be replaced in MnE by a periphrastic construction? By the simple indicative? Do you find any instances where in ME an indicative form is used to convey a subjunctive idea?

11. Does *may*, or its past-tense form *might*, always have the same meaning in Selections J and K that it has in MnE? Trace the relationship between *can*, *may*, and the inflected subjunctive form from ME to MnE.

Illustrative Selections from
MIDDLE ENGLISH

Selection E

Canterbury Tales, A 118–50

As the first specimen of Middle English, Chaucer's description of the Prioress, from the Prologue to the *Canterbury Tales*, is given here, accompanied by a phonetic transcription which is intended to represent in general the sounds of Chaucer's speech.

In this transcription, the symbol [x] represents a *voiceless velar fricative*. In making this sound, the vocal lips are open, the velum is retracted, the back of the tongue is placed lightly against the velum, and the breath stream escapes through the aperture formed by tongue and velum. Although this sound is no longer present in MnE, it is regularly found in Modern German, where it is spelled *ch; e.g. ich, ach.*

It is generally believed that at this time doubled consonants were pronounced in a manner quite distinct from single consonants. It is more than possible, however, that these consonants, rather than being actually doubled, were merely lengthened. Accordingly, in the phonetic transcription, these lengthened consonants are indicated in the conventional manner by the use of a colon [ː] after the symbol.

The spelling and punctuation of all but one of the selections from this period is that of the Oxford Edition of Chaucer's works, edited by Walter W. Skeat. Skeat's arrangement of the tales is here accepted as authoritative; all references to them consist of a letter indicating the particular group and the line number within that group. Observe the line reference at the top of this page.

Both the seven volume and the one volume Oxford editions of the *Complete Works of Geoffrey Chaucer* are supplied with a glossary which should be consulted for the meaning of unfamiliar words. The seven volume edition also contains a complete set of explanatory notes to the *Canterbury Tales* which will be helpful in explaining difficult constructions. Bradley's edition of Stratmann's *Middle English Dictionary* is also a useful aid in dealing with the language of this period.

Prologue, A 118–50

Ther was also a *Nonne*, a *Prioresse*,
θæːr wɑs ɑlsɔː ə nun ə priːɔrɛsːə

That of *hir smyling* was *ful simple and coy;*
θɑt ɔf ɪr smiːlɪŋg wɑs ful sɪmpl ɑnd kɔɪ

Hir gretteste *ooth* was *but* by *seynte* Loy;
ɪr grɛtːəst ɔːθ wɑs but bɪ sæɪntə lɔɪ

And *she* was cleped *madame* Eglentyne.
ɑnd ʃeː wɑs kleːpəd mɑdɑm ɛgləntiːnə

Ful wel she song the *service divyne*,
ful wɛl ʃeː sɔŋg θə sɛrvɪsə dɪviːnə

Entuned in hir *nose* ful *semely;*
ɛntɪunəd ɪn ɪr nɔːz ful seːməlɪ

And Frensh she spak ful faire and fetisly,
ɑnd frɛnʃ ʃeː spɑk ful fæɪr ɑnd fɛtɪslɪ

After the *scole* of Stratford atte Bowe,
ɑftər θə skoːl ɔf strɑtfɔrd ɑtːə bɔːuə

For Frensh of Paris was *to hir unknowe.*
fɔr frɛnʃ ɔf pɑrɪs wɑs toː hɪr ʊnknɔːʊə

At mete wel y-taught was she *with-alle;*
ɑt mæːtə wɛl ɪtɑuxt wɑs ʃeː wɪθ ɑlːə

She leet *no morsel* from hir *lippes falle,*
ʃeː leːt nɔː mɔrsəl frɔm ɪr lɪpːəs fɑlːə

Ne *wette* hir *fingres* in hir *sauce depe.*
nə wɛtː ɪr fɪŋgrəs ɪn ɪr sɑusə deːpə

Wel coude she carie a *morsel,* and *wel kepe,*
wɛl kuːd ʃe kɑrɪ ə mɔrsəl ɑnd wɛl keːpə

That *no drope* ne fille up-on hir *brest.*
θɑt nɔː drɔp nə fɪlː upɔn ɪr brɛst

In curteisye was *set* ful *muche* hir lest.
ɪn kuːrtæɪsɪ wɑs sɛt ful mutʃ ɪr lɛst

Hir *over lippe wyped* she *so clene,*
ɪr ɔːvər lɪpːə wiːpəd ʃeː sɔː klæːnə

That in hir *coppe* was no *ferthing sene*
θɑt ɪn ɪr kupːə wɑs nɔː fɛrðɪŋ seːnə

Of *grece,* whan she *dronken hadde* hir draughte.
ɔf græːsə ʍɛn ʃeː druŋkən hɑd ɪr drɑuxtə

Ful *semely after* hir *mete* she raughte,
ful seːməlɪ ɑftər ɪr mæːɪt ʃeː rɑuxtə

And sikerly she was of greet *disport,*
ɑnd sɪkərlɪ ʃe wɑs ɔf græːɪt dɪspɔrt

And ful *plesaunt,* and *amiable* of *port,*
ɑnd ful plɛzɑunt ɑnd ɑːmɪɑːbl ɔf pɔrt

And *peyned* hir to *countrefete chere*
ɑnd pæɪnəd hɪr toː kuːntrəfeːtə tʃeːrə

Of court, and *been estatlich* of *manere,*
ɔf kuːrt ɑnd beːn ɛstɑːtlɪtʃ ɔf mɑneːrə

And to *ben* holden digne of *reverence.*
ɑnd toː beːn hɔːldən diːn ɔf rɛvərɛnsə

But, for to *speken* of hir *conscience,*
but fɔr toː spæːkən ɔf ɪr kɔnsɪɛnsə

She was so charitable and so *pitous*,
ʃeː wɑs sɔː tʃɑrɪtɑːbl ɑnd sɔː pɪtuːs

She wolde *wepe*, if that she *sawe* a *mous*
ʃeː woːldə weːp ɪf θɑt ʃeː sɑu ə muːs

Caught in a *trappe*, if it were deed or *bledde*.
kɑuxt ɪn ə trɑp ɪf it wæːr dæːd ɔr blɛdːə

Of *smale houndes* had she, that she *fedde*
ɔf smɑlə huːndəs hɑd ʃeː θɑt ʃeː fɛdːə

With rosted flesh, or *milk* and wastel-breed.
wɪθ rɔːstəd flɛʃ ɔr mɪlk ɑnd wɑstəl bræːd

But *sore* weep she if oon of hem were deed,
bʊt sɔːr weːp ʃeː ɪf ɔːn ɔf hɛm wæːr dæːd

Or if *men smoot* it with a *yerde smerte:*
ɔr ɪf mɛn smɔːt ɪt wɪθ ə jɛrdə smɛrtə

And *al* was *conscience* and *tendre herte*.
ɑnd ɑl wɑs kɔnsɪɛns ɑnd tɛndər hɛrtə

Selection F

Prologue, A 587–614

The Reve was a sclendre colerik man,
His berd was shave as ny as ever he can.
His heer was by his eres round y-shorn.
His top was dokked lyk a preest biforn.
Ful longe were his legges, and ful lene,
Y-lyk a staf, ther was no calf y-sene.
Wel coude he kepe a gerner and a binne;
Ther was noon auditour coude on him winne.
Wel wiste he, by the droghte, and by the reyn,
The yelding of his seed, and of his greyn.
His lordes sheep, his neet, his dayerye,
His swyn, his hors, his stoor, and his pultrye,

Was hoolly in this reves governing,
And by his covenaunt yaf the rekening,
Sin that his lord was twenty yeer of age;
Ther coude no man bringe him in arrerage.
Ther nas baillif, ne herde, ne other hyne,
That he ne knew his sleighte and his covyne;
They were adrad of him, as of the deeth.
His woning was ful faire up-on an heeth,
With grene treës shadwed was his place.
He coude bettre than his lord purchace.
Ful riche he was astored prively,
His lord wel coude he plesen subtilly,
To yeve and lene him of his owne good,
And have a thank, and yet a cote and hood.
In youthe he lerned hadde a good mister;
He was a well good wrighte, a carpenter.

Selection G

Monkes Tale, Prologue, B 3087–3102

By goddes bones! whan I bete my knaves,
She bringth me forth the grete clobbed staves,
And cryeth, 'slee the dogges everichoon,
And brek hem, bothe bak and every boon.'
And if that any neighebor of myne
Wol nat in chirche to my wyf enclyne,
Or be so hardy to hir to trespace,
Whan she comth hoom, she rampeth in my face,
And cryeth, 'false coward, wreek thy wyf!
By *corpus* bones! I wol have thy knyf,
And thou shalt have my distaf and go spinne!'
Fro day to night right thus she wol biginne; —
'Allas!' she seith, 'that ever I was shape
To wedde a milksop or a coward ape,
That wol be overlad with every wight!
Thou darst nat stonden by thy wyves right!'

Selection H

The Nonne Preestes Tale, B 4011–4054

A Povre widwe, somdel stape in age,
Was whylom dwelling in a narwe cotage,
Bisyde a grove, stonding in a dale.
This widwe, of which I telle yow my tale,
Sin thilke day that she was last a wyf,
In pacience ladde a ful simple lyf,
For litel was hir catel and hir rente;
By housbondrye, of such as God hir sente,
She fond hir-self, and eek hir doghtren two.
Three large sowes hadde she, and namo,
Three kyn, and eek a sheep that highte Malle,
Ful sooty was hir bour, and eek hir halle,
In which she eet ful many a sclendre meel.
Of poynaunt sauce hir neded never a deel.
No deyntee morsel passed thurgh hir throte;
Hir dyete was accordant to hir cote.
Repleccioun ne made hir never syk;
Attempree dyete was al hir phisyk,
And exercyse, and hertes suffisaunce.
The goute lette hir no-thing for to daunce,
N'apoplexye shente nat hir heed;
No wyn ne drank she, neither whyt ne reed;
Hir bord was served most with whyt and blak,
Milk and broun breed, in which she fond no lak,
Seynd bacoun, and somtyme an ey or tweye,
For she was as it were a maner deye.
  A yerd she hadde, enclosed al aboute
With stikkes, and a drye dich with-oute,
In which she hadde a cok, hight Chauntecleer,
In al the land of crowing nas his peer.
His vois was merier than the mery orgon
On messe-dayes that in the chirche gon;

Wel sikerer was his crowing in his logge,
Than is a clokke, or an abbey orlogge.
By nature knew he ech ascencioun
Of equinoxial in thilke toun;
For whan degrees fiftene were ascended,
Thanne crew he, that it mighte nat ben amended.
His comb was redder than the fyn coral,
And batailed, as it were a castel-wal.
His bile was blak, and as the jeet it shoon;
Lyk asur were his legges, and his toon;
His nayles whytter than the lilie flour,
And lyk the burned gold was his colour.

Selection I

The Clerk's Prologue, E 1–56

'Sir clerk of Oxenford,' our hoste sayde,
'Ye ryde as coy and stille as dooth a mayde,
Were newe spoused, sitting at the bord;
This day ne herde I of your tonge a word.
I trowe ye studie aboute som sophyme,
But Salomon seith, "every thing hath tyme."
  For goddes sake, as beth of bettre chere,
It is no tyme for to studien here.
Telle us som mery tale, by your fey;
For what man that is entred in a pley,
He nedes moot unto the pley assente.
But precheth nat, as freres doon in Lente,
To make us for our olde sinnes wepe,
Ne that thy tale make us nat to slepe.
  Telle us som mery thing of aventures;—
Your termes, your colours, and your figures,
Kepe hem in stoor til so be ye endyte
Heigh style, as whan that men to kinges wryte.
Speketh so pleyn at this tyme, I yow preye,
That we may understonde what ye seye.'

This worthy clerk benignely answerde,
'Hoste,' quod he, 'I am under your yerde;
Ye han of us as now the governaunce,
And therefor wol I do yow obeisaunce,
As fer as reson axeth, hardily.
I wol yow telle a tale which that I
Lerned at Padowe of a worthy clerk,
As preved by his wordes and his werk.
He is now deed and nayled in his cheste,
I prey to god so yeve his soule reste!

Fraunceys Petrark, the laureat poete,
Highte this clerk, whos rethoryke sweete
Enlumined al Itaille of poetrye,
As Linian dide of philosophye
Or lawe, or other art particuler;
But deeth, that wol nat suffre us dwellen heer
But as it were a twinkling of an yë,
Hem bothe hath slayn, and alle shul we dyë.

But forth to tellen of this worthy man,
That taughte me this tale, as I bigan,
I seye that first with heigh style he endyteth,
Er he the body of his tale wryteth,
A proheme, in the which discryveth he
Pemond, and of Saluces the contree,
And speketh of Apennyn, the hilles hye,
That been the boundes of West Lumbardye,
And of Mount Vesulus in special,
Where as the Poo, out of a welle smal,
Taketh his firste springing and his sours,
That estward ay encresseth in his cours
To Emelward, to Ferrare, and Venyse:
The which a long thing were to devyse.
And trewely, as to my jugement,
Me thinketh it a thing impertinent,
Save that he wol conveyen his matere:
But this his tale, which that ye may here.'

Selection J

Wycliffe's Translation of Matthew viii

1. Forsothe when Jhesus hadde comen doun fro the hil, many cumpanyes folewiden hum.

2. And loo! a leprouse man cummynge worshipide hym, sayinge, Lord, ȝif thou wolt, thou maist make me clene.

3. And Jhesus, holdynge forthe the hond touchide hym, sayinge, I wole, be thou maad clene. And anoon the lepre of hym was clensid.

4. And Jhesus saith to hym, See, say thou to no man; but go, shewe thee to prestis, and offre that ȝifte that Moyses comaundide, into witnessing to hem.

5. Sothely when he hadde entride in to Capharnaum, centurio neiȝide to hym, preyinge hym.

6. And saide, Lord, my child lyeth in the hous sike on the palsie, and is yuel tourmentid.

7. And Jhesus saith to hym, I shall cume, and shall hele hym.

8. And centurio answerynge saith to hym, Lord, I am not worthi, that thou entre vnder my roof; but oonly say bi word, and my child shal be helid.

9. For whi and I am a man ordeynd vnder power, hauynge vnder me kniȝtis; and I say to this, Go, and he goth; and to an other, Come thou, and he cometh; and to my seruaunt, Do thou this thing, and he doth.

10. Sothely Jhesus, heerynge these thingis, wondride, and saide to men suynge hym, Trewly I saye to ȝou, I fonde nat so grete feith in Yrael.

11. Sothely Y say to ȝou, that manye shulen come from the est and west, and shulen rest with Abraham and Ysaac and Jacob in the kyngdam of heuenes;

12. Forsothe the sonys of the rewme shulen be cast out in to vttermest derknessis; there shall be weepynge, and beetynge togidre of teeth.

13. And Jhesus said to centurio, Go, and as thou hast

bileeued, be it don to thee. And the child was helid fro that houre.

14. And when Jhesus hadde comen in to the hous of Symond Petre, he say his wyues moder liggynge, and shakyn with feueris.

15. And he touchide hir hond, and the feuer lefte hir; and she roose; and seruyde hem.

16. Sothely whan the euenyng was maad, thei brouȝte to hym many hauynge deuelys, and castide out spiritis by word, and helide alle hauynge yuel;

17. That it shulde be fulfilled, that thing that was said by Ysaie the prophete, sayinge, He toke oure infirmytees, and bere oure sykenessis.

18. Sothely Jhesus seeynge many cumpanyes about hym, bad his disciplis go ouer the water.

19. And oo scribe commynge to, saide to hym, Maistre, I shal sue thee, whider euer thou shalt go.

20. And Jhesus said to hym, Foxis han dichis or borowis, and briddis of the eir han nestis, but mannes sone hath nat wher he reste his heued.

21. Sotheli an other of his disciplis saide to hym, Lord, suffre me go first, and birye my fadir.

22. Forsothe Jhesus said to hym, Sue thou me, and late dede men birye her dead men.

23. And Jhesus steyinge vp into a litle ship, his disciplis sueden hym.

24. And loo! a grete steryng was maad in the see, so that the litil ship was hilid with wawis; but he slepte.

25. And his disciplis camen niȝ to hym, and raysiden hym, sayinge, Lord, saue vs; we perishen.

26. And Jhesus seith to hem, What ben ȝee of litil feith agast? Thanne he rysynge comaundide to the wyndis and the see, and a grete pesiblenesse is maad.

27. Forsothe men wondreden, sayinge, what manere man is he this, for the wyndis and the see obeishen to hym?

28. And whan Jhesus hadde comen ouer the water in to the cuntre of men of Genazereth, twey men hauynge deuelis runnen

to hym, goynge out fro birielis, ful feerse, or wickid, so that no man miʒte passe by that wey.

29. And loo! thei crieden, sayinge, What to vs and to thee, Jhesu, the sone of God? hast thou comen hidir before the tyme for to tourmente vs?

30. Sothely a floc or droue of many hoggis lesewynge was nat fer from hem.

31. But the deuelis preyeden him, seyinge, ʒif thou castist out vs hennes, sende vs in to the droue of hoggis.

32. And he saith to hem, Go zee. And thei goynge out wente in to the hoggis; and loo! in a greet bire al the droue wente heedlynge in to the see, and thei ben dead in watris.

33. Forsothe the hirdes fledden awey, and cummynge in to the citee, tolden alle these thingis, and of hem that hadden the fendis.

34. And loo! al the citee wente aʒeinis Jhesu, metynge hym; and hym seen, thei preiden hym, that he shulde passe fro her coostis.

Selection K

Chaucer's Translation of Boethius' *Consolation of Philosophy* (Book III, Metre XII)

Blisful is that man that may seen the clere welle of good; blisful is he that may unbinden him fro the bondes of the hevy erthe. The poete of Trace, *Orpheus*, that whylom hadde right greet sorwe for the deeth of his wyf, after that he hadde maked, by his weeply songes, the wodes, moevable, to rennen; and hadde maked the rivers to stonden stille; and hadde maked the hertes and the hindes to joignen, dredeles, hir sydes to cruel lyouns, for to herknen his songe; and hadde maked that the hare was nat agast of the hounde, which that was plesed by his songe: so, whan the moste ardaunt love of his wif brende the entrailes of his brest, ne the songes that hadden overcomen alle thinges ne mighten nat asswagen hir lord *Orpheus*, he pleynede him of the hevene goddes that weren cruel to him; he wente him to the houses of helle. And there he temprede hise blaundisshinge songes by resowninge strenges, and spak and song in wepinge al that ever he hadde received and laved out of the noble welles of his moder *Calliope* the goddesse; and he song with as mochel as he mighte of wepinge, and with as moche as love, that doublede his sorwe, mighte yeve him and techen him; and he commoevede the helle, and requerede and bisoughte by swete preyere the lordes of sowles in helle, of relesinge; that is to seyn, to yilden him his wyf.

Cerberus, the porter of helle, with his three hevedes, was caught and al abayst for the newe song; and the three goddesses, *Furies*, and vengeresses of felonyes, that tormenten and agasten the sowles by anoy, woxen sorwful and sory, and wepen teres for pitee. Tho ne was nat the heved of Ixion y-tormented by the overthrowinge wheel; and Tantalus, that was destroyed by the woodnesse of longe thurst, despyseth the flodes to drinke; the fowl that highte voltor, that eteth the stomak or the giser of Tityus, is so fulfild of his song that it nil eten ne tyren no more. At the laste the lord and juge of sowles was moeved to misericordes and cryde, 'we ben overcomen,' quod he; 'yive we to Orpheus his wyf to bere him companye; he hath wel y-bought hir by his song and his ditee; but we wol putte a lawe in this, and covenaunt in the yifte: that is to seyn, that, til he be out of helle, yif he loke behinde him, that his wyf shal comen ayein unto us.' But what is he that may yive a lawe to loveres? Love is a gretter lawe and a strenger to him-self than any lawe that men may yeven. Allas! whan Orpheus and his wyf weren almest at the termes of the night, that is to seyn, at the laste boundes of helle, Orpheus lokede abakward on Eurydice his wyf, and loste hir, and was deed.

This fable aperteineth to yow alle, who-so-ever desireth or seketh to lede his thought in-to the soverein day, that is to seyn, to cleernesse of soverein good. For who-so that ever be so overcomen that he ficche his eyen into the putte of helle, that is to seyn, who-so sette his thoughtes in erthely thinges, al that ever he hath drawen of the noble good celestial, he leseth it whan he loketh the helles,' that is to seyn, in-to lowe thinges of the erthe.

VI

Old English

45. Backgrounds of Old English

Behind all the specific problems in phonetics and grammar we have been considering, there loom the ever important questions of the origin of language and the relationship of the languages of the world to one another. Linguistic science has not been able to give a positive answer to the first of these questions, but through comparative study of existing languages, earlier forms of those languages, and records of languages no longer spoken, the reconstruction of a number of parent languages has been made possible.

Of all these parent languages, the one called Indo-European [20] is of most interest to us, because it is the ancestor not only of English but of most of the languages of the western civilized world. It is supposed to have been spoken in the neolithic period by somewhat nomadic but primarily pastoral peoples with some primitive agricul-

[20] This term is generally used by American and English scholars in preference to *Indo-Germanic* or *Aryan.*

ture. We know nothing of the racial characteristics of the Indo-Europeans — which is another way of saying that the term *Indo-European* has no ethnological implications. The original home of the Indo-Europeans has not been located beyond the possibility of dispute; one widely accepted present theory places it between the Dnieper and Vistula rivers. Nor has present scholarship been able to form a very definite idea of the date at which these people lived as a unified or coherent community, a life which may have extended over many centuries. The end of their common existence, which implies the beginning of the differentiation of Indo-European into a number of dialects, is often placed around 2500 B.C.

Indo-European is considered to have been a highly inflectional language. It had three numbers, three genders, and eight cases of the noun, and a highly complicated verbal structure based upon aspect rather than upon tense. Accent or stress was free or shifting as in Latin, not fixed as in the Germanic languages. Word order was rhetorical rather than grammatical, no word having a fixed place in the sentence. Ancient Greek probably preserves the vowel system of Indo-European better than any other language which has come down to us.

It is believed that this parent language, after a time, developed into a number of dialects, each one through progressive differentiation becoming the ancestor of a whole group of closely related languages. For example, one of the Indo-European dialects or branches, Italic, developed into Oscan, Umbrian, and Latin, and the last was in turn to become the ancestor of modern Italian, Spanish, Portuguese, French, and Rumanian.

The chief branches of Indo-European are: (1) Indian, (2) Iranian, (3) Armenian, (4) Albanian, (5) Balto-Slavonic, (6) Hellenic, (7) Italic, (8) Celtic, and (9) Teutonic. The present-day languages which have sprung from each of these branches are listed in §§ 2–7, p. lxxxii of Webster's *New International Dictionary*.

Of the nine branches of Indo-European, the Teutonic or Germanic is naturally of the greatest interest to us, because the English language has descended from it. Two important changes served to differentiate Teutonic from other Indo-European dialects. One of these, sometimes called the Great (or First) Consonant Shift, consists of a symmetrical series of changes affecting the Indo-European stops and aspirates. Details of this sound change are given in § 14, p. lxxxiii of the Webster's dictionary; it is sufficient to say here as illustration that it is this change which is responsible for the initial [f] in English *father*, German *Vater*, and Dutch *vader* as opposed to Latin *pater* and Greek *patēr*, and for initial [h] in English heart, German *Herz* in contrast to Latin *cor*(*d*), Greek *Kardia*.

The other important change was a shift in the position of the word stress, which has already been described as free or shifting in Indo-European. In Teutonic the stress became fixed upon the root syllable, and this has remained as a characteristic of all the languages of this group. Within the English language itself we can usually distinguish words which are native from those which have been borrowed from some non-Teutonic language by observing the behavior of the word stress when derivative prefixes and suffixes are added. Compare, for example, *glad* (native), ˈ*gladly*, ˈ*gladden*, ˈ*gladdness*, ˈ*gladsome* with ˈ*transit* (Latin), ˌ*tran*ˈ*sition*, ˈ*transitive*, ˌ*transi*ˈ*tivity*.

Other distinguishing characteristics of Teutonic were (1) the development of a weak verb conjugation, (2) a twofold (strong and weak) adjective declension, and (3) the almost complete disappearance of inflected forms for the active and middle voices. For further details see §§ 15–23, p. lxxxiii of Webster's *New International Dictionary*.

Like Indo-European before it, Teutonic also divided into a number of dialects which in turn became the ancestors of the modern Germanic languages. The first division is into East, North, and West Teutonic. The principal representative of East Teutonic is Gothic, no longer spoken but important to linguistic science because of the fourth-century translation of the Gospels by Ulfilas, the most extensive of the early records of this family of languages. North Teutonic is represented today by the languages of Iceland, Norway, Sweden, and Denmark. West Teutonic is the parent of modern German, Flemish, Dutch, Frisian, and English.

Before they invaded the island of Britain in the fifth century, the Angles, Saxons, and Jutes lived on the continent, presumably in what are now the territories of Schleswig, Holstein, and Jutland. Their language was naturally much like that of their continental neighbors; it was very close to Old Frisian, which was spoken along the whole northern coast of Germany from the Elbe westward, and to Old Saxon (the parent language of modern Low German), which was spoken between the Rhine and the Elbe, south of the Frisian territory.

Naturally enough, the invading peoples brought their language and their customs with them, and this language became the standard speech of England. Few written records of this language earlier than the late ninth century have been preserved, although some of these were composed possibly two centuries earlier. Strictly speaking, however, our first hand knowledge of English goes back just about one thousand years.

Old English, in its sounds, grammar, and vocabulary, is quite different from Modern English, and at first sight, a mastery of it may appear somewhat difficult. You will find, however, that your familiarity with Middle English will help you in overcoming many apparent difficulties. As you proceed in your study of this stage of our language, try always to see all the possible connections and relationships between Old English and Modern English, and with Modern German as well, if you happen to be familiar with that language.

Remember always that you are studying Old English chiefly that you may have a better understanding of the English you yourself use in your everyday speech and writing. In the time which you will be able to devote to a study of this stage of the English language, you may not, for example, be able to acquire a complete knowledge of its vocabulary, particularly of those words which subsequently ceased to be in active use. For your present purpose, however, it is more important that you develop the ability to recognize in Old English context those words which are still used in Modern English, and to trace and to account for the changes in sound and meaning which they have since undergone. The same applies to the problems of inflections and syntax. To form a conception of a developing and evolving language is here, as before, our chief objective.

For this reason, the illustrative selections for this period of the language are chosen for the most part from various translations of the Gospels. From the point of view of subject matter these are not always the best possible representatives of the Old English vocabulary, nor is the syntax always free from the influences of the original. The advantage of using them lies in the fact that modern versions of the Bible always afford a ready help in translating them; since our primary purpose is analytic examination rather than rote memory of the inflectional and lexical details of this stage of the language, the employment of such ready-made help is wholly within the spirit of the purposes of the assignments.

Additional Reading:

Baugh, *History of the English Language*, Chapter II.
Emerson, *History of the English Language*, Chapter I, II.
Graff, *Language and Languages*, Chapter X.
Jespersen, *Growth and Structure of the English Language*, Chapters II, III.
Webster's *New International Dictionary*, §§ 1–24, pp. lxxxii–lxxxiv.

Exercise XLVIII

Old English Spelling

1. Old English spelling is extremely consistent, much more so than at any subsequent period in the history of the language, and the determination of the phonetic values of the various letters is a task which you may profitably perform without help. Read Selection L aloud.

Make a list of the Old English vowel characters and through examination of the phonetic transcription determine their phonetic value. Be careful to distinguish between the so-called long vowels indicated by a macron and the vowels not so distinguished. Continue this process with the diphthongs.

2. Make a list of the OE consonant characters and determine their phonetic value. Distinguish between the characters *c* and *g* and those with the dot superimposed (*ċ*), (*ġ*). What is the value of the combinations *cg*, *sc*, and *ng*?

3. What values do you find for *f*, *s*, *þ*, *ð*? What phonetic relationship is there between the values you find for each of these characters? Can you come to any conclusion about the nature of the phonetic situation in which these values occur? What phonetic process is involved?

4. What values do you find for *h*? Can you come to any conclusion as to the phonetic situation in which these values occur? How was *hw* pronounced?

5. Can you see any relationship between the occurrence of the sounds [tʃ] and [k] and the phonetic environment in which these sounds are found? Explain. Answer the same question in respect to [j] and [ɡ].

6. What is the value of doubled consonants in Old English?

7. What is your conclusion as to the position of word stress in OE? Does this conclusion hold generally for native English words in MnE? Does it always hold for borrowed words? Take the native English word *holy* and make as many derivatives as you can from it. Where is the stress in each case? Do the same with the word *moral*. What happens to the stress?

8. Be able to indicate in outline or diagram form the relationship of English to the other Teutonic languages; the relationship between the Teutonic and other branches of the Indo-European group.

9. What are the features which set the Teutonic languages apart from other Indo-European tongues? At what approximate date is Indo-European believed to have become differentiated into its various derivative languages?

Exercise XLIX

Old English Stressed Vowels

1. Applying the results of your analysis of Old English spelling, put the first paragraph of Selection M into phonetic transcription.

2. Make a list of the stressed vowel sounds and diphthongs which you found to occur in OE. What stressed vowels and diphthongs are found in ME which did not occur in OE? What stressed vowels and diphthongs were present in OE but not in ME? Is the change between the two periods most pronounced in long vowels, short vowels, or diphthongs?

3. Determine the relationship of the stressed vowel sounds of Old English to those of Modern English. Use the sixteen column arrangement suggested in Exercise XXXVI; place the words in their Old English transcription in the column headed by the present pronunciation of their stressed vowel or diphthong. Use as evidence only those words which are italicized in Selection M.

4. Expand the table you have already made in connection with Exercises XLI and XLII to include the OE equivalents for MnE [i, ɪ, ɛ, æ, u, ʊ, o, ʌ, ɑɪ, ɑʊ].

5. What were the OE sources of ME [i] and [ɪ]? What phonetic process is involved in the development of OE [yː] and [ʏ] in Middle English?

6. What are the OE sources of ME [ɑ]? What phonetic process is indicated by the ME development of OE *æ*?

7. What instances do you find of OE vowels identical in quality but different in quantity, and having a different

subsequent development in ME? What phonetic process is indicated by the ME development of OE *ā*?

8. Can you suggest an explanation for not finding an equivalent for MnE [ɔɪ]? Observe some of the Middle English words in which this sound occurred. From what source did they come into the language?

46. The Development of Unstressed Vowels

You will recall that in the transcriptions of Middle English, the unstressed vowels were generally spelled *e* and almost always transcribed as [ə]. In striking contrast to this situation, unstressed vowels in Old English are spelled with all the vowel letters (gebidd*a*ð, heof*o*n*u*m, sōðlīċ*e*) and from the transcription, appear to have had the full value demanded by their particular spellings.

It is clear, therefore, that some time between the years 900 and 1400 there must have been a sweeping movement toward the centralization of unstressed vowels, that OE unstressed or lightly stressed [ɛ, ʊ, ɔ, ɑ] became [ə].[21] In fact, this change seems to have taken place during the eleventh century, beginning in the north of England and gradually extending southward.

At the same time, two very important changes were also affecting the consonants *m* and *n* when they occurred at the end of a word. First of all, final *m* became *n*, and even before this first change was completed, final *n* began to be lost completely from words in which it occurred. The extent to which these developments in unstressed vowels and final consonants altered the structure of many

[21] The ME development of OE unstressed [iː], [ɪ], and occasionally [ɛ], was [ɪ].

English words may be shown by tracing the development of some of the words in Selections L and M:

	OE	>	ME	>	MnE
nama, L9:	[nɑmɑ]		[nɑːmə]		[nem]
heofonum, L10:	[hɛovɔnum]		[hɛvənə(n)]		[hɛvən]
gyltas, L11:	[gʏltɑs]		[gɪltəs]		[gɪlts]
sunne, M2:	[sunːɛ]		[sunːə]		[sʌn]
betwēonan, M2:	[bɛtweːonɑn]		[bɪtweːnə(n)]		[bɪtwin]

The effects of these changes upon the inflectional system were very profound and will be taken up in detail as we consider the Old English inflectional patterns for each of the parts of speech. It may be pointed out here, however, that the loss of final *e*, which occurred in the late Middle English or Early Modern English period, is but the final step in the history of these unstressed vowels throughout their several centuries of development.

ADDITIONAL READING:

Baugh, *History of the English Language*, pp. 194–200.
Emerson, *History of the English Language*, pp. 220, 221.
Webster's *New International Dictionary*, §§ 31, 32, pp. lxxxiv, lxxxv.

EXERCISE L

Special Developments in Old English Sounds

1. Indicate in phonetic transcription the successive stages from OE to MnE in the pronunciation of the following words from Selection M. Be careful to include also the relevant information about unstressed vowels and final consonants: *eorþan* M 2, *ūrum* M 5, *mōnað* M 9, *wætere* M 15, *mōnan* M 16.

2. What would have been the ME pronunciation of MnE *child*, *field*, *pound?* Compare these ME forms with those which occurred in OE as they are given in the *Oxford English Dictionary* or Webster. In each instance, what must have happened to the stressed vowel between the OE and ME periods? For a complete description of this change, consult Wyld, *Short History of English*, § 114, and the table at the bottom of p. xxiii of Webster's *New International Dictionary*. Before what kind of consonant combinations did this change occur? Note particularly the date at which this change is placed.

3. What would have been the ME pronunciation of the MnE words *five* and *fifty?* Compare the vowels of the OE forms of these words as they appear in Selection M, lines 28, 29. Which word must have undergone some kind of change between the Old and Middle English periods? Make a similar comparison of *south* and *southern*, *goose* and *gosling*, *clean* and *cleanser*, using a dictionary to determine the OE forms. For an explanation of this change consult Wyld, *Short History of English*, § 175, and Tables 2 and 3 on p. xxiv of Webster's *New International Dictionary*. The OE vowel ǣ was sometimes shortened to ME [ɑ] and sometimes to [ɛ]. Does this throw any light on the pronunciation of *wrestle* as [ræsl]?

4. What would have been the ME pronunciation of MnE *name?* What do you find, from Selection L, to have been the OE form of the word? What would have been the ME forms of MnE *eat* (infinitive), *broken* (past participle)? Consult a dictionary for the OE forms of these words. In each instance, what must have happened to the stressed vowel between the OE and ME periods? For a complete description of this change, consult Wyld, *Short History of English*, § 173.2, and Table 4 on p. xxiv of Webster's *New International Dictionary*. Be able to explain, also, the development of *waniende*, Selection M, line 17.

5. What was the ME pronunciation of MnE *day*, *maiden* and *rain?* Compare the OE forms as given in Selection M. Account for the development of the ME diphthong on phonetic grounds. What other vowel-consonant combinations produced the same sound in ME? See Wyld, *Short History of English*, § 171, and Table 5, p. xxiv of Webster's *New International Dictionary*.

6. Apply the preceding questions to MnE *snow* and its OE form in Selection M, line 38, to MnE *show* and the related OE form in L 28, to MnE *own* and *bow* (the weapon) and their OE forms as indicated by a dictionary. What kind of vowel and consonant combination produced this ME diphthong? What is the OE form of MnE *bought?* How and why does this differ in behavior from the preceding words?

7. Apply the preceding questions to MnE *new*, *shrew*, *you*. Does the development of ēa before *w* appear to have been consistent? Can you explain the apparent discrepancy between the MnE spelling and pronunciation of *sew?* Can you account for the earlier spelling of *show* as *shew?*

8. What appear to have been the principal OE sources of ME [ɑː, æɪ, ɔːu, ɔu, ɪu]? What did these ME sounds become in MnE? Complete the table you began in Question 4 of the preceding exercise.

9. What was the ME development of such consonant combinations as initial *hr* in *hrycg?* What was the OE form of MnE *follow*, *drawn*, *fowl?* What did OE intervocalic *g* tend to become in ME?

Exercise LI

Personal Pronouns

1. Construct a paradigm of the personal pronouns in Old English, using as evidence the underlined forms in Selections N and O, and supplementing your evidence

with Selection L. Use the arrangement recommended in Exercise XXXVII, p. 217 but distinguish between the direct object function and the indirect object and the object of prepositions. Label the direct object column *accusative* and the column for the indirect object and the object of a preposition *dative*.

2. Make a list of those pronominal forms the pronunciation of which in Middle English was the same as that in Old English. Disregard differences in spelling.

3. Make a list of those forms of the personal pronoun which show a change between the Old and Middle English periods. From this list select those in which the Middle English form may be explained by the normal process of sound change. (You may consider the disappearance of final [tʃ] and the lengthening of the preceding vowel as one of these changes.) Which pronouns acquired their ME forms through normal phonetic developments?

4. What are the ME equivalents for the pronouns *hīe* (accusative) and *hine?* Which case form replaced them? What is the ME form for the third person singular, neuter dative? Which case form replaced it? Consult the *Oxford English Dictionary*, s.v. *me*, *thee*, *you*. Do you find any evidence of an early Old English distinction between accusative and dative in these pronouns? In each instance note which of the two case forms survived.

5. What is the origin or derivation of the pronouns *she* and *they?* From what you know of the development of OE sounds in ME, why was it likely that both the OE pronouns *hīe* and *hēo* would have acquired a new form in ME?

6. What change took place in the third person singular neuter nominative and accusative pronoun? Can you explain why this change might have occurred? Do you know any forms of present-day English where the OE form is still retained?

47. Old English Gender

On the basis of the examination we have just made, it appears that the case forms for the accusative singular of the third personal pronoun were: masculine, *hine;* feminine *hīe;* neuter *hit.* It is of interest, however, to examine verses 43–7 from Selection O, and to observe the nature of the antecedents of these pronouns.

In verse 47, *hit* has for its antecedent the Old English form for the noun *eye*, which is just what we would expect in Modern English. In verse 45, however, *fōt* is referred to by the masculine pronoun *hine*, and in verse 43, the feminine pronoun *hīe*, in the same construction, has as its antecedent the OE noun *hand.* It appears then that *foot* demands a masculine pronoun in Old English, *hand* a feminine pronoun, and *eye*, one of neuter gender. To those who are familiar with German, this situation immediately suggests the forms *der Fuss*, *die Hand*, *das Auge* in that language. Likewise in Latin it will be recalled that *pēs* (foot) is a masculine noun and *manus* (hand) is feminine.

This points to the fact that Old English, like Latin and German, has what is called grammatical gender, in contrast to the logical gender which prevails in the language at present. That is to say, in OE nouns were arbitrarily placed into one of the three gender categories without reference to any fundamental quality or characteristic of sex. It is true that the nouns *man*, *boy*, *knave*, *lord*, *ox*, *buck*, all of which would be considered masculine in MnE, are likewise masculine in Old English. *Woman*, *lady*, *queen*, *cow*, *ewe*, and *hen* were feminine in Old English. Yet *horse*, *sheep*, *maiden*, and *wife* were all neuter. Moreover, the most noticeable difference from the logical gender of Modern English lay in those objects without sex-defining characteristics which according to our present classification would be considered neuter. The earth and sun were feminine, the moon masculine; day was masculine but night was feminine. Summer was masculine but winter might be neuter; wheat was masculine, oats feminine, and corn neuter. In short, the connection between any essential quality of the object designated and the grammatical gender to which the word for it belonged was generally accidental.

Exercise LII

Strong Noun Declensions

1. Construct a paradigm of the italicized nouns in Selections P and Q, classifying them according to number and case use. Recognize the same four case functions as with the pronouns in Exercise LI. Include the definite article with the noun whenever it appears.

2. In which case and number combinations do you find all nouns and articles inflected similarly? Where do you find differences of inflection?

3. Construct a paradigm of the article alone. Compare this paradigm with that of the third personal pronoun made in connection with the previous exercise. Do you see any similarity of form or of ending between the articles and the pronouns? In which genders do these similarities occur?

4. What is the dative singular ending for these nouns? How does it compare with the endings for the nominative and accusative singular? Was there such a difference of inflection in Middle English? Can you recall what happened in ME to the similar distinction between dative and

accusative in the OE pronoun? Would sound change or analogy be the more likely explanation for this change in the noun declension? Why?

5. Do the plural inflections of these nouns appear to vary according to case use? Was this true of the plural inflections in Middle English? Which of the OE plural inflections could have given rise to the ME regular plural through normal processes of sound change?

6. Do you find in your paradigm any instances of a plural form without an inflection?

7. Examine the instances of the inflected genitive in Selections P and Q, and compare them with the translations given in the King James version of the Bible. List the constructions where the OE inflected genitive is translated periphrastically in the King James version. The nouns *daga* and *nihta* in Selection P, verse 2, are genitive plurals. What is their function?

8. Look up the preposition *of* in the *Oxford English Dictionary*. What was its meaning in OE? Read through the various definitions and attempt to determine at what time it began to be used as a substitute for the inflected genitive.

9. Point out in each of the two selections (P and Q) five departures from what would be considered normal MnE word order in relation to the position of subject, verb, and object. What word order patterns do you find here?

48. Masculine and Neuter Noun Declension

In the third question of the preceding exercise, it was suggested that the forms of the article found in Selections P and Q be compared with those for the third personal pronoun. Actually there is, of course, a striking likeness in these endings as may be seen from the following tabulation:

	PRON.	ART.	PRON.	ART.	PRON.	ART.
	Masc. Sg.		*Neut. Sg.*		*Plural*	
Nom.	hē	sē	hit	þæt	hīe	þā
Gen.	his	þæs	his	þæs	heora	þāra
Dat.	him	þǣm	him	þǣm	heom	þǣm
Acc.	hine	þone	hit	þæt	hīe	þā

Notice the similarity of detail: the vowels of *hē* and *sē* are alike; the consonant endings of *hit : þæt*, *his : þæs*, *him : þǣm*, *heom : þǣm*, and the final syllable of *hine : þone* and *heora : þāra* correspond function by function. The masculine and neuter forms of the pronoun and article are alike in those very functions where no differentiation was found in the nouns: namely, in the genitive and dative singular and plural. Observe, moreover, that in the plural article as in the plural pronoun, there is no differentiation in form between nominative and accusative, *þā* and *hīe* serving for both case functions respectively. On this basis, therefore, we may consider the nouns which are declined with the various forms of the article *sē* as masculine in gender, and those which are declined with various forms of the article *þæt* as neuter, corresponding to the genders which have been assigned to the pronouns *hē* and *hit*. This gives us, then, the following two noun declensions:

	MASCULINE	NEUTER
Nom. Sg.	sē stān	þæt wīf
* *Gen. Sg.*	þæs stānes	þæs wīfes
* *Dat. Sg.*	þǣm stāne	þǣm wīfe
Acc. Sg.	þone stān	þæt wīf
Nom. Acc. Pl.	þā stānas	þā wīf, bearn, scipu, rīcu
* *Gen. Pl.*	þāra stāna	þāra wīfa
* *Dat. Pl.*	þǣm stānum	þǣm wīfum

*Identical forms for both genders.

Among the neuter nouns there was some variation in the manner of forming the nominative and accusative plural. In the preceding selections, both *bearn* and *rīcu* were found in these functions. In general, the basis of distinction between the *-u* inflection and no ending at all was the length of the root syllable: Monosyllabic nouns with a long root syllable remained uninflected, as *wīf* or *scēap* (sheep); nouns with a short root syllable had the *-u* inflection in these functions, as in *scipu*. Two additional bits of information are apropos. A short vowel or diphthong followed by two consonants behaved like a long vowel in this respect, so that we find neuter nouns such as *bearn*, *þing*, or *hors* without the inflection here. Moreover, a disyllabic word ending in *-e* also behaved like a word with a short root syllable, which explains the inflection on *rīcu*, nom. sg. *rīċe*.

Exercise LIII

Noun Inflections (continued)

1. Construct a paradigm of the italicized nouns in Selection R, including the definite article whenever it is present, and using the classification employed in the two foregoing exercises.

2. Construct a paradigm of the article alone. Compare it with the paradigm for the third personal pronoun which was determined in connection with Exercise LI. Do you see any similarity of ending between the article and the pronoun? With which gender are we presumably dealing here?

3. How would the neutralization of unstressed vowels, the change of final *m* to *n*, and the loss of *n* have affected each of the forms of this OE noun declension? Of the

nouns in Selection R, at least three survived in ME: *sin*, *offring*, and *ax*. What was the ME form of these nouns in the genitive singular and in the plural? How must they have acquired these endings?

4. How would the neutralization of unstressed vowels, change of final *m* to *n*, and the loss of *n* have affected the forms of the definite article for all three genders in ME? In working this out, assume that any form of the article was sufficiently unstressed that its vowel might be neutralized.

5. What was the ME definite article? From which of the forms of the OE article might it have developed through normal processes of sound change? What change in initial consonant would have had to take place in certain of the forms? In this connection consult Wyld, *Short History of English*, §§ 289–94.

6. What forms for the nominative singular of the noun did you find in this declension? Is the variation in form reminiscent of anything you have encountered in previous declensions? In view of the phonetic value of *x*, can you explain why *æx* behaves like *sprǣc* rather than like *ġiefu?*

7. Is there any variation in the plural article for the various genders? Was there any in the personal pronoun? In which case functions do you find a variation in the form of the noun plural?

49. The Definite Article and Its Functions

In view of the similarity between the nominative singular *hēo* and *sēo*, and between the genitive and dative singular forms *hiere* and *þǣre*, it is scarcely necessary to explain that the nouns considered in the preceding exercise belong to the feminine gender. One other point of similarity between the personal pronoun and the article remains to be pointed out: namely, that the article has the form *þā* in those situations where the personal pronoun is *hīe*, that is, in the feminine accusative singular and in the nominative and accusative plural for all genders.

These correspondences have been indicated primarily for the purpose of illustrating that even in a reasonably complicated inflectional system, the variation in form is not purely arbitrary, but is rather a design or pattern which can usually be discerned if the student will take the trouble to look for it.

The function of the definite article in Old English was not quite the same as its Modern English descendant. In the first two verses of Selection R, to choose a random example, it is difficult to conceive of Modern English getting along without the definite article before the words *beginning* (OE *frymðe*) and *time* (OE *tīman*). On the other hand, the article preceding *stānas* in Selection P, verse 3, is translated by a demonstrative in the King James version of the Bible. In fact, one of the functions of the Old English article was that of our present demonstrative *that* and in translating from Old English we are not always certain whether the OE article should be rendered in MnE by *the* or *that*. See, for example, Selection R, ii: 40, where *þæt ċild* might permit either form in a modern version.

When the Middle English definite article *the* came to replace the many forms of the Old English article, the neuter singular *þæt* retained its demonstrative function, and the form was extended to all cases and genders of the singular. Likewise the OE nominative, accusative plural form *þā*, with the regular phonetic change of [ɑː] to [ɔː], emerged as the Middle English form *tho*, the demonstrative form for all cases and genders of the plural. For the development of *tho* into MnE *those*, see Question 8, Exercise XLV. Moreover, the article was capable of being used as a demonstrative pronoun in a primary as well as in a secondary function. See Selection R, i : 2, *ðā þe hit of frymðe ġesāwon* (those who saw it from the beginning).

The Old English definite article also had a relative function, as illustrated by Selection R, ii : 4, *sēo is genemned Bethleem* (which is called Bethlehem). Naturally, the definite article used in this function was in formal agreement with its antecedent in number and gender but employed the case form demanded by its own function in the clause. The indeclinable particle *þe* was also commonly used in a relative construction, as in R, xv : 12, *þe tō mē ġebyraþ* (which belong to me), or as in R, iii : 9. Finally the combination of the article and the particle *þe* (*sē þe*, *þone þe*, etc.) was sometimes used, especially in situations where Modern English would employ a compound construction such as *he who.*

Exercise LIV

Weak Noun Declension

1. Classify the italicized nouns in Selection S according to case, number, and gender, using the article as a guide to the gender whenever possible. Supplement these paradigms with all the forms of the nouns *sunne*, *eorðe*, *mōna*, and *wǣta* in Selection M. Consider the form *eorðan*, M 4, as the accusative object of the preposition *ymb*, and the form *wucena*, M 29, as the partitive genitive plural; also that the nominative and accusative plural forms are identical.

2. What gender appears to be lacking from your paradigms?

3. How would the neutralization of unstressed vowels, the change of final *m* to *n*, and the loss of final *n* have affected the forms of this declension in ME? What would you have supposed the ME declension of *sun*, *moon*, and *bridegroom* to have been? How must they have acquired their ME forms for the genitive singular and for the plural?

4. Do you recall from Exercise XLIV any ME nouns which did have a plural in *(e)n?* Consult a dictionary for the OE forms of these nouns. To what extent does the MnE noun *ox* preserve the forms of the OE weak declension? Are any of the MnE inflectional forms of this noun the result of analogy?

5. Judging from Selection S, verse 2, what parts of speech must the words *dysiġe* and *glēawe* have been originally? In what function are they principally used throughout the selection? Does this suggest a general principle concerning the type of inflectional pattern assumed by words which undergo functional change? In MnE, do verbs which are formed from other parts of speech generally adopt the weak or strong pattern? What does the term *weak* signify as it is applied to this OE noun declension?

50. Weak Noun Declension

The references given in the preceding exercise were sufficiently numerous to give a fair idea of the general nature and behavior of the weak nouns. Some details were unavoidably lacking and for this reason a complete paradigm for each of the genders is given on page 298.

	MASCULINE	FEMININE	NEUTER
Nom. Sg.	nama (name)	heorte (heart)	ēaġe (eye)
Gen. Sg.	naman	heortan	ēagan
Dat. Sg.	naman	heortan	ēagan
Acc. Sg.	naman	heortan	ēaġe
N. A. Pl.	naman	heortan	ēagan
Gen. Pl.	namena	heortena	ēaġena
Dat. Pl.	namum	heortum	ēagum

Little supplementary explanation is necessary. Observe that the masculine weak nouns end in *-a*, the feminine in *-e*. This is invariable, and, moreover, *any* masculine noun ending in *-a* in the nominative singular will belong to the weak declension; any feminine noun ending in *-e* in the nominative singular will likewise be weak.

The preceding selection contained no instances of the weak neuter nouns, and indeed the nouns for *eye* and for *ear* (OE *ēare*) were the only two commonly used OE neuter nouns which were weak, the former of which retained its weak plural form until very late in the Middle English period. The neuter weak pattern differs from the masculine and feminine in one respect, that the accusative singular has the inflection *-e* instead of *-an*. It should be recalled that identity in form of nominative and accusative is a distinguishing mark of the neuter gender in many languages. It has already been evident in the OE personal pronoun (nom. acc. sg. *hit*) and in the definite article (*þæt*). We need only to recall Latin *donum* or German *das Buch* to remind ourselves that this is not a peculiarly English characteristic.

The definite article, of course, has the same forms with the weak declensions as with the strong.

Exercise LV

Adjective Inflections

1. Construct a paradigm of the italicized adjectives in Selection T, classifying them according to the case, number, and gender of the noun they modify. Consult Clark Hall's *Anglo-Saxon Dictionary* for the gender of the nouns about which you are uncertain.

2. Is the pattern of these inflectional endings similar to any other inflectional patterns you have encountered in OE? Judging from the distinctiveness of the endings, would you call this a weak or a strong declension? What adjective ending appears to correspond to *hīe* and *þā* in the pronoun and article inflectional patterns?

3. Had verse iii. 7 read 'a certain multitude,' it would have been *sumu menigu*. If verse xii. 19 were to read 'some children,' it would be *sumu bearn*. On the other hand the nominative plural of 'high cliffs' would be *hēah clifu*. In view of these facts, what do you conclude about the relationship of the *u* inflection on the feminine nominative singular or the neuter nominative accusative plural of the adjective to that on the noun, in these constructions? Considering the inflected adjective stems *sum*, *nān*, *miċel*, and *hēah*, upon what would the presence of the *u* in the adjectives seem to depend?

4. What was the inflection of the adjective in ME? Review the conclusions reached in Question 7, Exercise XLIV. Taking into consideration the neutralization of unstressed vowels, the change of final *m* to *n*, and the loss of *n*, which of the ME forms could be derived from the OE declension through normal processes of sound change? See also in this connection Wyld, *Short History of English*, §§ 323–30.

5. What does the italicized form in v. 30 suggest about the inflection of the genitive pronoun used adjectivally?

Consult your paradigm of personal pronouns to see what other persons and numbers of the genitive pronoun were similarly inflected. What bearing does xii. 19 seem to have on this question?

6. Observe the inflection of the adjectives *unclǣna*, i. 26, *nīwe*, i. 27, and *Hālgan*, iii. 29. How do these compare with the inflections you have already classified? What part of speech precedes the adjectives which have been listed above? How does this compare with the construction of the italicized adjectives? Judging from verse iv. 5 does the declension (strong or weak) to which the noun belongs appear to affect the inflection on the adjective?

7. Observe the forms *þēos*, i. 27 and *þisre*, xiv. 4. What do these forms suggest about the general pattern of the demonstrative pronoun?

8. Observe the dative adjective-noun constructions in verses i. 26, and i. 36. What device would MnE use to indicate the same relationship?

51. Adjective Declensions

The paradigm of adjective inflections constructed from the italicized forms in Selection T has already been seen to have a number of similarities to the declension of the third personal pronoun and the article. It is necessary to mention only such distinctive endings as the masculine accusative singular *-ne*, the feminine genitive and dative *-re* and the genitive plural *-ra* as illustrations of this point. In the sense that this inflectional pattern contains such inflections specifically associated with certain case and gender forms, it is a 'strong' declension.

The adjective inflections referred to in Question 6 of the preceding exercise suggest a quite different pattern, that of the weak noun declension. Observe that we found the ending *-a* for a masculine nominative singular adjective, *-an* for the accusative singular of the same gender, and *-e* for a feminine nominative singular. In fact the weak adjective declension corresponds point for point with the weak noun declension, even to the distinctive *-e* form in the neuter accusative singular, so that it is wholly unnecessary to reproduce it here.

Our next task is to determine the purpose of the two adjective declensions. Since *Hālgan* (iii. 29) was one of the adjectives to which the weak inflectional ending was applied, and since it also appears among the adjectives with strong inflectional endings (i. 8, i. 10) it is clear that unlike the nouns, the same adjective may be declined either way. Therefore something in the construction or position of the adjective must determine which declension is to be employed.

We may best approach this problem by raising anew the question of the purpose of inflectional patterns and inflectional endings.

Inflections exist primarily to indicate relationship. In our study of the inflections of OE nouns and of the definite article, we have found the inflectional pattern of the article to be more highly differentiated than any one noun declension. We observed also (in Question 6 of the preceding exercise) that the strong, or highly differentiated adjective inflection was used when the article did not precede the noun, and that on the three occasions when the weak adjective inflection was employed, the adjective was preceded by the definite article or by a demonstrative.

Here then is the clue to the use of the two OE adjective inflections: the strong declension is used when the adjective alone must bear the primary burden of indicating the construction of the noun; the weak or non-distinctive inflection is employed when an article, a demonstrative adjective, or a possessive has already performed the office of case, number and gender indication:

He ġeseah Hāligne gāst.
He ġeseah þone Hālgan gāst.

This same principle forms the basis of the strong, weak, and mixed adjective declensions in Modern German: compare *alter Mann* (old man) with *der alte Mann* (the old man). Generally in Old English the strong declension is used with a predicative adjective or when a pre- or post-substantive adjective is not accompanied by an article, a demonstrative, or a possessive pronoun. The weak declension is used when such distinctive forms do accompany the adjective; when the adjective modifies a noun used in direct address; when the adjective is already inflected for degree; and frequently in poetry where the strong declension would be used in prose.

It is clear therefore that the principle explained above, which may be called the *economy of distinctive inflection*, was not always maintained in actual practice. For example, the genitive pronouns of the first two persons had the same inflection as the strong adjectives; the corresponding pronouns of the third persons were not declined. Yet we find the weak adjective used after *all* the genitive pronouns:

Iċ ġeseah mīnne ealdan fæder (I saw my old father).
Iċ ġeseah his ealdan fæder (I saw his old father).

These incidental inconsistencies, however, do not affect the validity of the general principle. If a copy of the Old

English version of the Gospel of St. Mark is available, you will find it helpful to analyze and account for the adjective inflections in verses i. 11, ii. 21, v. 7, v. 12, vii. 31, ix. 25, ix. 31, xii. 24, xiv. 24, xiv. 39, xiv. 58.

If we apply to the weak adjective declension our general rules for the neutralization of unstressed vowels and loss of final *n*, the normal processes of sound change would have converted all these Old English forms into a single Middle inflection, namely [ə]. It will be recalled in this connection that we did find in Middle English a number of adjectives which did have final *e* in the singular. This final *e* can now be understood as the vestigial remnant of the Old English weak declension, which permits us to organize our Middle English adjectives on something like the following basis:

	STRONG	WEAK
Sg.	good man	the goode man
Pl.	goode men	the goode men

Little need be said about the comparison of Old English adjectives except to point out that the endings *-ra*, comparative, and *-est* (*-ost*) superlative, were regularly employed and that periphrastic comparison was as yet unknown.

Exercise LVI

Verb Inflections

1. Classify according to person, number, tense (and mood, if possible) all the forms of the verb in Selection U. To find forms for those indicative categories which do not occur in this selection, or occur only once or twice, read in Selections M, N, and O, until your conjugations are

completed. In addition, try to obtain a complete conjugation for the present and past tenses of the verb *to be*.

2. What endings do you find for the three persons of the present indicative singular? Do you find more than one inflectional ending for any one of these three persons? Can the ME forms be derived from the OE by normal processes of phonetic change? Explain.

3. What endings do you find for the present indicative plural? What was the ME inflection for the present indicative plural? Could it have developed from the OE form as a result of phonetic change? If not, how might it have arisen? Consult Wyld, *Short History of English*, § 335.

4. How many forms do you find for the present indicative conjugation of the verb *to be?* If your reading has not furnished you with a complete conjugation, complete it by reference to the *Oxford English Dictionary*, s.v. *be*. How does the OE conjugation of this verb compare with the ME? How late do you find *bēo*, *bist*, and *bið*, or variants of these, used for the present indicative (with present or future meaning)? According to the Oxford Dictionary statement and citations, how long in the ME period was the present plural form *sindon* used? See also Wyld, *Short History of English*, § 365.

5. How many types of endings do you find used to indicate the past tense of weak verbs? How many were there in ME? Can you account for the differences in form between the two periods?

6. Read, in Wyld, *Short History of English*, §§ 343–64, the discussion of strong verbs. How many principal parts did strong verbs have in OE? How many have they in MnE? What is meant by a 'class' of strong verbs? From Selection U, pick out one verb illustrative of each of the strong verb classes, including the reduplicating verbs as a seventh group. What factors operated to reduce the number of principal parts in the strong verb during the ME period?

7. What happened in ME to the form *slēp*, Selection U, verse 24? According to the *Oxford English Dictionary*, how early does the weak past tense of this verb occur? How late did the strong past tense remain in the language? Is the same degree of overlapping to be found in the past participle as in the past tense? Apply the same questions to the forms of the verb *sow*.

8. Judging from Selection U, what were the OE forms of the infinitive and present participle respectively? What were the ME forms? Can the ME form of the infinitive be explained by the operation of phonetic change? Read Webster and the *Oxford Dictionary* concerning the origin of the *-ing* form of the present participle. Do the two dictionaries agree in their accounts? See also Wyld, *Short History of English*, § 337.

9. Using the paradigms given in Wyld, *Short History of English*, § 334, compare the personal endings of the subjunctive and indicative in OE, both in the present and the past tense. At what, and in how many, places in the present conjugation are the OE subjunctive and the indicative identical in form? How many points of identity are there in MnE? Answer the same question for the past tense. Would sound change or analogy have been primarily responsible for the subsequent development of the OE subjunctive conjugations? Explain. What subjunctive forms do you find in Selection U?

Exercise LVII

Syntax of the Verb

1. Extract from Selection U all the negative and all the interrogative forms of the verb. Put into two brief statements your conclusions concerning the formation of the negative and the interrogative in OE. Do you find any differences between OE and ME in the way in which questions and denials were expressed? How many nega-

tives are contained in the verbal construction in Selection S, verse 3?

2. Selections J and U are Middle and Old English versions respectively of the same chapter of Matthew. Review the list you made in connection with Exercise XLVII, of the verbal constructions with *shall* and *will* in Selection J. Find the corresponding passages in Selection U for each of these constructions. How was future time indicated in Old English? Consult the *Oxford English Dictionary*, s.v. *shall*, definitions 8–10. What are the earliest records of the use of *shall* as a future auxiliary? Answer the same question concerning *will*.

3. Review the list you made in connection with Exercise XLVII of the verbal constructions expressing condition contrary to fact, condition possible in the future, exhortation, wish or desire, concession, improbability, supposition. Find the corresponding constructions in Selection U. How do they differ from the ME version? What can you find in the *Oxford English Dictionary* concerning the date of the earliest uses of *should*, *may*, and *might* as periphrastic subjunctive auxiliaries?

4. From Selection J collect all the instances of verbs in the present perfect and past perfect tenses. Find the corresponding constructions in Selection U. How do they compare?

5. Collect all the verbal constructions in the passive voice in Selection J and compare them with the corresponding constructions in the OE version. What auxiliary, no longer used in ME was sometimes used for the passive in OE? Consult the *Oxford English Dictionary* to determine how long it continued to be used in this function.

52. Conclusion

We have completed our survey of the development of the English language throughout the last thousand years.

In the space which could be given to it, many topics were necessarily treated inadequately; others were left out entirely. Nevertheless, the main lines of the development of our language have been set forth.

We have seen in operation, especially in the transition from the Old to the Middle English period, tendencies toward the loss of inflection and toward the development of function words and the fixation of word order as devices for indicating various kinds of relationships. The ways in which phonetic changes operated in conjunction with the loss of inflection and the creation of numerous analogical forms within the English inflectional patterns have also been noted. Finally, the most important points of contact of English with other languages, and the influences of those languages upon our own, have been considered.

We began, however, with Modern English, and now after our millennial excursion, we must return to it with the question of applicability. We have seen how a language develops, how it may change from period to period. What has all this to do with the English we use every day? How can it help us to decide what is good, what is effective English?

This question may be approached in various ways. That a knowledge of the history, development, and mechanism of a tool of communication and expression increases our mastery of it has already been pointed out, and need not be discussed in detail a second time.

The experience of having traced the changes in those forms of English which were, from one period to another, accepted as the standard language will also contribute materially to the essential health and sanity of our attitude toward what constitutes 'correct' or 'acceptable' or 'good' English today. The Old English texts which we read, and in fact most of the material from that period which has been preserved, are all in the West-Saxon dialect, that spoken south and west of the Thames. This was standard English a thousand years ago chiefly because at that time the West Saxon kingdom under a few powerful rulers, the most able of whom was Alfred, had achieved a political, cultural, and social hegemony over the rest of the island. The confusion of dialects during the early centuries of Norman French dominion, and the ultimate emergence of the London dialect as a standard in late Middle English have already been told in some detail. Modern sequels to all this may be found in the divergent developments of British and American English and the conflict among three types of regional speech within this country itself.

We have seen enough of the relationships between dialects and the ways in which they differ from one another, to realize that the acceptance as a standard of one type of speech over another is based not upon linguistic considerations but rather upon political, cultural, and economic factors. As a tool of expression, London speech was probably no better, neither more efficient nor more effective, than Gloucester speech, Nottingham speech, or Canterbury speech. It happened to be the plant which was sown in the good earth; circumstances favored its growth and gave it a heightened social utility.

The same point of view is equally applicable to those forms of English which are today considered as standard forms of the language. They have become so because of the fact of widespread usage, due in large part to extra-linguistic factors. Particularly in connection with the spoken standard, there can be little reason for an undiscriminating admiration and zeal for some regional form of the language which is foreign to you. London English is a satisfactory standard for most southern English speakers, but there is no excuse for its adoption in New York, Chicago, Atlanta, or San Francisco, when these cities in themselves constitute powerful centers which affect in many ways the behavior and culture of the inhabitants within their spheres of influence. Many Americans, Middle Westerners in particular, are likely to have a feeling of inferiority about their native regional speech. Although this attitude is understandable in terms of the cultural and settlement history of the region between the Alleghanies and the Rockies, there is little justification for it so far as purely linguistic considerations enter into the question.

Our analyses and observations should also have taught us that frequently what comes to be adopted as the standard is not always the most logical or systematic arrangement of linguistic elements. We have already seen that from the point of view of systematization, certain sub-standard paradigms, particularly those of the reflexive pronoun and the absolute genitive form of the personal pronoun, are definitely more regular than our own. On the other hand, many standard English constructions seem to be put together with greater regard for logic than the corresponding sub-standard expression: compare, for example, *as far as* with *all the farther*. Yet in neither case does logic or regularity constitute a valid argument for acceptance or adoption; the essential question is which form or construction is actually used in standard English.

We have also learned something about the historical relation of dialects to one another, and of standard to sub-standard speech. The doubled verbal negative which was standard English as well as sub-standard in Chaucer's time, has only the latter status today. On the other hand, the sub-standard participial forms *broke* and *tore* represent a reduction to a two part verb which has not yet taken place and may never take place in the standard language. Sub-standard or regional [sæs] for *sauce* is an archaism, but on the same speech level the pronunciation [sʌt] for *soot* is a step in advance of standard English [sut] or [sʊt]. From one point of view, many of the differences between standard and sub-standard English are differences in the rate of speed of language changes.

These considerations have not been pointed out for the purpose of making the mastery of standard English seem less important than it really is. As an educated member of your community, it is desirable, important, possibly even necessary, that you express yourself in what is accepted by your associates and neighbors as standard speech. But nevertheless it is a mistaken attitude to ascribe to that standard any logical, aesthetic, or functional virtues which it does not possess. Quite possibly, a frank recognition of and an interest in the relationship of various forms of the language to each other will make you the more capable and adept in your daily use of the standard language. Certainly it will not operate adversely.

We have seen too that the only way in which anyone,

even the most distinguished of linguistic scholars, can determine precisely what the usages of standard English are, is through the scientific method of painstaking and unbiased observation. This is important, for there has been in the past a tendency in this country, and particularly in its schools, to disregard the facts of the language in favor of certain traditional but not always scientifically correct notions of what constitutes correct English. Again such an attitude is understandable in the light of our cultural history during the past century, but this does not constitute an excuse for the continued acceptance of rationalization after the fact, pseudo-psychology, and the attempted application of the rules of Latin grammar to the English language.

In practice, of course, it is scarcely possible for every speaker of English to make of himself a linguistic scientist, or to engage in first hand research either into the extensive fields of present-day usage or into the historical ramifications every time he wants to decide a simple question of syntax or of pronunciation. What he can do, however, is to discover for himself the results of the research of others, such results as are contained in the authoritative dictionaries and the competent grammars of the English language. This implies an intelligent use of the dictionary, interpreting its findings in the light of the purposes and working methods of its compilers. It implies also an intelligent discrimination between grammars which are based upon first hand, scholarly observation of the language and those which merely repeat without investigation or verification whatever someone else has written before. It is with this end in view that you have been given constant practice in the use of the dictionary, and that you have been introduced to many of the reliable and scientific treatments of various phases of English. For the same reason, there has been a constant insistence throughout this book upon the fundamentally scientific basis of grammar and language study, and upon the organic relationship between the science of language and all other intellectual disciplines which seek to record and to understand the activities of the human mind and spirit in terms of their traditional heritage and their environment.

Additional Reading:

Wyld, *Short History of English*, §§ 60–75, 146–9, 208–11.
Fries, *Teaching of the English Language* (also published under the title *What Is Good English?*), Chapters I–IV.

Exercise LVIII

1. Be able to name and locate the regions in which the various dialects of Old English were spoken. Which of them might be called the linguistic standard of the time? Why?

2. Which dialect became the standard of Middle English speech and writing? Account for the change from the Old English period.

3. What evidence can you cite concerning the existence of a linguistic standard in the Early Modern English period?

4. What factors other than geography must be taken into account in a consideration of standard Modern English?

5. Explain the origin, and trace the development and transmission of the ideas of 'correctness' which appear in

many of our common-school textbooks. How valid are they? Give reasons for your answer.

6. Illustrate how a knowledge of the history of the language may be of service when applied to any specific problem of grammar.

7. What are the most frequently consulted authorities in matters of pronunciation? How valid are they? What do you think would constitute a reasonable and defensible standard of pronunciation?

8. What are the most frequently consulted authorities in questions of word meaning? How valid are they? What do you think would constitute a reasonable and defensible standard in this phase of language?

Illustrative Selections from OLD ENGLISH

Selection L

MATTHEW vi. 9–16, 28

As the first specimen of Old English, the West Saxon version of Matthew vi, which contains the Lord's Prayer, has been selected. As usual it is accompanied by a phonetic transcription which is intended to represent the pronunciation of the time.

In this transcription the symbols [yː], and [ʏ] represent the high front and lower high-front rounded vowels. The sound [j] when final represents a voiced palatal fricative. In the first six verses, the stress of all plurisyllabic words is marked.

9. Eornostlīċe ġebiddaÐ ēow Ðus Fæder ūre þū þe eart
ˈɛornɔstliːtʃɛ jɛˈbɪdːɑθ eːow θʊs ˈfædɛr ˈuːrɛ θuː θɛ æərt

on heofonum, sīe ðīn nama gehālgod.
ɔn ˈhɛovɔnʊm siːə θiːn nɑmɑ jɛhɑːlgɔd.

10. Tō-cume þīn rīċe. Ġeweorðe ðīn willa on eorðan swā
toː'kumɛ θiːn 'riːtʃɛ jɛ'wɛorðɛ θiːn 'wɪlːɑ ɔn 'ɛorðɑn swɑː

swā on heofonum.
swɑː ɔn 'hɛovɔnum.

11. Ūrne ġedæghwǣmlīcan hlāf sele ūs tō-dæġ.
'uːrnɛ jɛ'dæjʍæːmliːkɑn xlɑːf 'sɛlɛ uːs toː'dæj.

12. And forġief ūs ūre gyltas swā wē forġiefað ǣlcum
ɑnd fɔr'jɪəf uːs 'uːrɛ 'gʏltɑs swɑː weː fɔr'jɪəvɑθ 'æːlkum

þāra þe wið ūs āgyltað.
'θɑːrɑ θɛ wɪθ uːs ɑː'gʏltɑθ

13. Ne ġelǣd þū ūs on costnunge ac ālīes ūs of yfele.
nɛ jɛlæːd θuː uːs ɔn 'kɔstnuŋgɛ ɑk ɑː'liːəs uːs ɔf 'ʏvɛlɛ.

14. Witodlīċe ġif ġē forġiefað mannum heora synna, þonne
'wɪtɔdliːtʃɛ jɪf jeː fɔr'jɪəvɑθ 'mɑnːum 'hɛorɑ 'ʂʏnːɑ 'θɔnːɛ

forġiefeð ēower sē heofonlīca fæder ēow ēowre gyltas.
fɔr'jɪəvɛθ eːowɛr seː 'hɛovɔnliːkɑ 'fædɛr eːow 'eːowrɛ 'gʏltɑs.

15. Ġif gē sōþlīċe ne forġiefað mannum, ne ēower fæder
jɪf jeː soːðliːtʃɛ nɛ fɔrjɪəvɑθ mɑnːum nɛ eːowɛr fædɛr

ne forġiefeð ēow ēowre synna.
nɛ fɔrjɪəvɛθ eːow eːowrɛ sʏnːɑ.

16. Sōðlīċe þonne ġē fæsten, nellen ġē wesan swylċe lēase
soːðliːtʃɛ θɔnːɛ jeː fæstɛn nɛlːɛn jeː wɛzɑn swʏltʃɛ læːəzɛ

liċetteras. Hīe fornimað heora ansīena, þæt hīe ætīewen
lɪtʃɛtːɛrɑs hiːə fɔrnɪmɑθ hɛorɑ ɑnsiːənɑ θæt hiːə ætiːəwɛn

mannum fæstende. Sōðlīċe iċ secge ēow þæt hīe onfēngon
mɑnːum fæstɛndɛ soːðliːtʃɛ ɪtʃ sɛdʒɛ eːow θæt hiːə ɔnfeːŋgɔn

heora meda.
hɛorɑ meːdɑ

* * *

28. Ond tō hwȳ sindon ġē ymbhȳdiġe be rēafe; bescēawiaꝺ
ɔnd toː ʌyː sɪndɔn jeː ʏmbhyːdɪjɛ bɛ ræːəvɛ bɛʃæːəwɪɑθ

æceres lilian, hū hīe weaxaþ; ne swincaꝺ hīe ne hīe ne spɪnːɑθ.
ækɛrɛs lɪlɪɑn huː hiːə wæəksɑθ nɛ swɪŋkɑθ hiːə nɛ hiːə nɛ spinnaꝺ.

Selection M

De Temporibus

This is a highly simplified version of Bede's *De Temporibus*, a practical treatise on astronomy and related matters. Words and constructions which are not immediately self-explanatory are glossed at the end of the passage. You may find it advantageous to begin compiling a glossary of your own on small cards and continue it as you go on to more complicated material. Clark Hall's *A Concise Anglo-Saxon Dictionary*, will also be useful for further reference.

Be þǣre sunnan

Sēo *sunne* gǣþ *betwēonan heofone* and eorꝺan: *on* dæġ *bufan* eorþan, and on niht *under þisse* eorþan. Ǣfre hēo biþ iernende ymb þās eorþan, and ealswā leohte *scīnꝺ* under ꝺǣre eorþan on niht swā *swā* hēo on dæġ dēþ bufan *ūrum* hēafdum.

On þā *healfe* þe hēo scīnꝺ, þǣr biꝺ dæġ; and on þā healfe þe hēo ne scīnꝺ, þær biþ niht. *Wē* hātaꝺ ānne dæġ from sunnan ūpgange oþ *ǣfen*.

Ǣlċe mōnaꝺ sēo sunne iernꝺ under ān ꝺāra *tācna*. Ān þāra tācna is ġehāten ARIES, *þæt* is *ramm;* ōꝺer TAURUS, þæt is *bula;* ꝺridda GEMINI þæt sind getwisan; fēorꝺa CANCER, ꝺæt is *crabba;* fifta LEO; siexta VIRGO, þæt is mæġden; seofoꝺa LIBRA, þæt is *pund* oꝺꝺe wǣġė; eahtoꝺe SCORPIUS; nigoꝺa SAGITTARIUS; tēoꝺa is CAPRICORNUS, þæt is *buccan horn;* endlyfta is AQUARIUS, þæt is wæter ġyte; twelfte is PISCES, þæt sind *fiscas*.

Be þǣre mōnan

Dæġhwǣmlīce ðæs *mōnan* leoht bit *weaxende* and waniende. Simle hē went his *hrycg* to ðǣre sunnan. Hwonne he weaxeð, is *hē full*. *Sōð*līċe ðæs mōnan *ġēar* hæfð *seofon* and *twentiġ* daga and eahta *tīda;* þonne hē underiernð ealla þā *twelf* tācna þe sēo sunne undergǣð twelf mōnað.

Be þǣre nihte

Niht is ġesett mannum to *reste* on þissum middanġearde. Soþlīċe þēah ðe hit wundorlīċ þynċe, nis þēos woroldlīċe niht nān þing būtan ðǣre eorðan *sceado* betwēonan þǣre sunnan and mancynne.

Be ðǣm ġēare

On þǣm ġēare sind getealde twelf mōnþas, and twā and fīftiġ wucena, þrēo hund daga and *fīf* and siextig daga and ðǣr tō ēacan siex tīda.

Be þǣre lyfte

Þēos lyft ðe wē on libbaþ is ān ðāra fēower ġesceafta. Nis nān *þing* þe næbbe þā fēower ġesceafta *him* mid: ðæt is lyft, and *fȳr*, and eorþe, and wæter. Reġnas *cumaþ* of ðǣre lyfte þurh Godes mihte. Sēo lyft *liccað* and ātīehð ðone wǣtan of ealre eorðan and of ðǣre *sǣ* and *ġegaderað* to *scūrum*. Hagol cymð of reġndropum ðonne hīe bēoþ ġefrorene up on ðǣre lyfte and swā siððan feallað. Snāw cymþ of ðǣm *ðynnum* wǣtan ðe bið ūp atogen mid ðǣre lyfte.

Lyft is swīðe þynne. Sēo ofergǣð ealne middangeard, and ūp-āstīgþ oð ðone mōnan. On þære flēogað fuglas swā swā fiscas *swimmað* on wætere.

GLOSSARY

2 *bufan*, above

3 *biþ iernende ymb*, is running about, revolves

4 *þās*, this

4 *ealswā swā . . . swā*, just as . . . so. *Ealswā* = MnE also, as. Swā = MnE so.

5 dēþ, does

5 *hēafdum*, heads

6 *healfe*, side, half

7 *hātað*, reckon, call

9 *tācna*, genitive plural of *tācen*, token, sign. *Aries*, *Taurus*, *Gemini*, etc., are the Latin names for the signs of the zodiac.

10 *ōðer*, second, other
11 *ġetwisan*, twins
13 *wǣġe*, scales
15 *ġyte*, pouring forth, shedding
18 *simle*, ever, always
18 *went*, syncopated form of *wendeð*, turns
18 *hrycg*, back, ridge
19 *ġēar*, year, season
20 *tīda*, hours, tides
20 *underiernð*, runs through
23 *ġesett*, established
23 *middanġearde*, middle earth, that is, the territory between heaven and hell. Compare the *Midgard* of Norse mythology.
24 *þēah ðe*, although
24 *nis*, contraction of *ne is*, is not
24 *þynċe*, may seem
25 *būtan*, except, but
29 *ðǣr tō ēacan*, in addition thereto
31 *lyft*, air
32 *ġesceafta*, elements
33 *næbbe*, contraction of *ne hæbbe*, has not
35 *ātīehð*, draws
35 *wǣtan*, moisture
36 *hagol*, hail
37 *ġefrorene*, frozen
38 *siððan*, afterward
40 *swīðe*, very
41 *ūp-āstīġþ*, climbs up, ascends

Selection N

Old English Gospels, Matthew i. 18–25

i : 18. Ṡōþlīce þus wæs Crīstes cnēoriss: þā þæs Hælendes mōdor Marie wæs Iosepe beweddod, ǣr hīe tōsomme becōmon, hēo wæs ġemēt on innoðe hæbbende of þǣm Hālgan Gāste.

19. Sōðlīċe Iosep hire wer, ðā hē wæs rihtwīs and nolde ġewīdmǣrsian, hē wolde hīe dīeġellīċe forlǣtan.

20. Him þā sōðlīċe þās þing ðenċendum, Dryhtnes engel on swefnum ætīewde and him tō cwæð: 'Iosep, Dauides sunu, nelle þū ondrǣdan Marian þīne gemæċċan tō onfōnne. Þæt on hiere ācenned is, hit is of þǣm Hālgan Gāste.

21. Witodlīċe hēo cenð sunu and þū nemnest his naman Hǣlend. Hē sōðlīċe his folc hāl ġedēð from heora synnum.'

22. Sōþlīċe eal þis wæs ġeworden þæt ġefylled wǣre þæt from Dryhtne ġecweden wæs þurh þone wītegan.

23. Sōðlīċe sēo fæmne hæfð on innoðe, and hēo cenð sunu, and hīe nemnað his naman Emanuhel, þæt is gereht on ūre geþēode, 'God mid ūs.'

24. Ðā ārās Iosep of swefene, and dyde swā Dryhtnes engel him bebēad, and hē onfēng his gemæċċan.

25. And hē ne grētte hīe. Hēo cende hiere frum-cennedan sunu and nemde his naman Hǣlend.

vii. 22–7

vii : 22. Maniġe cweþað on ðǣm dæġe tō mē, 'Dryhten, Dryhten, hū ne wītegode wē on þīnum naman, and on þīnum naman wē ūt āwurpon dēoflu, and on þīnum naman wē worhton miċle mihta?'

23. Þonne cweðe ic tō heom, 'Þæt iċ ēow nǣfre ne cūðe; ġewītað fram mē, ġē þe worhton unrihtwīsnesse.'

24. Eornostlīċe ǣlċ þāra þe ðās mīne word ġehīerð, and þā wyrċð, bið gelīċ þǣm wīsan were sē his hūs ofer stān ġetimbrode.

25. Þā cōm þǣr reġn and miċele flōd, and þǣr blēowon windas, and āhruron on þæt hūs, and hit nā ne fēoll; sōðlīċe hit wæs ofer stān getimbrod.

26. And ǣlċ þāra þe gehīerþ ðās mīne word, and þā ne wyrċð, sē bið geliċ þǣm dysigan men þe ġetimbrode his hūs ofer sand-ċeosol.

27. Þā rīnde hit and þǣr cōmon flōdas and blēowon windas and āhruron on þæt hūs and þæt hūs fēoll and his hryre wæs miċel.

xxi. 19

xxi : 19. And hē ġeseah ān fīctrēow wið þone weġ, þa ēode hē to him, and ne fand on him būtan þā lēaf āne; ðā cwæð hē, 'Ne weorþe nǣfre wæstm of þē ācenned. Þā sōna forscranc þæt fīctrēow.

GLOSSARY

i : 18 *cnēoriss*, birth, generation
18 *Hǣlend*, Saviour, literally 'Healer'
18 *tōsomne*, together
18 *ġemēton innoðe hæbbende*, found having within
19 *nolde*, contraction of *ne wolde*, would not, did not wish
19 *ġewīdmǣrsian*, to make or become notorious
19 *dīeġellīċe*, secretly
20 *him . . . ðenċendum* (ablative or dative absolute construction), to him then thinking these things
20 *swefnum*, dreams

20 *nelle*, contraction of *ne wille*, will not
20 *ġemæċċan*, mate, wife
20 *onfōnne*, receive
21 *cenð* (present used with future meaning), will bear, bring forth
21 *hāl*, whole, sound
21 *ġedēþ* (present of verb 'to do' used with future and causative meaning), he shall make . . . whole
22 *wæs ġeworden*, was come to pass
22 *ġecweden*, said
22 *wītegan*, prophet
23 *hæfð on innoðe*, will have within, *i.e.* will be with child
23 *ġereht*, interpreted
23 *ġeþēode*, language
24 *him bebēad*, commanded to him. The pronoun is dative in construction.
25 *grētte*, greeted, approached
vii : 22 *Dryhten*, Lord
22 *wītegode*, prophesied, cf. i : 22
22 *mihta*, mighty works
23 *cūðe*, knew
23 *gewītað*, depart
24 *ǣlc þāra þe*, each of those who
25 *āhruron*, rushed, beat
26 *dysigan*, foolish, MnE dizzy
26 *men* (dative singular), man
26 *sandċeosol*, gravel
27 *hryre*, fall, destruction
xxi : 19 *ēode* (irregular past tense of *gān* 'to go'), went
19 *wæstm*, fruit
19 *forscranc*, shrank, withered

Selection O

Old English Gospels, Mark ix. 31–48

ix : 31. Sōðlīċe hē lǣrde his leorningcnihtas and sægde, 'Sōþlīċe mannes sunu bið ġeseald on synfulra handa þæt hīe hine ofslēan; and ofslagen, þǣm þriddan dæġe hē ārīst.'

32. Đā niston hīe þæt word, and hīe ādrēdon hine āxiende.

33. Đā cōmon hīe to Capharnaum; and þā hīe æt hām wǣron, hē ācsode hīe, 'Hwæt smēaġde gē be weġe?'

34. And hīe swīgodon; witodlīċe hīe on weġe smēaġdon hwylċ heora ieldost wǣre.

35. Þā hē sæt, hē clipode hīe twelfe, and sæġde heom, 'Ġif ēower hwylċ wile bēon fyrmest, bēo sē ēaðmōdost, and ēower ealra þeġn.'

36. Þā nam hē ānne cnapan, and ġesette on heora middele; þā hē hine beclypte, hē sæġde heom:

37. 'Swā hwylċ swā ānne of þus ġerādum cnapum on mīnum naman onfēhð, sē onfēhð mē; and sē þe mē onfēhð, hē ne onfēhð mē ac þone þe mē sende.'

43. And ġif þīn hand þē swicað, ċeorf hīe of; betere þē is þæt þū wanhāl to līfe gā, þonne þū twā handa hæbbe, and fare on helle and on unācwenċedlīċ fȳr;

44. Þǣr heora wyrm ne swilt, and fȳr ne bið ācwenċed.

45. And ġif þīn fōt swicað þē, ċeorf hine of; betere is þē þæt þū healt gā on ēċe l f, þonne þū hæbbe tweġen fēt, and sīe āworpen on helle unācwenċedlīċes fȳres;

46. þǣr heora wyrm ne swilt, and fȳr ne bið ācwenċed.

47. Ġif þīn ēaġe þē swicað, weorp hit ūt; betere þē is mid ānum ēagan gān on Godes rīċe þonne twā ēagan hæbbende sīe āworpen on helle fȳr;

48. þǣr heora wyrm ne swilt, ne fȳr ne bið ācwenċed.

GLOSSARY

ix : 31 *lǣrde*, taught
31 *leorningcnihtas*, disciples
31 *synfulra* (genitive plural), of the sinful
31 *ofslagen* (past participle in absolute construction), and being slain
32 *niston*, contraction of *ne wiston*, knew not
32 *hīe . . . axiende*, they feared asking him
33 *cōmon*, they came
33 *smēaġde*, discussed, deliberated, inquired
34 *swīgodon*, were silent
34 *ieldost*, oldest, most important
35 *clipode*, called
35 *hīe twelfe*, literally 'them twelve,' all twelve of them
35 *ēower hwylċ*, which of you. *Ēower* is genitive plural
35 *fyrmest*, foremost
35 *ēaðmōdost*, most humble
35 *þeġn*, servant
36 *cnapan*, boy
36 *beclypte*, embraced
37 *swā hwylċ swā*, whosoever
37 *þus ġerādum cnapum*, such children
37 *onfēhð*, receives
37 *sē þe*, whosoever, that one who
43 *swicaþ*, offend
43 *ċeorf*, cut, carve
43 *þē* (dative singular), for you
43 *wanhāl*, unsound, unhealthy, maimed
43 *unācwenċedlīċ*, unquenchable
44 *þǣr*, where

44 *swilt* (present tense of *sweltan*), dies

45 *ēċe*, eternal

45 *unācwenċedlīċes fȳres* (genitive singular), of unquenchable fire

Selection P

Old English Gospels, Matthew iv. 1–8

iv : 1. Þā wæs sē Hǣlend ġelǣd fram þǣm Gāste on þæt wēsten þæt hē wǣre fram þǣm dēofle ġecostnod.

2. And þā þā hē fæste fēowertiġ daga and fēowertiġ nihta, þā ongan hine siððan hyngrian.

3. And þā ġenēalǣhte sē costniend and cwæð: 'Ġif ðū Godes sunu sīe, cwæð þæt þās stānas to hlāfe ġeweorðan.'

4. Þā andswarode sē Hǣlend: 'Hit is āwriten, ne liofað sē man be hlāfe ānum ac be ælcum worde þe of Godes mūðe gæð.'

5. Þā ġebrōhte sē dēofol hine on þā hālgan ċeastre and āsette hine ofer þæs temples hēahnesse.

6. And cwæð tō him: 'Ġif þū Godes sunu eart, send þē þonne niðer; sōðlīċe hit is āwriten þæt hē þā englas bebēad be ðē, and hīe þē on heora handum beren, þe læs þe þīn fōt æt stāne ætspurne.'

7. Þā cwæð sē Hǣlend eft tō him: 'Hit is āwriten, ne costna þu ðone Dryhten, þīnne God.'

8. Eft sē dēofol hine ġenam and lǣdde hine on swīðe hēahne munt and ætīewde him ealle þā rīcu middanġeardes and heora wuldor.

GLOSSARY

iv : 1 *wēsten*, wilderness, waste

1 *wǣre* (subjunctive), might be

1 *ġecostnod*, tempted

2 *ongan hine . . . hyngrian* (impersonal construction), it began to hunger him

3 *ġenēalǣhte*, approached

3 *hlāfe*, bread, MnE 'loaf'

3 *ġeweorðan*, become, be made into

4 *liofað*, lives

4 *ānum*, alone

5 *ċeastre*, city

6 *hē . . . bebēad*, He commanded the angels concerning you

6 *hīe . . . beren*, they should bear

8 *rīcu* (nominative singular, *rīċe*), kingdoms

Selection Q

Old English Gospels, Matthew xiii. 31–40

xiii : 31. Hē rehte heom þā ġīet ōþer bīspell þus cweðende:
'Heofona rīce is ġeworden ġelīċ senepes corne þæt sēow sē man
on his æcere.
32. Þæt is ealra sǣda lǣst; sōðlīċe þonne hit weaxeþ, hit is
ealra wyrta mǣst, and hit wierþ trēow, swā þæt þā fuglas þāra
heofona cumaþ and eardiaþ on þǣm bōgum.'
33. Hē spræc tō heom ōþer bīspell and þus cwæð: 'Heofona
rīce is gelīċ þǣm beorman þone þæt wīf onfēng and behȳdde on
þrīm ġemetum meluwes, oð hē wæs eall āhafen.'
34. Ealle þās þing sē Hǣlend spræc mid bīspellum to þǣm
werodum, and nān þing ne spræc hē būtan bīspellum.
36. . . . þā ġenēalǣhton tō him his leorningcnihtas and
cwǣdon: 'Āreċe ūs þæt bīspell þæs hwǣtes and þæs cocceles.'
37. Þā andswarode hē heom: 'Sē þe sēow þæt gōde sǣd, sē is
mannes sunu.
38. Sōþlīċe sē æcer is þēs middanġeard; þæt gode sǣd þæt
sindon þā bearn þæs heofonlīcan rīċes; sē coccel sindon sōþlīċe
þā mānfullan bearn.
39. Sē unholda man sē þe þone coccel sēow, þæt is dēofol;
sōþlīċe þæt rīp is þǣre worulde endung; þā rīperas sindon englas.
40. Eornostlīċe, swā swā sē coccel bið ġegaderod, and on
þǣm fȳre forbærned, swā biþ on worulde endunge.'

GLOSSARY

xiii : 31 *bīspell*, parable
31 *heofona* (genitive plural), 'heavens' is the more frequent construction in OE
31 *is ġeworden ġelīċ*, literally 'is become like,' is likened to
31 *corne*, grain
31 *senep*, mustard
32 *lǣst*, least
32 *wyrta*, herb, root
32 *mǣst*, most, greatest
32 *fuglas*, birds, fowls
32 *eardiaþ*, dwell
32 *bōgum*, boughs
33 *beorman*, leaven, yeast
33 *meluwes* (nominative singular, *melu*), meal
33 *āhafen*, raised

34 *werodum*, hosts, multitudes
34 *būtan bīspellum*, except in parables
36 *hwǣtes*, wheat
36 *cocceles*, tares
38 *bearn*, children
38 mānfullan (adjective), evil, wicked
39 *unholda*, wicked
39 *rīp*, harvest

Selection R

OLD ENGLISH GOSPELS, LUKE: various verses

i : 2. Swā ūs betǣhton ðā þe hit of frymðe ġesāwon, and *bǣre sprǣċe* þeġnas wǣron.

i : 10. Eal werod þæs folces wæs ūte ġebiddende on *þǣre offrunga* tīman.

ii : 4. Ðā fērde Iosep fram Galilea of *þǣre ċeastre* Nazareth on Iudeisce *ċeastre* Dauides, sēo is ġenemned Bethleem, for þǣm hē wæs of Dauides hūse and hirede.

ii : 40. Sōðlīċe þæt ċild wēox and wæs gestrangod, wīsdōmes full, and Godes *ġiefu* wæs on him.

iii : 3. And hē cōm intō eal Iordanes rīċe bodiende *dǣdbote* fulwiht on *synna forġiefenesse*.

iii : 9. Nū is *sēo æx* āsett to þæs trēowes wyrtruman; witodlīce ælċ trēow þe ne bringð gōdne wæstm bið forcorfen and on fȳr aworpen.

v : 15. Witodlīċe þæs þē mā *sēo sprǣc* be him fērde; and miċele menigu cōmon þæt hīe ġehīerdon and wurdon ġehǣlede fram heora *untrumnessum*.

v : 37. Ne nān man ne sent nīwe wīn on ealde bytta; elles þæt nīwe wīn bricð *þā bytta* and þæt wīn bið āgoten, and *þā bytta* forweorðað.

vi : 41. Hwȳ ġesiehst þū *þā eġle* on þīnes brōþor ēagan and ne ġesiehst þone bēam on þīnum ēagan?

viii : 4. Sōþlīċe þā miċel menigu cōm and of *þǣm ċeastrum* tō him efston, hē sæġde heom ān bīspell.

xv : 12. Þā cwæð sē ġingra tō his fæder, 'Fæder, sele mē mīnne dǣl *þāra ǣhta* þe tō mē ġebyraþ.' Þā dǣlde hē him his *ǣhta*.

GLOSSARY

i : 2 *betǣhton*, delivered, committed
2 *frymðe*, beginning
2 *þeġn*, minister, servant
10 *ġebiddende*, praying
ii : 4 *ċeastre*, city
4 *hirede*, household, family
iii : 3 *bodiende*, preaching, announcing
3 *dǣdbote*, repentance
3 *fulwiht*, baptism
9 *wyrtruman*, roots
9 *wæstm*, fruit
v : 15 *þæs þē mā*, so much the more
15 *spræc*, speech, talk
15 *menigu*, multitude, hosts
15 *untrumnessum*, weaknesses, infirmities
37 *sent*, puts
37 *bytta*, bottles
37 *bricð*, breaks
37 *āgoten*, spilled
37 *forweorðað*, perish, be destroyed
vi : 41 *eġle*, mote
viii : 4 *efston*, hastened
xv : 12 *sele*, give, sell
12 *dǣl*, share, deal
12 *ǣhta*, possessions
12 *ġebyraþ*, pertain, belong

Selection S

Old English Gospels, Matthew xxv. 1–12

xxv : 1. Þonne biþ heofona rīċe gelīċ *þǣm* tīen *fǣmnum* þe ðā leohtfatu nāmon and fērdon onġēan *þone brȳdguman* and þā brȳde.

2. Heora fīf wǣron dysiġe and fīf glēawe.

3. Ac *þā* fīf *dysigan* nāmon lēohtfatu and ne nāmon nānne ele mid heom.

4. Ðā *glēawan* nāmon ele on heora fatum mid þǣm lēohtfatum.

5. Ðā *sē brȳdguma* ielde, þā hnappodon hīe ealle and slēpon.

6. Witodlīċe tō middre nihte man hrīemde and cwæþ: 'Nū *sē brȳdguma* cymð; farað him tōġēanes.'

7. Þā ārison ealle *þā fǣmnan* and glengdon heora lēohtfatu.

8. Ðā cwædon *þā dysigan* to *þǣm wīsum:* 'Sellaþ ūs of ēowerum ele, for þǣm ūru lēohtfatu sindon ācwenċte.'

9. Ðā andswarodon *þā glēāwan* and cwǣdon: 'Nese, þē lǣs þe wē and ġē næbben ġenōh. Gāþ tō þǣm ċīependum, and bycgað ēow ele.'

10. Witodlīce þā hīe fērdon and woldon bycgan, þā cōm *sē brȳdguma*, and þā þe ġearwe wǣron ēodon in mid him tō þǣm ġiftum; and sēo duru wæs belocen.

11. Đā æt nīehstan cōmon *þā* ōðre *fǣmnan* and cwǣdon, 'Dryhten, Dryhten, lǣt ūs in.'

12. Đā andswarode hē heom and cwæð: 'Sōþ iċ ēow secge, ne cann iċ ēow.'

GLOSSARY

xxv: 1 *fērdon onġēan*, went toward. Notice that this preposition with a verb of motion governs the accusative case.
2 *dysiġe*, foolish
2 *glēawe*, wise
3 *ele*, oil
4 *fatum*, vessels. MnE 'vat'
5 *ielde*, delayed
5 *hnappodon*, slumbered, napped
6 *man hrīemde*, one cried out. *Man* is an impersonal pronoun.
6 *farað* (imperative plural), go
6 *tōġēanes*, toward
7 *glengdon*, trimmed
9 *ċiependum*, merchants
10 *ġearwe*, ready
10 *ġiftum*, ceremonies
11 *æt nīehstan*, thereupon, later, next
12 *cann*, know

Selection T

Old English Gospels, Mark: various verses

i : 8. Ic fulwie ēow on wætere; hē ēow fulwað on *Hālgum* Gaste.

10. And sōna of ðǣm wætere he geseah *opene* heofonas, and *Hāligne* Gāst swā culfran āstīgende and on him wuniende.

26. And sē unclǣna gāst, hine slītende and *miċelre* stefne clipiende, him of ēode.

27. Þā wundrodon hīe ealle swā þæt hīe betweox heom cwædon: 'Hwæt is þis? Hwæt is þēos nīwe lār, þæt hē on anwealde *unclǣnum* gāstum bebīet, and hīe hīersumiað him?'

36. And hē maniga ġehǣlde þe *missenlīcum* ādlum ġedrehte wǣron, and *maniga* dēofolsēocnessa hē ūt ādrāf, and hīe sprecan ne lēt, for þǣm hīe wiston þæt hē Crīst wæs.

iii : 7. And þā fērde sē Hǣlend tō þǣre sǣ mid his leorning-cnihtum; and *miċel* menigu him fyliġde fram Galilea and Iudea.

28. Sōðlīċe iċ ēow secge þæt *ealle* synna sindon manna bearnum forġiefene, and bismerunga þǣm ðe hīe bismeriað.

29. Sōðlīċe iċ ēow secge: 'Sē þe ðone Hālgan Gāst bismerað, sē næfð on ēċenesse forġiefenesse, ac biþ *ēċes* gyltes *scyldiġ*.'

iv : 5. Sum fēoll ofer stānscyligan þær hit næfde *miċele* eorþan, and sōna ūp ēode; and for þǣm hit næfde eorðan þiċnesse.

11. And hē sæġde heom: 'Ēow is geseald tō witanne Godes rices gerȳnu; þǣm þe ūte sindon *ealle* þing on bīspellum ġeweorþað.'

31. Swā swā senepes sǣd, þonne hit bið on eorðan ġesāwen, hit is *ealra* sæda lǣst þe on eorðan sindon.

32. And þonne hit āsāwen bið, hit āstīhþ, and bið *ealra* wyrta mǣst, and hæfð swā *miċele* bōgas þæt heofonas fuglas eardian magon under his sceade.

v : 30. And þā sē Hǣlend oncnēow on him selfum þæt him mæġen of ēode, hē cwæð bewend tō þǣre menigu: 'Hwā æthrān *mīnes* rēafes?'

vi : 7. And him twelf tō ġeclipode, and ongan hīe sendan twām and twām; and heom anweald sealde *unclǣnra* gāsta.

x : 8. And beoð twēġen on *ānum* flǣsce; witodlīċe ne sindon nā twēġen, ac *ān* flǣsc.

xi : 16. And hē ne ġeþafode þæt *ǣniġ* man *ǣniġ* fæt ðurh þæt templ bǣre.

xii : 19. Lārēow, Moyses ūs āwrāt, ġif hwæs brōðor *dēad* bið, and lǣfð his wīf, and næfð nān bearn, þæt his brōðor nime his wīf, and his brōðor sǣd weċċe.

xiv : 4. Sume hit unweorðlīċe forbǣron and betweox heom selfum cwǣdon: 'For hwȳ wæs *þisre* sealfe forspilledness ġe-worden?'

xv : 3. Ðā wrēġdon hine þā hēahsācerdas on *manigum* þingum.

GLOSSARY

i : 8 *fulwie*, *fulwað*, baptize
10 *opene* (adjective), open
10 *āstīġende*, descending
10 *wuniende*, dwelling, remaining
26 *slītende*, tearing
27 *anweald*, authority, power
27 *bebīet*, commands (with dative object)
34 *missenlīcum*, various
34 *ġedrehte*, afflicted, troubled
iii : 28 *bismerunga*, *bismeriað*, blasphemy, blaspheme
29 *nǣfð* — ne hæfð
29 *ēċenesse*, *ēċes*, eternity, eternal
29 *scyldiġ*, guilty
iv : 5 *stānscyligan*, stony ground
11 *witanne*, know
11 *ġerȳnu*, mystery
32 *āstīhþ*, climbs, grows
v : 30 *oncnēow*, perceived, knew
30 *mæġen*, power
30 *bewend* (past participle), turned
30 *æthrān*, touched (with genitive object).
30 *rēafes*, garment (singular)
xi : 16 *ġeþafode*, permitted, allowed
xii : 19 *lārēow*, master, teacher
19 *hwæs*, someone's
19 *weċċe*, bring forth, produce
xiv : 4 *hit . . . forbǣron*, behaved unworthily about it
4 *þisre*, applies to 'ointment' and not to 'waste.'
xv : 3 *wrēġdon*, accused

Selection U

OLD ENGLISH GOSPELS, MATTHEW viii. 1–34

viii : 1. Sōþlīċe þā sē Hǣlend of þǣm munte nyþer āstāh, þā
fyliġdon him miċele menigu.
2. Þā ġenēalǣhte ān hrēofla to him, and hine tō him ġeēaðmēdde, and þus cwæð: 'Dryhten, ġif þū wilt, þū miht mē
ġeclǣnsian.'
3. Ðā āstrehte sē Hǣlend his hand, and hrepode hine, and þus
cwæð: 'Iċ wille; bēo ġeclǣnsod.' And his hrēofla wæs hrædlīċe
ġeclǣnsod.
4. Ðā cwæð sē Hǣlend to him: 'Warna þē þæt þū hit nǣne-
gum men ne secge; ac gang, ætīewe þē þǣm sacerde, and bring
heom þā lāc þe Moyses bebēad on heora ġecȳðnesse.'

5. Sōþlīċe þā sē Hǣlend in ēode on Capharnaum, þā ġenēalǣhte him ān hundredes ealdor, hine biddende,
6. And þus cweðende: 'Dryhten, mīn cnapa liġð on mīnum
hūse, lama and mid yfle ġeðrēaġd.'
7. Ðā cwæð sē Hǣlend tō him: 'Iċ cume and hine
ġehǣle.'
8. Ðā andswarode sē hundredes ealdor and ðus cwæð:
'Dryhten, ne eom iċ wierðe þæt þū in gange under mıne þeċene;
ac cweð þīn ān word, and mīn cnapa biþ ġehǣled.'
9. 'Sōðlīċe, iċ eom man under anwealde gesett, and ic
hæbbe þeġnas under mē, and iċ cweðe tō þissum, "Gang," and
hē gǣð; and ic cweðe to ōðrum, "Cum," and hē cymð; tō
mīnum ðēowe, "Wyrċ þis," and hē wyrċð.'
10. Witodlīċe, þā sē Hǣlend þis ġehīerde, þā wundrode hē,
and cwæð tō þǣm ðe him fyliġdon: 'Sōþ iċ secge ēow, ne ġemētte
iċ swā ġelēafan on Israhel.
11. Tō sōþum iċ secge ēow þæt maniġe cumað fram ēastdǣle
and westdǣle, and wuniað mid Abrahame, and Isahace, and
Iacobe on heofona rīċe.
12. Witodlīċe þises rīċes bearn bēoð āworpene on þā ȳtemes-
tan þēostro; ðǣr bēoð wōp and tōða grīstbītung.'
13. And sē Hǣlend cwæð tō þǣm hundredes ealdre: 'Gā, and
ġeweorþe þē swā swā þū ġelīefdest.' And sē cnapa wæs ġehǣled
on þǣre tīde.
14. Ðā sē Hǣlend cōm on Petres hūse, þā geseah hē his
sweġre licgende, and hriþiende.
15. And hē æthrān hiere hand, and sē fēfor hīe forlēt; þā
ārās hēo and þeġnode him.
16. Sōþlīċe þā hit ǣfen wæs, hīe brōhton him maniġe dēofol-
sēoce; and hē ūt ādrǣfde ðā unclǣnan gāstas mid his worde, and
hē ealle ġehǣlde þā yfel hæbbendan.
17. Þæt wǣre ġefylled þæt ġecweden is þurh Esaiam þone
wītegan, þus cweðende, 'Hē onfēng ūre untrumnessa, and hē
ābær ūre ādla.'
18. Ðā ġeseah sē Hǣlend miċle menigu ymbūtan hine, þā hēt
hē hīe faran ofer þone mūðan.

19. Đā ġenēalǣhte him ān bōcere, and cwæþ: 'Lārēow, iċ fyliġe þē swā hwæder swā þū færst.'

20. Đā cwæð sē Hǣlend tō him: 'Foxas habbað holu, and heofenan fuglas nest; sōðlīċe mannes Sunu næfð hwǣr hē his hēafod āhielde.'

21. Đā cwæð tō him ōþer of his leorningcnihtum: 'Dryhten, ālīefe mē ǣrest tō farenne and bebyrġian mīnne fæder.'

22. Đā cwæð sē Hǣlend tō him: 'Fyliġ mē, and lǣt dēade bebyrġian heora dēadan.'

23. And hē āstāh on scip, and his leorningcnihtas him fyliġdon.

24. Đā wearð miċel styrung geworden on þǣre sǣ, swā þæt þæt scip wearð ofergoten mid ȳþum; witodlīċe hē slēp.

25. And hīe ġenēalǣhton, and hīe āwehton hine, þus cweðende: 'Dryhten hǣle ūs; wē mōton forweorþan.'

26. Đā cwæð hē to heom: 'Tō hwȳ sindon ġē forhte, ġē lȳtles ġelēafan? Đā ārās hē, and bebēad þǣm winde and þǣre sǣ; and þǣr wearð ġeworden miċel smiltness.

27. Ġewisslīċe þā men wundrodon and ðus cwǣdon: 'Hwæt is ðēs þæt windas and sǣ him hīersumiað,'

28. Þā sē Hǣlend cōm ofer þone mūþan on Geraseniscra rīċe, þā urnon him tōġēanes twēġen þe hæfdon dēofolsēocnesse, of byrġenum ūt gangende; þā wǣron swīðe rēþe, swā þæt nān man ne mihte faran þurh þone weġ.

29. And hīe hrīemdon and cwædon: 'Lā Hǣlend, Godes Sunu, hwæt is þē and ūs ġemǣne? Cōme þū hider ǣr tīde ūs to þrēaġenne?'

30. Đǣr wæs sōþlīċe unfeorr ān heord manigra swīna lǣswiende.

31. Đā dēofla sōplīċe hine bǣdon þus cweþende, 'Ġif þū ūs ūt ādrīfst, āsende ūs on þās swīna heorde.'

32. Đā cwæð hē to heom: 'Faraþ.' And hīe þā ūt gangende fērdon on þā swīn, and þǣrrihte fērde eall sēo heord miclum onrǣse niwel on þā sǣ, and hīe wurdon dēade on þǣm wætere.

33. Þā hyrdas witodlīċe flugon, and cōmon on þā ċeastre, and cȳðdon ealle þās ðing, and be ðǣm þe þā dēofolsēocnessa hæfdon.

34. Ðā ēode eall sēo ċeasterwaru tōġēanes þǣm Hǣlende; and þā þā hīe hine ġesāwon, þā bǣdon hīe hine þæt hē fērde fram heora ġemǣrum.

GLOSSARY

viii : 2 *hrēofla*, leper
2 *hine ġeēaðmēdde*, humbled himself
3 *hrepode*, touched
3 *hrædlīċe*, quickly, immediately
4 *warna* (imperative)
4 *ætīewe þē*, show yourself
4 *lāc*, gift
4 *ġecȳðnesse*, testimony
6 *lama*, lame, crippled, paralytic
6 *geðrēaġd*, afflicted
8 *þeċene*, roof
9 *wyrċ*, do, make, perform
10 *ġelēafan*, belief, faith
11 *wuniað*, dwell, remain
12 *þēostru*, darkness
12 *grīstbītung*, gnashing
13 *ġeweorþe* (subjunctive), let it become
14 *sweġre*, mother-in-law
14 *hriþiende*, shaking, feverish
15 *þeġnode*, served
16 *onfēng*, received
17 *mūþan*, mouth of a river, estuary. Observe that OE *mūþ*, MnE 'mouth' belongs to the strong declension.
21 *ālīefe*, permit, allow
24 *ofergoten*, overwhelmed
24 *ȳðum*, waves
25 *mōton forweorþan*, are likely to perish
26 *wearð ġeworden*, was become
26 *smiltness*, quietness, peace, calm
27 *ġewisslīċe*, certainly, truly
28 *urnon* (infinitive *irnan*), ran
28 *byrġenum*, tombs, burial places
28 *rēþe*, fierce
29 *hrīemdon*, cried
29 *hwæt . . . ġemǣne*, what is common to you and to us? *i.e.* what have we to do with each other?
30 *lǣswiende*, grazing, feeding
32 *þǣrrihte*, thereupon
32 *onrǣse*, rush
32 *niwel*, headlong
33 *cȳðdon*, made known, told
34 *ċeasterwaru*, citizens (collective noun)
34 *ġemǣrum*, borders, coasts

Suggestions for Review

You have studied the history of the English language literally by going backward, beginning with the most recent developments in the language and concluding with the earliest known stage of English. In review it will undoubtedly prove advantageous to see in chronological sequence the same developments with which you have been concerned throughout your study.

A subject as complex as this deserves a systematic review. A division of the material into the four main topics of *sounds*, *inflections*, *syntax*, and *vocabulary*, followed by arranging in chronological order the chief facts under each topic, should prove helpful.

Sounds

As a further aid to the student in refreshing his memory of the more important phonological developments, a working list of words has been prepared. In each instance, the Old English form is given below. You are expected to convert the Old English form (preferably reproduced in phonetic transcription) through its successive Middle English and Early Modern English developments into Modern English. If necessary, consult an Old English dictionary to discover if the MnE form you have arrived at is the correct one.

Example: OE stɑːn > ME stɔːn > EMnE stoːn > MnE stoːn

singan
mēd
tūn
hȳrling
bēam
fēond
feld
tiġel
fuġlere
scōgan
blāwan
warnung
hand
stamerian
heofon
synn
hōc
fæst
ðunrian
scamful
nāht
hwǣġ
fāh
dīċere
hūsbonde

ċeorfan
halt
fāh
þōht
rūmian
tēgan
heard
sīde
mǣnliċ
fæġer
lagu
trēawa
hīw
spadu
Crīstnung
nīwe
ġēol
fēgan
setol
molde
lōcian
crabba
swogen
tācen
nēh

niht
treġan
awel
top
rest
fann
hāl
hǣðen
tōl
Crīstennes
flǣsc
hlūd
ēaht
gnagan
burg
þanc
wrong
scōh
crāwa
hwīting-trēow
slēacnes
swolgen
hæġl
sēowian
rōwan

INFLECTIONS

Put the successive stages in the inflectional system of each of the major parts of speech, nouns, pronouns, adjectives, and verbs, side by side. Note in each case the relative importance of sound change, analogy, or any other causes in explaining the changes in inflection from one period to another. Observe carefully the chronology of such developments as the establishment of *the* as the definite article, or *-es* in the third person singular, present indicative of verbs, which will help you identify the date of some document you may be asked to analyze.

Syntax

The facts about syntax are more elusive and abstract than those about sounds or inflections. It is in connection with this division of the subject that you will form your broader conceptions of the direction in which our language is tending. Keep clearly in mind the changes from Old English to Modern English in respect to the following linguistic features:

The break-down of the inflectional system; where it is most marked.
Development of function words, particularly in replacing case and tense forms.
The fixation or word order patterns.
Expression of negation and interrogation.
Expression of gender.
Development of the pronoun of address.

Vocabulary

Summarize the chief sources of influence upon the English vocabulary. Note in each case the time at which borrowings were most numerous, the kinds of words borrowed, the extent to which derivatives have been formed, the extent to which the borrowed words have changed in pronunciation and meaning.

List of References

Aiken, Janet R. *A New Plan of English Grammar.* New York, Henry Holt & Co., 1933.

Baugh, Albert C. *History of the English Language.* New York, D. Appleton-Century Co., 1935.

Bloomfield, Leonard. *Language.* New York, Henry Holt & Co., 1933.

Curme, George O., and Kurath, Hans. *A Grammar of the English Language.* D. C. Heath and Co., 1931–5. 3 vols. Vol. II, *Parts of Speech and Accidence;* Vol. III, *Syntax.* (Volume I of this series has not yet appeared.)

Emerson, Oliver F. *History of the English Language.* New York, Macmillan, 1922.

Fries, Charles C. *Teaching of the English Language.* New York, Thomas Nelson and Sons, 1927. Part of this book has been recently reissued with the title *What Is Good English?* Ann Arbor, 1940.

Fries, Charles C. *American English Grammar.* New York, D. Appleton-Century Co., 1940. English Monograph No. 10, National Council of Teachers of English.

Graff, Willem L. *Language and Languages.* New York, D. Appleton & Co., 1932.

Grattan, J. H. G., and Gurrey, P. *Our Living Language.* New York, Thomas Nelson & Sons, 1935.

Greenough, James B., and Kittredge, George L. *Words and Their Ways in English Speech.* New York, Macmillan, 1920.

Hall, J. Lesslie. *English Usage.* Chicago, Scott, Foresman & Co., 1917.

Jespersen, Otto. *Philosophy of Grammar.* New York, Henry Holt & Co., 1924.

Jespersen, Otto. *Growth and Structure of the English Language.* 4th ed. New York, D. Appleton & Co., 1929.

Jespersen, Otto. *Modern English Grammar.* Heidelberg, Carl Winter, 1928–31. 4 vols.

Jespersen, Otto. *Essentials of English Grammar.* New York, Henry Holt & Co., 1933.

Jones, Daniel. *Outline of English Phonetics.* 6th ed. New York, Dutton & Co., 1940.

Jones, Daniel. *Phonetic Transcriptions of English Prose.* 2nd ed. Oxford, Clarendon Press, 1914.

Kennedy, Arthur G. *Current English.* Boston, Ginn & Co., 1935.

Kenyon, John S. *American Pronunciation.* 6th ed. revised. Ann Arbor, George Wahr, 1935.

Krapp, George P. *The Pronunciation of Standard English in America.* New York, Oxford University Press, 1919.

Leonard, Sterling A. *Current English Usage.* Chicago, Inland Press, 1932. English Monograph No. 1, National Council of Teachers of English.

McKnight, George H. *English Words and Their Background.* New York, D. Appleton & Co., 1929.

Marckwardt, Albert H., and Walcott, Fred. *Facts About Current English Usage.* New York, D. Appleton-Century Co., 1938. English Monograph No. 7, National Council of Teachers of English.

Moore, Samuel, and Knott, Thomas A. *Elements of Old English.* 8th ed. Ann Arbor, George Wahr, 1940.

Perrin, Porter G. *An Index to English.* Chicago, Scott, Foresman & Co., 1939.

Robertson, Stuart. *Development of Modern English.* New York, Prentice-Hall, 1934.

Sapir, Edward. *Language.* New York, Harcourt, Brace & Co., 1921. See also his article 'Language' in the *Encyclopedia of Social Sciences.*

Serjeantson, Mary S. *History of Foreign Words in English.* London, K. Paul, Trench, Trubner & Co., 1935.

Sturtevant, Edgar H. *Linguistic Change*. Chicago, University of Chicago Press, 1917.

Summey, George. *Modern Punctuation*. New York, Oxford University Press, 1919.

Sweet, Henry. *New English Grammar*. Oxford, Clarendon Press, 1924. 2 vols.

Wright, Joseph, and Elizabeth Mary. *Elementary Middle English Grammar*. 2nd ed. London, Oxford University Press, 1928.

Wyld, Henry Cecil. *Short History of English*. New York, Dutton & Co., 1929.

Dictionaries

Clark Hall, John R. *A Concise Anglo-Saxon Dictionary*. 3d ed. Cambridge University Press, 1931.

Fowler, H. W. *Dictionary of Modern English Usage*. Oxford, Clarendon Press, 1926. Reprinted with corrections, 1930, 1937.

Horwill, H. W. *Dictionary of Modern American Usage*. Oxford, Clarendon Press, 1935.

Murray, James A. H., Bradley, Henry, Craigie, W. A., Onions, C. T. *Oxford English Dictionary*. Corrected re-issue. Oxford, Clarendon Press, 1933. 12 vols. and supplement. (Originally issued as *A New English Dictionary on Historical Principles*. 1884–1928. 10 vols.)

Skeat, Walter W. *Etymological Dictionary of the English Language*. 4th ed. Oxford, Clarendon Press, 1910.

Stratmann, Francis Henry. *Middle English Dictionary*. Re-edited by Henry Bradley. Oxford, Clarendon Press, 1891.

Webster's New International Dictionary. 2nd ed. Springfield Mass., G. & C. Merriam Co., 1934.

Weekley, Ernest. *Etymological Dictionary of Modern English*. New York, Dutton & Co., 1921.

Wright, Joseph. *English Dialect Dictionary*. London, Frowde, 1898–1905. 6 vols.

Index

Throughout the index, references are to page numbers. In general the phonetic symbols have been placed at the beginning of each letter. In addition, the symbols [ɑ], [æ], [ɑɪ] and [ɑʊ] will be found at the beginning of the *A*'s; [dʒ] and [ð] at the beginning of the *D*'s; [ɛ] and [ə] at the beginning of the *E*'s; [ɪ], [ɨ], and [ɪu] at the beginning of the *I*'s; [ŋ] at the beginning of the *N*'s; [ɝ], [ɜ], and [ɚ] at the beginning of the *R*'s; [ʃ] at the beginning of the *S*'s; [tʃ] and [θ] at the beginning of the *T*'s; [ʊ] and [ʌ] at the beginning of the *U*'s; [ʍ] at the beginning of the *W*'s.

The text for this book has been set in 11 point Monotype Caslon #337 with 3 points leading. It was designed by William Caslon in England about 1722 and it is said to have been based upon type purchased in the Netherlands by Bishop Fell for the Oxford University Press. The type used for the chapter openings is Garamont, a design by the famous American designer Frederic Goudy, based upon the type cut by Claude Garamond in 1540 (?). The composition, printing, and binding were done by the Norwood Press, Norwood, Massachusetts. The paper is Warren's #1854 manufactured by S. D. Warren Company. The book is bound in Bancroft Oxford #37. The format was designed by John Begg.

Illustrative Selections

EARLY MODERN ENGLISH

MIDDLE ENGLISH

OLD ENGLISH